THE SAFETY BUBBLE

A PRACTICAL GUIDE TO KEEPING YOUR CHILDREN SAFE AND SOUND

DR VICTORIA ATKINSON

MICHELLE ANDERSON PUBLISHING

First published in Australia 2012 by
Michelle Anderson Publishing Pty Ltd
P O Box 6032 Chapel Street North South Yarra 3141
Melbourne, Australia
Email: mapubl@bigpond.net.au
Website: www.michelleandersonpublishing.com
Tel: 61 3 9826 9028
Fax: 61 3 9826 8552

Copyright © Victoria Atkinson 2012
Cover design: Chameleon Print Design
Typeset by Midland Typesetters, Maryborough Vic
Printed by: Toppan Security Printing Pte. Ltd., Singapore

National Library of Australia Cataloguing-in-Publication entry
Author: Atkinson, Victoria
Title: The safety bubble : a practical guide to keeping children safe and sound / Victoria Atkinson.
ISBN: 9780855724269 (pbk.)
Subjects: Children's accidents—Prevention.
            Home accidents—Prevention

Dewey Number: 363.137

Table of Contents

Acknowledgments vi
Foreword ix

Part 1: Home   xiii

1. **Nursery** 1
   • Nursery layout • Cot • Bassinette • Bedding and sleepwear • Baby monitor • Change table • Storage and toybox • Windows and doors • Portable cots • Moving from cot to bed • Bunk beds • Secondhand furniture
2. **Bathroom** 16
   • Bath shower • Bath toys • Cabinets • Floors • Toilets • Cleaning
3. **Kitchen & Laundry** 25
   • Bench tops and storage • Appliances • Garbage
4. **Living and Dining Room** 34
   • Furniture • Lamps and ornaments • Fireplaces • Electricity and appliances • Windows, doors and stairs • Plants
5. **Home Office & Computer** 45
   • Access • Cords and outlets • Appliances and stationery • Furniture • Computer hardware • Software
6. **Parents' Bedroom** 53
   • Floors and surfaces • Bedside table • Beds • Co-sleeping • Wardrobes and drawers • Ensuite
7. **Windows, Doors and Stairs** 58
   • Windows • Doors • Stairs
8. **Dogs and Cats** 65
   Dogs
   • Reasons dogs bite • General guidelines • Behavioural training • What to teach your dog • Puppies • What to teach your child • Guidelines for children • Outside the home • Hygiene • Bringing home baby • Buying a dog
   Cats
   • Pregnancy • Bringing home baby • Older children • Cats and disease • Cat breeds

9. Television. 86
  • Television screen time recommendations • Violence • Ethnic and gender stereotypes • Sexual themes • Developmental impact • Benefits • Parental controls • Television and entertainment system

10. Poisoning 92
  • Medicines • Essential oils and rubs • Recreational • Household poisoning prevention • Plants and poisonous plants guide • Safe plants guide • Poisoning first aid

Part 2: Outdoors   109

11. Backyard and Playgrounds. 110
  Playground
  • Surfacing • Equipment • Playground use • Arsenic treated wood • Garden and plants • Water • Barbeque area • Decking and balconies
  Backyard
  • Fences, gates and doors • Garden shed • Mowers • Chemicals and cleaning • Plants

12. Pools and Ponds 124
  • Pool gate • Access from house • Pool fence • Pools and ponds • Supervision • covers • Pool surrounds • Pool toys • Pool chemicals • Spa pools • Public pools

13. Garage 133
  • Garage doors • Tools and equipment

14. Fences, Gates and Balconies 142
  • Gates • Access from house • Fence • Balconies and decking

15. Barbeque. 148
  • Barbeque grill • Tools and accessories • Supervision • Table full of food • Fire and fuel • Barbeque fire safety • Burns first aid

16. Cars and Car seats. 154
  • Buying a safe car • Creating a childproof car • Hot cars • Hyperthermia • Travelling in hot weather • Driver distraction • Flying objects • Power windows • Driveways • Seatbelts and restraints • Australian child restraint law changes
  Carseats 168
  • Car seat installation • When to replace • Rear-facing car seat or capsule • Convertible rear to forward facing car seat • Booster seat • Lap belts • Is your child ready for adult seatbelt • Car seats at a glance

Part 3: Baby Equipment and Toys   177

17. Indoor Baby Equipment.........................178
• High chairs • Bouncers • Baby walkers • Jolly jumper • Baby gates • Dummies • Playpens

18. Out and About Baby Equipment...................196
• Prams • Jogging prams • Harnesses and slings • Portable restaurant chairs

19. Toys..211
• Batteries • Strings • Cords • Balls • Plush toys • Magnets • Balloons • Noisy toys • Bath toys • Water toys • Guns • Chemistry set • Sports equipment • Computer and online gaming • Toy storage • Trains • Chemicals in toys and bottles • BPA • Phthalates • Lead • Age appropriate toy buying guide

20. Bikes and Trikes...............................225
• Bicycles • Bike-buying guide • Fit • Safe riding • Rules to teach children • Bike maintenance • Helmets • Clothing • Child bike seats • Bike trailers • Tricycles • Balance bikes

Part 4: Travelling   237

21. Grandparents & Visiting.......................238
22. Travel.......................................241
• Flying with children • Airports • Aeroplanes • Hotels

Appendices
i. Paediatric CPR guide............................. 247
ii. The Choking Child Guide......................... 248
iii. SIDS Guidelines................................ 249

Resources, References and Links.................... 250

Acknowledgements

The writing of a book can be an agonisingly long and solitary process, but when fatigue and disillusionment creep in, it is the support of others which can pick you up, brush you off and allow you to carry on. In my case, it has only been through the belief and encouragement of those mentioned here which has allowed me to finish what I set out to do.

So thank you to those who have helped me stay focussed and to those who have distracted me when required, you have all helped me persevere, especially when I was on the verge of giving up.

Firstly, to my publisher Michelle Anderson who looked into the bubble and dared to see what I see, I will be eternally grateful for your vision and for your leap of faith; I hope to repay you in kind.

To my dear friend Amy Rogers who has been a gift in my life, thank you for your enthusiasm and your friendship. To my one woman cheer squad Robyn Gillies who has my back in and out of the operating room and who I lean on more than I probably should; I hope to return the favour more often. And to Jo Nolte whose laughter and encouragement has always seen me through the toughest of moments, I hold our times dear lovey. Ladies, you have always backed me and I love you for it.

A special thank you to Dr. Mark Umstad, whose gentle strength and skill safely delivered my three babies to me; an incredible gift which also began this literary journey.

It is with great gratitude that I acknowledge Dr Mark Stokes who agreed to turn his considerable expertise to reviewing the manuscript and bought invaluable perspective, insight and gravitas to the project. Thank you for taking the time from your Easter holiday to read the book.

Just when you become dispirited by humanity, someone comes along to tip the balance a little and Lisa Wilkinson is just such a person. This incredibly busy lady, who is pulled in a million directions took the time to read a random letter from a stranger and then made a phone call. Thank you for your support of a then unpublished manuscript and for your voice on such an important subject.

Thank you to my brother Richard who has been looking out for me since the school bus; I may not say it often enough but your support means everything.

To my husband Noel; how do you thank the love of your life for letting you be who you are and who supports every crazy vision you have? You are my all and I adore you Micks.

And finally to the reason this book holds so dear to my heart; my three incredible children Flynn, India and Emerson. I try my best everyday to let you grow and flourish in happiness, but always know that I am there to tend any bumps and bruises you receive as you venture outside my safety bubble. I love you guys endlessly, so thanks for dropping into my world and making it so much bigger.

Dedication

For everyone trying to keep their children safe, and for those I hold dearest, Micks, Flynn, India and Eme; may you always be safe and happy within the bubble.

Foreword
Dr Victoria Atkinson

Every parent wants their child to be happy, healthy and safe, and with 250,000 Australian children per year requiring medical attention after unintentional accidents, it is not always easy to keep a child from harm.

In fact, after the first year of life, injury is the leading cause of death for children with 41% of deaths in the 0–14 age group compared to only 6% deaths in those aged over 15 years.

Most childhood injuries requiring hospital admission are from falls with crushed digits or limbs following close behind and child deaths are most commonly related to babies who suffocate or strangle in cots or prams.

When my first child was born, so too was my fierce need to protect him from danger. I just couldn't believe how small he was and so how vulnerable he must be in such a busy, grown-up world. My first instinct was to wrap him up and hold him close, but I also knew that this was hardly a realistic long-term strategy, and so began my search for the best and most complete approach to childproofing his expanding world.

Childproofing is a state of mind, a new way of seeing and experiencing a space and in time, it becomes completely instinctual; I walk into a room with a different set of eyes when I have my three young children with me, than I do when I am alone. Instead of noticing the gorgeous art deco table lamp, I instead note the dangling cord, heavy wrought iron base and the exposed power point. I will move the handbag off the ground without thinking, unconsciously push the coffee cup to the back of the countertop and automatically close the stair gate and laundry door. There are literally hundreds of such manoeuvres I perform everyday that have become second nature, as I have learnt, tested and then integrated, child safe strategies into our family life.

Children will have accidents as they learn new skills and push to evolve, but with a sound approach to child safety, the number and severity of such accidents can be minimised. Effective childproofing does not have to be about buying expensive gadgets, much can be achieved by being thoughtful and thorough and by never underestimating your children; they are always smarter, faster and more determined than you realise.

This book is the result of five years of research, experience and mothering, it will provide you with your own pair of childproofing glasses and will change your view of the world forever. It will help you to build your very own safety bubble.

The top 10 most important childproofing rules are:

1. There is no childproof device that replaces good adult supervision. Life can change in a split second so watch, watch, watch! In particular never leave a child alone in the bathroom or kitchen where there is a concentration of hazards.
2. When childproofing, change your perspective. By getting on the floor you will see what your child sees and spot potential hazards you never knew existed. You'd be amazed how different everything looks from down there. What's within reach? What looks tempting? Where would you go if you could crawl, toddle, or walk? As he starts walking and climbing, you'll have to re-evaluate again, looking higher each time.
3. Power points should all be fitted with childproof guards and concealed from view where possible. Out of sight out of mind.
4. In every room, be on constant lookout for choking hazards which may have

been left on a low surface or have fallen on the floor. Do surface 'sweeps' throughout the day especially before baby wakes from a nap. As a general guide, any object which fits inside a cardboard toilet roll inner is a definite choking hazard. Larger objects may also have small components which can come loose.
5. Make sure all adult carers have completed a certified first aid and CPR course appropriate for your child's age group. You will need it when you least expect it and minutes can make the critical difference in treating injuries.
6. All medications, cleaning products, and animal products should be placed in high cupboards or in drawers or cupboards with childproof locks in place
7. Buy furniture that has an Australian safety standards sticker or local equivalent.
8. Adjust water heater temperature to <50°C/120°F which is hot enough for an adult shower but not hot enough to scald a child. At 60°C it takes only one second for water to cause a full thickness burn compared with 5 minutes at 50°C.
9. Prepare for an emergency; have the phone numbers for key people like doctors, emergency services and Poisons information close by. Know where the fire blanket and fire extinguishers are as well as how to use them.
10. Some childproofing requires only common sense however; childproofing can be enhanced through the use of safety devices. Expensive is not always best. Keep it simple and do your research before buying equipment.

It is important to remember that just as your children change and evolve, so too should your childproofing evolve to keep one step ahead of their developing skills. Review your childproofing strategies every six months to ensure children have not outgrown or outsmarted them.

PART 1

Home

CHAPTER 1

Nursery

There is no more enjoyable part of pregnancy than shopping for and preparing the nursery. This room will be the greater part of your baby's world for years to come and therefore must be as childproof as possible. From purchasing sound furniture to establishing a safe nursery floorplan, there is much to consider. It is essential that sound childproofing principles are applied to any nursery construction, with the aesthetics falling in behind.

In Australia two children lose their life in a home accident every single week and one in five injuries to children under five is associated with nursery furniture. Most injuries requiring hospital treatment are as a result of falls from furniture or equipment, and include closed head injuries, fractures and lacerations. Falls account for two thirds of nursery-related injuries with other common injuries including crushed digits or limbs. Tragically, some injuries prove fatal and are generally related to babies who suffocate or strangle in their cots.

The many options available for fitting out a nursery can be overwhelming for new parents, but researching the crucial safety features required of this equipment can help parents navigate the nursery maze. As a general guide, it is important to check all baby furniture and equipment for an Australian safety standard sticker and to look for sturdy, easy-to-use designs.

Excited parents-to-be may be dazzled by the many impressive-sounding features offered by modern baby equipment, but it is important to maintain a primary focus on safe design and function. In truth, many impressive-sounding gadgets are nothing more than gimmicks in disguise.

General Nursery Layout

Consider the floor-plan of your nursery and keep all baby furniture clear of hazards such as windows, curtains, heavy shelves and pictures. Consider the function of furniture within the room, for instance, it makes sense for the cot to be as close as possible to the change table to minimise carrying distance.

It is best for the nursery to have carpeting or rugs rather than hard floors as this minimises the risk of slipping whilst carrying baby and is a softer landing in the event of a fall. Any rugs should have non-slip backing with no fringing or edging which is easy to trip on.

All electrical outlets within the nursery must be covered by approved safety plugs which most often take the form of a simple plastic cover that fits into the socket directly; they are cheap and effective. Electrical cords from lamps or appliances should be tethered out of sight and out of reach. Dangling wires are irresistible to babies and they may become entangled risking strangulation or alternatively, may pull heavy objects onto themselves.

There should never be a radiator in a child's room as they can lead to serious burns. Heaters must not be within a metre of beds, cots, or curtains as they can become fire hazards. Beware of overheating your baby, and aim for an ideal nursery temperature of 16–20°C/61–68°F.

Smoke detectors are proven life-savers and should be installed outside all sleeping areas, test them once a month and change the batteries at the beginning of each season.

Cot

Purchasing a cot with a child-proof structure and design is at the core of a safe and secure nursery. Half of all cot injuries involve the child climbing or falling out of their cot, while other accidents involve failure of the cot sides or base. Strangling deaths can occur from something as simple as the cot bars being spaced incorrectly or from the cot being placed near a dangling cord.

The cot lies at the heart of any childproof nursery as babies will spend such a large amount of time sleeping over their first few years of life. Consequently, a cot must be the safest place in the house for a baby and parents-to-be need to learn the key features of a safe cot prior to purchase.

One of the quickest checks to make when purchasing a cot is for the label showing it complies with the Australian Standard (AS 2172), which sets the minimum requirements for materials, design, construction, performance, testing and labelling.

A number of basic design necessities should be checked off next, with one of the mainstays being that the spaces between the vertical slats should be between 50–85mm apart to prevent baby slipping his head through and strangling. It is best to carry a tape measure when shopping and confirm important measurements manually.

There should be no cut outs on a solid headboard or footboard

The Five Ticks standards mark

which may catch head and limbs or be used as a foothold for climbing. If the cot has corner posts, they must either be flush with the top of the headboard and footboard or very tall; over 41 centimetres. Anything in between is a potential strangulation hazard.

If assembling a cot yourself, it is essential that all screws and bolts be well-tightened. They should then be checked regularly to ensure they have not loosened or dislodged completely, as this can make the structure unstable and also poses a choking hazard. Recessed screws are preferable to avoid snagging or tampering.

Choosing an appropriate mattress is a critical part of building a safe cot. The mattress must be firm and should fit snugly all the way around the cot or bassinet, with no gaps larger than an index finger at any point. A firm, well fitted mattress is one of the main factors in reducing the risk of Sudden Infant Death Syndrome or SIDS (see appendix for more SIDS guidelines).

There should be a minimum of 50cm (preferably 60cm), between the top of the mattress and the top of the cot sides. If the cot has an adjustable mattress level, it must be dropped to its lowest level once a baby is sitting up to ensure he does not pull himself up and over the side of the cot. Remove all plastic wrappings which may cover new cot mattresses, knot them and dispose of them immediately as they can cause suffocation.

The cot must have a sturdy base, and may have up to four castor wheels but at least two of these must be lockable, and must stay locked unless moving the cot.

The firmness of a baby's mattress is paramount in minimising SIDS and suffocation risks, it is dangerous therefore, to place baby to sleep on waterbeds or beanbags.

Most modern cots have drop-sides and these should never be left down when baby is asleep in the cot, no matter their age and perceived mobility. Cot side rails or tracks should be concealed from prying fingers which can become trapped, and the mechanism for the drop-side should be sturdy and impossible for a child to activate from inside or outside the cot.

Check all nursery furniture regularly for snags, splinters or protrusions which may catch on clothing or little heads. If any defects are noted they should be professionally repaired as amateur modifications may inadvertently create new dangers.

Thoughtfully planning the layout of a nursery is essential for effective childproofing. The first step is to create a safety zone around the cot; it should not be positioned under windows, heaters, curtains or cords as toddlers may pull themselves up and out of the cot, overheat, or strangle on such hazards. Look at the walls above the cot and ensure there are no heavy pictures or laden shelves which could fall and seriously injure a baby.

It can look somewhat unnerving to see your tiny baby all alone in a huge cot, but resist the temptation to fill the cot with bumpers, pillows or soft toys. They may look pretty and cosy but they will also increase the risk of suffocation and SIDS, and for older children may provide a foothold for climbing; baby should sleep alone.

Any mobiles should be hung completely out of reach, preferably from the ceiling rather than from the cot side. Toys must never be strung across the top of the cot, nor should they, or objects such as dummies, be tied to cot slats; all pose a serious strangulation risk.

Buying second-hand nursery furniture is certainly an economically sound choice, but from a safety point of view, extra vigilance is required to ensure it meets modern safety standards. Find out when the cot was purchased and beware of any cot made before 1980 as the paint may contain lead; this may be one time not to use the family heirloom. Any second-hand cots should be checked carefully for splinters, peeling paint, loose screws and instability. Buying used cots online makes a hands-on safety inspection difficult prior to purchase, therefore, if using this method check the returns policy should a fault be discovered later.

Bassinette

Many parents place their newborn in a bassinette before graduating them to a larger cot, either to sleep them in the parental bedroom initially, or to keep them cosy as a tiny newborn can seem lost in a large cot. Although most child safety experts recommend that babies are placed in standard cots from birth, if parents do choose to use a bassinette, there are a few simple safety tips to know.

The bassinette should be wide-based, sturdy and any castor wheels must be lockable with brakes kept engaged unless moving the bassinette. The sides should be at least 300mm higher than the top of the mattress and the mattress must be snug to the edge of the cot and less than 75mm thick to prevent suffocation.

If the bassinette has a frame with collapsible legs, these must be firmly locked and the base pressed on before placing baby.

Keep decorative bows and trim to a minimum as they can decrease air circulation around the baby and so risk overheating them; a risk factor for SIDS.

Long ribbons and the like also risk strangulation.

Do not use pillows or place toys in the bassinette as these can cause suffocation, and ensure the baby is slept away from all hazards such as curtains, windows, heaters etc.

It is critical to adhere to the manufacturer's height and weight recommendations for the specific bassinette and to transfer the baby to a cot when they exceed these limits or are close to rolling; if baby becomes to big, they can come into contact with the ends or sides of the cot and suffocate.

Bedding and Sleepwear

Every parent wants the nursery and cot to look spectacular despite the fact that babies are completely oblivious to most of the trimmings. This inevitably means that nurseries are often filled with all things soft and cuddly, but in baby-world fuzzy and cute can also mean dangerous.

When buying cot bedding, it is important to follow a few simple guidelines to optimise safety and minimise the risk of SIDS.

Cot bumpers (the padded border that lines the inside of the cot and ties to the slats) may look adorable and provide a soft haven for your baby, but that same softness can cause suffocation if a baby rolls and becomes trapped against the bumper. In addition, bumpers decrease ventilation and airflow around the baby which can lead to overheating, whilst the bumper ties can also cause strangulation. So despite the fact that many stores still sell them, and that many nursery sheet sets still include them, cot bumpers are not recommended and should not be fitted.

Any mattress cover should fit snugly without bunching or coming loose, with fitted covers offering the best stability. Use bedding specific to the cot model to guarantee a custom fit and never use adult sheets which have been gathered and tucked.

Do not place pillows, quilts, doonas, or soft toys within the cot as any of these may cause suffocation to a baby. Older children may use these items to climb and can topple out of the cot

A simple, light weight and breathable blanket and sheet are all that are needed, and these should be tucked tightly in order to minimise the chance of bedding migrating over a baby's face. In accordance with SIDS guidelines, babies should be slept on their backs, with their feet against the bottom of the cot so that they cannot slip under blankets.

Consider the use of a sleeping bag for baby as an alternative to sheets and blankets. They provide warmth, move with the baby, and cannot be kicked off or end up covering a baby's face. They are available in different sizes and temperature ratings, allowing for summer heat and winter cold.

Babies should always be dressed in non-flammable sleepwear and snug-fitting sleepwear is less likely to snag on something and also less likely to catch on fire. In addition, well-fitted clothing will burn less rapidly as there is less air between clothing and your baby's skin. These extra minutes can make the world of difference to the severity of a burn.

There are commercially available anti-roll pads into which you strap your baby and then lay them in the cot. These claim to hold the baby on their back and prevent face-down sleeping. Newborn babies cannot roll over and as they grow and start to roll it is hard to contain their sleep-time movements, but these devices may give you peace of mind.

Nursery temperature is a critical component of childproofing the space with the ideal nursery temperature being 16–20°C/ 61–68°F. Overheating a baby is particularly dangerous as they cannot regulate their own temperature efficiently. As a general guide, baby should be dressed in one extra layer to you but it is far easier to place a simple thermometer in the nursery to accurately monitor ambient temperature. Many baby monitors also have built-in thermometers.

Baby Monitors

Baby monitors allow sound (and vision if you choose) to be transmitted to a remote unit carried with a carer and allows for increased freedom of movement when baby is asleep. In smaller houses, where baby's cries can be heard from every room, these monitors may not be required, but in larger or split-level houses they are very useful.

Advancing technology,

however, has led to great evolution in baby monitors and the sheer number and complexity of features now available can leave parents overwhelmed by choice. So when purchasing a baby monitor look for a few essential components and then add other features according to your own circumstances.

The essential components

To make a monitor useful, it must have the following;
- Good volume, clear sound transmission with minimal static interference
- More than one channel for switching in case of static interference from the neighbours remote-controlled garage door. Some offer only 2 channels, while others have over 100 channels to counter a neighbourhood full of garage doors.
- As a rule, digital rather than analogue monitors have less interference, but are more expensive.
- Indicator lights which illuminate with increasing sound so that baby cries can be 'seen' over television or talking.
- Good range of transmission, which depending on the size of your house may mean greater than 100, 250 or 300 metres.
- Portability features such as belt clips are helpful.
- Good battery life with an AC adapter alternative, and a low battery indicator to protect against unrecognised shut-offs.

The optional extras

Most monitors offer the essentials, albeit to varying degrees of quality. The optional extras, however, cater to each parent's specific needs (and fears).
- Some models monitor baby movement or apnoea (breath holding). These have pressure plates which are placed under the mattress and sound a piercing alarm when no movement is sensed for a prescribed period. This allows parents to stimulate or resuscitate a baby. It should be clearly stated however, that there is *no scientific evidence* that apnoea monitors reduce the risk of SIDS, and as babies get older and move around the cot they can roll off the sensor pads triggering the alarm incessantly. Some babies, especially those born

prematurely require hospital-grade apnoea monitors for medical reasons, and will be prescribed these under medical advice.
- If you literally want to keep an eye on baby while he sleeps, some monitors offer a night vision camera in the nursery unit and a 2.5 inch LCD screen in the mobile unit.
- Temperature and/or humidity monitoring. As babies cannot efficiently regulate their own temperature, it is important to dress baby appropriately for bed. The ideal nursery temperature is recommended as 16–20°C and as overheating is a known SIDS risk, baby monitors with built-in thermometers make sense.

Change Tables

The majority of injuries from change tables involve the baby rolling or falling off and suffering head injuries and it should be noted that some safety organisations recommend against change tables altogether. Even small babies who have never rolled before can squirm their way off the table and it should go without saying that hands and eyes should never be taken off a baby whilst on the change table. This involves making sure that everything needed is close at hand and if not, that the baby is removed from the table before retrieving extra nappies and the like.

A change table should be sturdy with a broad, stable base and should contain compartments, drawers or pockets for safe storage. All potentially dangerous baby accessories and lotions must be stored well out of reach of little hands to lessen the risk of swallowing or injury. The table ought to be at a convenient working height for carers and any wheels should be lockable.

There are many different variations on change table design and many are incorporated into another piece of furniture, e.g. atop a chest-of-drawers, or on rails over the cot. It is important that safety has not been compromised in the design of a change table to allow for integration into another piece of furniture and these pieces should be appraised with the same childproofing eye as dedicated change tables; do not trade safety for convenience.

Sound change table design will include ends at least 10cm

high and raised sides or rails to minimise any rolling risks. These risks can be further reduced by the addition of a hollow-shaped change mat, preferably with a fitted restraint belt. The restraint mechanism should be easy to use one-handed e.g. Velcro.

For a particularly wriggly older baby the safest option may be to bypass the change table completely and to place the change mat directly onto the floor; this will negate any chance of rolling from a height.

Storage and Toyboxes

As a matter of course, there never seems to be enough storage in a child's room and this is particularly true of toy storage; no matter how many shelves, cupboards and tubs there are, the toys just refuse to stay put. It may not be obvious how simple storage units can become child hazards, but to an inquisitive child determined to reach its contents, a toy box can be an irresistible danger. Children will climb in, on and under just about anything and all storage must be adapted to this likelihood.

All free-standing storage units such as shelves, chest-of-drawers and wardrobes should be bolted securely to the wall. This is done simply and cheaply with an L-shaped metal bracket available at any hardware store. Older children will often attempt to climb up a set of shelves leading to possible falls but even younger babies can pull poorly fixed shelf or storage units over on themselves, causing serious injury. Store the books and toys most used by younger children on the lower shelves to discourage them from climbing or reaching. Store older children's toys at a higher level not easily accessible to a younger sibling

The open drawers of a dresser or storage stack make perfect stairs, so keep drawers closed and secured with childproof locks where possible. Locking drawers with childproof devices such as magnetic locks can avoid curious fingers becoming trapped. Foam doorstoppers or a rolled up towel draped over the drawer can be used temporarily as a buffer to stop the drawer being slammed shut on little fingers, for e.g. whilst putting away clothes.

Many children's wardrobes have split hanging space, but if there is a choice, lower shelves and higher hanging space is preferable. All metal coat-hangers should be kept out of reach as they can cause serious injury to a child, especially to the eyes and face. Better yet, invest in plastic hangers with rounded ends.

Toyboxes should have slow-closing hinges which stop heads and fingers being slammed in the lid. There should always be cut-outs at both ends of the toy box to allow for ventilation should the child climb or fall in and they should not be lockable.

Plastic storage tubs are a convenient form of storage but avoid tubs with lids and clip-locks as they are a major suffocation risk if children climb in and have a helpful sibling lock it behind them. The safest way to store toys and other items is in an open-topped basket or plastic container with curved corners. As an alternative, select plastic containers with loose-fitting, non-sealing lids.

Windows and Doors

The danger of windows and doors lies mostly in those leading to the outside, especially those above the ground floor where the potential for falls and serious injury is significant. Whilst the dangers of windows and doors may not seem much to a newborn baby, it is amazing how quickly these helpless bundles become mobile danger-seeking machines. It is best to childproof the nursery as a complete and cohesive plan from the beginning and this should include childproofing windows and doors.

Toddlers enjoy playing with doors and windows and if given the chance are especially fond of slamming them shut. This leaves them vulnerable to finger and limb entrapment, crush injury and possible amputation.

Where possible, doors should have spring-loaded, slow-closing devices to negate the potential for slamming and if not already installed, these mechanisms are simple to fit retrospectively.

Various door-stopping devices are available to place over top of a door, providing a buffer to stop the door being completely closed. The simplest of these is a c-shaped piece of foam which fits around the door to intercede between door and frame; it is cheap and effective. As a temporary solution when working in a room around a hovering toddler, a rolled towel can be hung over the top of the door. The disadvantage of this type of doorstop is that the door cannot be closed until it is removed.

Floor-level stops behind doors should be a one-piece design and any rubber-tipped spring models should be replaced. Until this occurs, remove the rubber tips completely to decrease any choking risk to curious crawlers.

Doorknob covers can be installed to prevent a child opening a closed door and accessing potentially perilous areas of the house. Bear in mind that lever type door handles are harder to childproof than the classic rounded knob, but there are some childproof guards available. A cheaper option is to fit selected doors with handles that are placed high and out of reach to children.

Windows and doors including sliding doors to outside areas should be secured with locks, high door handles and childproof locks. Remove any keys from the lock and keep them somewhere out of reach in a childproof cupboard or drawer.

Windows, especially those at height, can be fitted with devices to limit the opening aperture. Any window opening should be from the top rather than the bottom and should be no greater than 10cm to prevent a child squeezing through.

Most toddlers are natural climbers and will make-shift stairs from any found object, so keep chairs and other potential climbing aids, away from windows.

Fit child safety window guards within window frames, and choose one with an emergency release latch where appropriate. Install childproof latches on all windows, and choose those with a built-in quick-release mechanism which an adult can open quickly as an emergency exit. It should be noted that fly screens, no matter how sturdy, are no substitute for proper window safety guards as they are not designed to withstand the force of a falling child.

With windows come blinds and with blinds come cords. It is critical that all curtain cords are secured well off the floor (higher than 1600mm) and out of reach of the cot; raise them or tie them up as necessary. Be especially cautious with looped curtain cords which can cause strangulation or hanging, so tie them well out of reach or if necessary, cut the loop in half and convert it to a couple of weighted, single cords.

It is important that curtains cover the windows in a measured way and do not sweep majestically to the floor; these can be climbed on or swung from, to reach a window. A baby or toddler entwined within long, heavy curtains also risks suffocation or strangulation, so keep curtains light and made-to-measure.

Portable Cots

Portable cots are designed for easy transport and therefore are completely collapsible with soft, mesh sides. Inevitably, this means that the major danger with any portable cot is collapse and trapping of a child. Unfamiliarity with cot assembly enhances the threat of collapse, as often these cots are used only on occasion for trips away or sleepovers. It is important to become intimately familiar with your portable cot by repeated assembly and collapse and to always read the instructions before the first use as some features may not be obvious.

It is preferable to take your own cot when travelling, but if this is not possible and you are using a strange cot (e.g. in a hotel), ask for the instructions or a demonstration of assembly; do not just assume that it assembles the same as your own cot.

Create a childproof zone around the cot when travelling by placing it away from windows, doors, tables, and dangling cords; be observant and considered.

When assembling a portable cot, the most important task is to ensure that the collapsible sides are fully engaged and clicked into place as described in the instructions. There should be at least two locking mechanisms to guard against sudden collapse and the cot should be checked for stability by pushing on the base before placing the baby inside. Any frame locking devices should be shielded or out of reach of babies to avoid them collapsing the frame or trapping fingers within the mechanism.

Regularly check the cot for any protrusions or snags and be constantly vigilant for worn or broken clasps.

Always use the mattress purchased with the portable cot to

ensure a custom fit with no gaps to potentially trap and suffocate a baby. These mattresses can seem quite hard and thin, but do not be tempted to pad it out by adding blankets or quilts. These form a base which is too soft and may smother a baby causing suffocation or overheating. The cot floor should not sag as baby can sink into it and potentially roll face down. The mesh on the cot sides should be taut, of fine knit and be free of holes which may catch fingers or buttons. Neither the cot sides nor the top should ever be covered with heavy, blackout material such as blankets, as this reduces air circulation and can lead to overheating. Alternatively, they may be pulled into the cot leading to smothering and suffocation.

Stop using the portable cot when your child can climb out or tip it over, for most brands this is usually when a child reaches approximately 86 centimetres in height.

Moving From Cot to Bed

When a child starts climbing out of a cot, it is time to move to a bed. This may begin occurring once a child is over 90 centimetres tall. In the interim until you buy a bed, it is safer to simply leave the cot sides down to allow children to get out themselves rather than to fall out.

A mattress placed on the floor next to the bed can be an intermediate step until a child gets used to sleeping in a bed.

Children's beds can temporarily be fitted with toddler guard rails to stop them rolling out while still allowing them to get in and out of bed themselves. These rails can aid the transition from cot to bed and prevent any unpleasant bumps in the night. Alternatively, many modern cots convert to a small toddler bed with side rails.

It should be noted that electric blankets are not recommended on a child's bed, especially if not consistently toileting at night, as this will avoid the risk of electrocution and fire.

Bunk Beds

Bunk beds can be a practical space-saver where children are sharing rooms but if used inappropriately, they can also present a number of hazards to young children. In general, bunk beds are not recommended for children under 6 years old and children should be over the age of 9 before moving to the top bunk.

Any top bunk should have side rails on all aspects to minimise the risk of falls and must be at least 2 metres below ceiling fans and light fittings. Do not allow children to play on the top bunk as this is when most falls occur.

A major source of injury using bunk beds originates from misuse of the ladder to the top bunk. Ensure ladders are firmly attached and particularly if there are young children around, the ladder should be removed during the day to stop them accessing or playing on the top bunk.

Second Hand Furniture

Baby equipment is used for a relatively short period of time and so much of it appears on the second-hand market but it is important to view and inspect any items carefully. Safety standards have changed over the years and older items may not conform to modern standards, so whilst a piece may be in good condition it may simply be out of date and unsafe. For example, any painted furniture made before 1980 may contain lead.

If buying a used cot always replace the mattress and ensure it is snug fitting and firm. If necessary, visit a foam rubber store and have them cut a mattress to size. It is essential to check older furniture for splinters, peeling paint or missing and loose screws. Inspect any wheels for intact brakes and locks.

Bathroom

For many parents bathtime represents one of the happiest parts of the day with the warm water seemingly able to re-animate even the tiredest baby. But with water comes a multitude of potential dangers, especially for young children and this makes vigilant childproofing of the bathroom essential.

Most home accidents occur between 5 and 6 pm when everyone is tired and distracted by pre-sleep activities such as homework, after-school activities or cooking dinner. For many families, this flurry of activity also includes bathing the children and it can be difficult at times to resist distraction and focus entirely on the task at hand.

Bathrooms contain a high concentration of child hazards with most bathroom accidents involving drowning, scalds from hot water or slipping on watery surfaces. It is not well appreciated that a baby or toddler can drown in as little as 3cms of water, and moreover that drowning happens quickly and silently.

Consequently the most important childproofing tool in the bathroom, is constant supervision; with no exceptions. Babies and young children should never be left alone in a bathroom or in the bath, not even for a minute.

General Bathroom Guidelines

Bathrooms have the ungainly combination of water and

electricity and all within a relatively confined space; adding children to this mix is potentially lethal. So it is essential that all power outlets are placed as far away from sinks and baths as possible and are not fitted at ground level where water and young children may mingle.

Ideally, all power points should be concealed and at height, perhaps within a high bathroom cabinet, as this will ensure that they are out of reach, out of sight and hopefully, out of mind to a child.

As always, power points should all be fitted with childproof guards or plugs and should be left switched off. All houses should be fitted with residual Current Devices (RCDs) in the meter box. These are different to surge protectors and detect any imbalance in electrical current and disconnect power within 10–50 milliseconds, preventing electrocution and fire. This is particularly important to prevent electrical shocks from water.

One of the most effective ways to childproof the bathroom is to restrict access, thereby ensuring that babies can access the bathroom only when accompanied by an adult and not when wandering the house looking for entertainment. Keep the bathroom door closed with a child safety latch, a high door handle and/or a door knob cover to stop such unsupervised access. Do not, however, install a formal bathroom door lock unless it can be unlocked readily from the outside as inevitably, a child will lock themselves inside.

Successful childproofing is all about changing your perspective. This means getting down onto those cold bathroom tiles to see things the way your child does. It is amazing how this simple manoeuvre will give you a unique point of view and may reveal a few hidden hazards.

Baths and Showers

Bath-time childproofing begins with *never* leaving your child unattended in the bath, not even for a minute. Supervising a young child in the water means staying within arms reach of them at all times, and does not mean casually observing them from across the room. This close proximity helps to guarantee rapid retrieval of any child who has slipped or fallen into the water.

This close supervision may mean that a forgotten towel or a ringing phone will have to be ignored, but these distractions pale into insignificance when compared with the potential harm to a child. So if the sound of a ringing phone annoys you, take it off the hook or let it go to the answering machine. Resist the temptation to answer a cordless or mobile phone in the bathroom as being immersed in a conversation will divert concentration away from the bathtub. If you feel it necessary to answer the door or the telephone, then remove baby from the bath and take them with you; they will be wet but safe.

It is equally dangerous to leave older siblings to supervise younger children in the bath. Even older children do not possess the cognitive maturity required to make sound judgements based on projected consequences and it is unfair to expect them to keep younger siblings safe in such a high risk environment.

Keep bath-time essentials close by creating space within reach of the bath to store towels, washers, soaps and anything else you may require. This ensures that any forgotten items can be safely retrieved whilst staying within arms length of a child.

Hot water burns account for a large proportion of bathroom accidents and it is generally recommended that all household water be no warmer than 50°C to minimise the risk of serious scalding. At 60°C it takes only one second for water to cause a full thickness burn compared with 5 minutes at 50°C. Adjust the thermostat on your water heater to a temperature of 50°C/120°F which is hot enough for an adult shower but not hot enough to scald a child. New houses are required to have water temperature limiters installed.

When running a bath fill it with cool water first and then add the hot water as desired. If using mixer taps, check the water temperature frequently as the water temperature may fluctuate. Do not place a child in the bath while the water is still running and never leave running water unattended.

Young children should not have a deep bath and water needs only to reach belly button height or 8–10cm for washing; remember that babies are top heavy and can drown in as little as 3cms of water especially if unable to right themselves.

The desired temperature for a baby's bath water is between 37° to 38°C (98.5°F–100°F) and it should not exceed 39°C/102°F. Bath thermometers are cheap and readily available at baby equipment or hardware stores and will take the guess work out of bath temperatures. Whether using a thermometer or not, water temperature should always be tested with your elbow before placing a baby in the bath. Elbows rather than hands should be used, as hands tend to acclimatise quickly to heat.

Children are fascinated by taps and should be taught from the youngest age that bath taps are strictly off-limits. Basin taps are a safer learning ground and this is where older children should be taught about the difference between hot and cold water taps, or about how to safely use mixer taps.

In addition, there are a number of simple manoeuvres which can limit the risks posed by bath taps. Once the bath is filled, run a small amount of cold water through the tap before placing a child in the tub as this cools the bath spout and prevents burns if it is touched. A soft cover over the bath spout can also protect kids against sharp edges and burns. These covers come in many colourful designs but if too enticing, they can also draw a child's attention to the spout and taps.

Always leave mixer taps pointed towards the cold setting in case they are activated and face your child away from the taps and spout as they are less likely to play with something they cannot readily see. Childproof tap covers are available to prevent children turning them however, it can be difficult to source covers for some of the more unusually-shaped mixer taps.

Adding babies to a bath full of water can create a very slippery customer, however the use of an adhesive mat or decals on the bottom of the bath can minimise slipping, especially when babies are learning to sit. Also designed to limit slippery accidents is the bath seat in which babies recline at 45° on a gripping backrest. These seats can give new parents confidence in the bath but are not designed as safety aids and babies should never be left sitting unattended as they can roll off or tip the seat and drown.

Remember to drain the bath immediately on finishing the bath as toddlers will return to play and may fall in.

Sunken baths or spa baths can pose a hidden obstacle for toddlers and should be fitted with a sturdy cover to stop children falling in. Bathtubs fitted with spa systems are not recommended for children as drowning and hair or limb entrapment are very real dangers. For more detailed information on spas see Chapter 12 on Pools and Ponds.

For young children who prefer showers rather than baths, many of the same childproofing rules apply. Mixer taps are often lower and more accessible than in baths and supervision of showering children can be more difficult depending on fogging and the type of shower screen installed. For these reasons many parents prefer to shower with their young children or alternatively, to shower them with the screen open.

Shower doors and cubicles should be fitted with toughened safety glass and decals applied at a child's eye-level to make the screen more visible, this will minimise the risk of children running into, or through, a glass pane.

Bath Toys

Bath toys should be fully washable with no small parts or sharp edges. Toys to be immersed should be sealed to stop water collecting inside as stagnant water leads to mould growth which can be harmful to young children. So what of the traditional squirty bath toy? As there is no way to adequately clean inside these toys they will inevitably collect mould and the only solution is to change them regularly. Hold these toys up to the light and discard any with tell-tale shadowing indicating internal mould growth, or similarly discard any toys which squirt brown or green particulate matter with the water. Discourage children from sucking on, or swallowing water from such toys.

Be aware that many squishy

bath toys contain phthalates which are oily, colourless, and odourless compounds which are used, primarily to make PVC more flexible.

The potential health effects of phthalates raised by scientists include early onset puberty, low sperm counts as well as in-utero effects such as abnormal genital development and premature delivery. The potential health effects of phthalates are particularly worrying in the case of baby toys, where constant mouthing of toys could lead to increased dose exposure. The European Union has banned phthalates in children's toys and in early 2009 the U.S. also banned these compounds in toys. In Australia the use of phthalates in toys is currently under review by the Australia's National Industrial Chemicals Notification and Assessment Scheme (NICNAS).

For more information see Chapter 19 on Toys.

Cabinets

Bathroom benches are notorious for accumulating all kinds of lotions and potions and to an inquisitive toddler they can be a wonderland of new experiences. So it is essential that all bathroom benches are kept as clear as possible and in particular that all potentially poisonous compounds and medications are stored in high cabinets; out of reach and out of sight. Too many accidents occur from underestimating the reach and determination of a curious toddler.

Bathroom cabinets should be fitted with locks or childproof latches and kept secured at all times. Some simple preparations are harmless when used externally but when ingested by a small child, these same substances can prove highly poisonous.

Consider changing to an electric razor for shaving to avoid the presence of open razor blades, and if not, store blades in a high, childproof cupboard.

Keep hair dryers and other electrical appliances unplugged and stored away from baths and sinks to prevent burns and electrocution. Dangling cords can prove an irresistible temptation to a toddler and can risk objects being pulled off benches onto little heads or into water.

Make sure all cabinets, mirrors and clocks are secured

properly to the wall and avoid the use of adhesive fixture alone as this may degrade in the damp conditions causing the object to fall.

All medication should be bought in childproof packaging and stored in this original packaging in a high, locked cabinet. Tablets in silver foil can look like lollies to a child and these should never be left on a bathroom bench. Keep a current list of any medications in case of accidental ingestion by a child and have the phone number for the local poisons information centre on an emergency list of numbers stored by the phone. For a more complete picture of childhood poisoning see Chapter 10.

Floors

Tiled floors can be slippery to an unsteady toddler especially when wet, so clean all water spills quickly. If renovating, look for tiles with an anti-slip coating and ask your tile store about the anti-slip rating of different tile types. There are also anti-slip coatings available for application to existing floors.

If using bathmats, make sure they have a non-slip backing and do not have raised or fringed edges which can cause tripping.

Babies need to be kept warm especially when bathing, but do not be tempted to use floor heaters or radiators in the bathroom as they are a burn and an electrocution risk. Instead, install ceiling heater lights or central heating ducts.

Bathroom garbage bins are a hidden safety risk and can be full of dangerous refuse. These should be removed from the bathroom floor and stored in a cupboard fitted with a childproof latch. In addition, any sharp or hazardous bathroom garbage should be disposed of in a secure bin out of reach, or out of the bathroom completely.

If using cloth nappies and nappy buckets filled with chemical solutions, do not keep them on the bathroom floor where they can be freely accessed by toddlers. Buy a nappy bucket with a tight, latched lid and keep it out of reach or in an 'off-limits' room such as the laundry.

Toilets

No one likes the thought of their child playing with the toilet, but play they will unless it is properly secured. Install a toilet lock to keep children from lifting the lid as it is both unhygienic and dangerous as toddlers risk falling in and drowning. At the very least, various objects will be posted into the toilet for amusement and no one wants to be fishing their toothbrush or worse, their mobile phone, out of the toilet bowl.

Avoid the use of detachable toilet fresheners or cleaners inside the bowl where they can be accessed and eaten by toddlers and always store the toilet brush out of reach, in a cupboard or off the floor. A friend recently found her 3 year old brushing his sister's hair with their particularly large toilet brush!

When toilet training, use a toddler seat attachment which makes the aperture smaller and prevents them falling in. Also, teach toddlers not to climb onto the toilet without an adult present.

Cleaning

It is best not to store cleaning products in a room accessed by children, instead store all cleaning products securely in an 'off-limits' room such as the laundry. If products are stored in the bathroom, ensure they are in a high cupboard, fitted with a childproof latch and keep it locked.

Store cleaning products in the original, childproof packaging and do not place non-food substances in old food containers, such as floor cleaner in an old jam jar. This can be confusing to a child and increases the risk of inappropriate ingestion.

Where possible, try to clean when children are napping, absent or occupied elsewhere with another adult, especially if using chemical cleaning agents; trying to supervise children and clean can be a recipe for disaster as they attempt to 'help'.

Never leave a bucket of water around when cleaning as toddlers can drown in as little as 3cm of water especially if stuck in a bucket head first. If the water is hot it can also pose a burns risk if pulled over, and as most will also contain cleaning solutions, it is also a poisons risk.

Do not leave spray bottles of cleaning chemicals on low surfaces or on the floor, and turn the spray nozzle to 'off' between squirts. Children love these bottles but instinctively tend to point the nozzle at their face or put it in their mouth before squeezing the trigger.

Consider switching from potentially harmful cleaning products such as chorine bleach and lye products to cleaner, greener alternatives such as vinegar and water for cleaning glass and surfaces. This approach also saves money and 'recipes' for making green cleaning solutions are freely available online.

Beware of plug-in air fresheners as a double danger; they present an electrocution danger if removed leaving an exposed power point, but can also contain poisonous chemicals if sucked on.

Kitchen and Laundry

Both the kitchen and laundry contain a high concentration of child hazards, from open flames and sharp utensils to poisonous cleaning agents and washing machines, these two rooms should never be under-estimated.

The main difference between these two however, is that while a modern kitchen often forms the hub of a home and is openly accessible to the whole family, the laundry should be the opposite; that is, used less frequently and accessible only to adults. Whilst the divergent roles of these two rooms dictate differing childproofing strategies, at their core are the common themes of education and supervision.

As with all childproofing, parents should begin by sitting on the floor and surveying the potential dangers, in particular power points, the contents of low shelves and cupboards, as well the accessibility of appliances and poisons. Understanding how much of the stovetop or bench space can be seen from the floor will help inform the use of such space as children are less likely to reach for something they cannot see.

Parents tend to underestimate the reach and ingenuity of a determined toddler as they stretch and climb their way into trouble. Consequently, thinking carefully about the content of cupboards, drawers, bench tops and shelves is central to making the kitchen and laundry as safe as possible.

These two rooms also contain a relative over-supply of power points and so require extra vigilance in the provision of childproof outlet covers and power points which contain Residual Current Devices (RCDs) to prevent electrical shocks from water. Where possible, power outlets and power boards should be concealed within cupboards or at the back of benches as this will discourage children's attention.

Both the kitchen and laundry are 'wet' areas and consideration must be given to the provision of non-slip flooring. Most tiles have an anti-slip rating which rate their performance in both wet and dry conditions and similar information is available for alternate flooring such as wood or linoleum. In addition, all spills should be cleaned immediately.

Kitchen

The recent popularity of open plan living means that the kitchen often forms the centre of a home and functions as a hub for activities within the home. This encourages children to gravitate towards parents as they prepare meals.

Most kitchen accidents involve burns from hot liquids or foods either dropping or being pulled down, as well as from children climbing to access appliances or knives. In addition, many accidents involving babies or toddlers occur between 5 and 6 pm when everyone is tired and distracted with evening activities such as cooking dinner.

As a primary strategy, consider the use of a childproof safety gate in the kitchen entrance to restrict access for young children when the kitchen is in use.

Do not let your child play on the floor while you are cooking as they can be hit by falling implements or hot food. Ideally, occupy them elsewhere either with another person, or another distraction e.g. a book or DVD.

If children are present in the kitchen, they must be closely supervised as they are often very keen to 'help', but equally when the kitchen is dormant, it must be packed away safely to protect the inquisitive baby.

Do not keep a step or stool in the kitchen, as this enables contact with any number of potential hazards, instead introduce such aids as required when an older child is to cook with you.

A fire extinguisher must be kept in the kitchen and you should know how to use it. It must be an extinguisher which is appropriate to use on electrical and fat fires and have a fire blanket readily accessible as a back-up. Have a family fire plan and drill young children regularly in what to do in the event of a fire.

Install a smoke detector near but not inside, the kitchen and if battery-operated check the battery every month. Some detectors come with lithium batteries which have a 10 year life-span, but they should still be checked monthly.

Bench Tops and Storage

Be alert for choking hazards which may have been left on a low surface or have fallen on the floor. As a general guide, any object which fits inside a cardboard toilet roll inner is a definite choking hazard but larger objects may also have small components which can be prised loose. Perform surface 'sweeps' throughout the day clearing away any dangerous objects and be especially attentive before your baby wakes from a nap.

Clear all benches at the completion of kitchen use and store small appliances and other permanent objects at the back of the bench top and out of reach of little hands.

If designing a kitchen, include bench tops with adequate depth to keep objects out of a child's reach and place the stove and sink close to each other to minimise the risk of carrying hot foods and liquids across the kitchen.

Childproofing cupboards and drawers is essential and relatively easy. There are a variety of cheap and effective childproof latches and locks available for all types of storage units; from external slide locks to tether cupboard door handles through to the more elaborate magnetic locks for drawers, there is a childproof lock for all situation and all budgets. These simple mechanisms, however, are absolutely pivotal in the childproofing of any home, and in particular of the kitchen.

Of greater importance is that these childproof latches and locks are actually kept latched and do not degenerate into useless pieces of plastic hanging impotently from cupboards and drawers. It is a sad fact that many people install these locks in a flush of initial enthusiasm but quickly tire of unlatching and re-latching them multiple times a day and so leaving them largely disengaged as dangerous monuments to convenience. Unfortunately, children rarely tire of exploring such places and it takes only one curious trip into the cutlery drawer to potentially end in tragedy. So install childproof latches and use them; every time.

With all cupboards sporting a childproof latch, it is a good idea to leave one low cupboard and/or a drawer unsecured and filled with plastic bowls, cups and other safe items for children to enjoy. This becomes a designated child's cupboard and they are free to open it and play whenever you are in the kitchen; this not only acts as a useful distraction but will also make children feel that they are helping. The allocated cupboard should be on the edge of the kitchen away from stoves, ovens and busy floor space.

Drawers should be secured with mechanical or magnetic locks and kept closed at all times as open drawers can be used as a toddler staircase to access high surfaces.

Large kitchen knives should be kept in a knife block or rack out of reach of children, at the back of the bench for example. Other sharp utensils such as peelers, graters and the like should be kept in one drawer and must be stored securely with a good quality drawer lock in place.

Store all crockery and glasses up high where possible and throw out any which are cracked or chipped.

Beware of the kitchen 'junk' drawer, usually filled with matches, batteries, elastic bands, toothpicks and all other manner of miscellaneous flotsam. Allocate a high drawer or cupboard to store these objects and be ever-vigilant about engaging childproof locks on this frequently used drawer.

Plastic bags seem to breed within modern households and

are the scourge of both the environment and child safety. These bags should be rounded up into one area and stored securely out of reach. Children are drawn to these scrunchy, crunchy bags and often their first instinct is usually to place it over their head risking rapid suffocation. If disposing of plastic bags, tie them in a knot before throwing them into the garbage.

It is an undeniable truth that curious babies and toddlers seem to find dirty pet bowls and pet food, irresistible, so keep food bowls off the floor between meals and put pet water bowls away from the kitchen to a less frequented area.

Appliances

Modern kitchens are rife with appliances programmed to perform all manner of little miracles, but the one thing that they have in common is that most are perilous to young children. In general, small appliances should be stored in locked cupboards or against the back of counters and away from sinks with their electrical cords rolled up and well out of reach.

Leave appliances unplugged when not in use so that children cannot operate them accidentally; this will also avoid shocks should a child pull one into a water-filled sink. Fill the kettle only with the water immediately required as it is easier to pour and minimises the amount of boiling water present in the case of any accident.

Older children should be taught about different appliances as appropriate for their age and can be shown how to use these devices safely and under supervision.

Refrigerators and dishwashers should be fitted with child-proof locks as they are sealed appliances and can lead to suffocation if a child climbs in and closes the door.

Certain items stored in the fridge such as alcohol, can be dangerous to children and are best stored up high and at the back of the shelf. Even a small amount of alcohol can be toxic to a child so do not place these bottles in the door of the fridge where they are well within reach. Alcohol not requiring refrigeration, such as spirits, should be stored securely in a high, locked cupboard. Similarly, ensure all breakable jars and bottles are not stored in the fridge door but on the top shelves.

Exercise extreme caution when using the stove around children and enforce a 'no go' zone or square around the stove about an arm's length in size and teach your child to stay outside this area. Teach kids from an early age not to touch the stove and install stove guards which fence the cook top and prevent curious hands from reaching up onto the burners. Additionally, use stove knob covers to stop children from accidentally turning on the hotplates or the gas.

Make it a habit to cook on the back burners with the pot-handles turned inwards and out of sight to avoid children reaching up and pulling pots off the stove; this is one of the commonest kitchen accidents. Wipe all spills immediately to prevent slipping, in particular, any oily or fatty spills should be cleaned using a detergent to negate any residual greasiness.

Prepare and plate food close to the stove so as to avoid carrying hot foods and liquids over distance but store food ingredients in a pantry well away from the stove to stop this area being the focus of a child's attention.

Late afternoon is a generally unsettled period for many babies and they are often soothed by being carried during this time. Unfortunately, this 'witching hour' often coincides with preparing dinner but it is imperative that children are not held whilst cooking, even in a sling or baby carrier. There is a very real risk of splatter burns or inadvertent contact with a hotplate or the like and older babies will instinctively reach for objects and may catch parents off-guard. For older children's early dinners, choose dishes which cook rapidly and when possible, pre-prepare ingredients perhaps during baby's nap-time. During the cooking process, place the baby in a swing or a high-chair and try to tune out any crying or grizzling; at the end of a long day it can be tempting to pick them up and soothe them, but the risk is simply not worth it.

Floor-level ovens pose a particular danger to curious children and it is imperative that they have an insulated door. Many current models have in-built door insulation, but for older ovens it will be necessary to install a door-guard to protect children from an overheated glass door.

This insulation should be coupled with an oven door lock which is kept engaged at all times to restrict access. Before opening an oven door, look around to ensure children are not in the vicinity as they may lunge enthusiastically for the pizza on a hot oven tray.

Microwave ovens can be a parent's best friend but they should also be used with extreme care when heating a child's bottle or meal as heat distribution can be uneven creating 'hot spots'. Be sure to stir or shake food and liquid heated this way and test it yourself before giving it to your child. Letting food rest for a few minutes before serving can also allow heat to dissipate.

If the microwave oven is positioned high, be careful not to tip hot contents when lifting containers from the oven as these can spill on children below. Ideally, position the microwave oven so that containers can remain level. Avoid opening microwave containers around curious children as the rush of steam can rapidly burn hands and faces.

Choose a dishwasher with a factory-fitted childproof door lock or alternatively, install an external lock to stop access to knives and other dangerous objects. Large knives should be placed on the top rack of the dishwasher rather than in the cutlery basket on the bottom rack where they are more easily accessed by children. Smaller knives and other sharp utensils should be loaded upside-down in the cutlery rack and the rack removed as soon as the cycle finishes.

Ideally, the dishwasher should be emptied at the completion of a cycle, however this may prove unrealistic, and so as a minimum remove the cutlery rack and any large knives or glassware.

Dishwashing detergent is extremely alkaline and can cause extensive burns to the mouth and gastrointestinal tract if ingested, so fill the detergent dispenser immediately before starting the cycle and do not leave a dishwasher sitting dormant with detergent loaded. Further, keep children away when adding detergent. When emptying a load, check for any leftover or undissolved powder. Choose a dishwasher with a built-in childproof lock, or buy an adhesive lock to ensure it cannot be opened by children; they can be poisoned, climb in and suffocate, or suffer burns if accessing the dishwasher mid-cycle. Any dishwasher powder or tablets should be stored in high, secure cabinets. Look for non-caustic detergents which are becoming increasingly available and which minimise the risk of serious injury if accidentally ingested. White vinegar may be used as a non-toxic alternative to commercial rinsing aids.

Garbage

The humble kitchen bin can harbour all manner of unpleasant surprises which range from the mere unsanitary to the frankly dangerous. Ensure all garbage bins are covered with a lid which can be secured, or install a childproof lid lock to prevent the lid being opened as easily. Better yet, keep the garbage out of sight in a cupboard with a safety latch as this will prevent children from foraging through potentially dangerous trash.

Dispose immediately of any broken glass or poisonous substances to a secured external bin rather than placing them in the kitchen garbage bin to await emptying. Consider wrapping all sharp waste in paper before disposal.

Place recyclables such as glass and opened tins in an off-limits recycling bin immediately after use, and keep these bins out of reach

Laundry

In proportion to the amount of time they are used, the bathroom and laundry are the most dangerous rooms in the house largely due to a combination of water, potential poisons and various appliances. The laundry must be kept off-limits using a gate, lock, high door handle and/or an automatic door closer but should also be adequately childproofed in the event of unrealised access. Any laundry chutes should be kept locked.

Place washing machines and tumble dryers off the floor where possible and have their doors secured with childproof locks;

both have sealed doors which can suffocate a child who climbs in. Even worse, is the possibility of another child activating the appliance with someone inside.

Children should not be allowed to play around the washing machine or dryer especially whilst in use as they may topple in and drown, or stick their hands into a spinning washing machine. In addition, there are some parts of a tumble dryer which become extremely hot during use and can cause extensive burns.

Along this same line, ensure that the household hot water thermostat is set no higher than 50°C, as this minimizes the risk of serious hot water scalds.

Make sure all appliances such as irons are kept unplugged and that their cords are not dangling. If possible, do the ironing when children are asleep to neutralise the risk of them pulling the iron onto themselves or being hit by a falling iron and never leave the iron on and unattended even for a moment. On finishing do not leave the iron to cool on the ironing board, instead wind up the cord and place the iron to the back of a high bench to cool. Fold the ironing board away immediately as children will climb and tip it over.

The laundry is a toxic playground with detergents, solvents and washing powders all posing a serious threat to a curious toddler. Store all potions in the original childproof packaging and place in a secure cupboard high off the ground. Avoid transferring poisonous solutions to old food containers such as jars or plastic bottles, as this not only removes the childproof packaging but can be confusing to children and so increase the risk of ingestion.

Consider switching from hazardous cleaning products such as chorine bleach and lye products to cleaner, greener alternatives such as vinegar or bicarbonate of soda as a glass and surface cleaner. This approach also saves money and 'recipes' for making cleaning solutions are freely available online.

Indoor clothes lines pose a strangulation risk for active children so when in use, make sure that they are at height. When not in use, lines should be retracted or wound up and stored in a childproof cupboard; never leave cords dangling.

Living and Dining Room

THE RECENT POPULARITY OF open-plan living has meant that the traditional living room is now more commonly configured as a living, dining and kitchen 'zone' and as such has become a major focal point within the home. As a busy family hub which figures prominently in a child's day-to-day routine, the modern living/dining area has many roles to fulfil; it is a family area, de facto playroom, entertainment centre and eating zone. As such it must therefore work safely as a multi-function space which accommodates children's play, adult activities, electronic entertainment, meals and at times, visitors. With careful childproofing the living and dining area can be transformed into a safe and useful space for all age groups.

In most homes, the living room is filled with heavy furniture as well as a vast array of ornaments, lamps and other electronics and as a result, most living room accidents involve falls from furniture or being struck by toppling ornaments or lamps. According to the US Consumer Product Safety Commission (CSPC) over 5000 children under the age of 10 attend the emergency room each year with injuries caused by the tipping of TVs, bookcases and other furniture.

It is essential that parents begin the childproofing process by crawling around these rooms on all fours, paying close attention to the position of power points, dangling cords as well as to the contents of shelves, cupboards and table tops. In particular, care must be taken to clear surfaces of choking hazards and frequent checks of the floor and other low surfaces should be performed throughout the day. As a general guide, any object which fits inside a cardboard toilet roll inner is a definite choking hazard, however, however, be aware that larger objects may also pose a threat through the production of smaller components.

Living Room

Furniture

The dining-room table forms the centrepiece of many living rooms and consequently may place a dangerous arrangement of potential hazards within arms reach of a toddler. Apart from the sharp utensils and hot foods associated with meals, the dining table is invariably used as a collecting surface for all manner of miscellaneous objects. The resultant accumulation of small, sharp, toxic or heavy objects may be pulled down by an inquisitive toddler and makes it essential that the table is regularly vetted for such material.

Children must never be left alone with a laden dining table for fear of pulling knives, hot food and drinks down onto themselves. All food and drinks should be placed near the centre of a table and handed to a child once seated.

When setting the table, avoid the use of table-cloths and instead use slip-resistant table mats with rubber backing; a table-cloth will hang tantalisingly over the edge of the table and can be slid easily pulling with it any hot drinks or food.

Adjust seating to ensure that children are placed at the correct height for the table and are not reaching awkwardly for things; this will protect against tipping and spills. Young children still in highchairs should be positioned slightly away from the table to stop them grabbing at objects and to prevent them pushing off from the table and rolling or tipping the chair. High chair castor wheels should be locked and babies must be secured in the seat all times with a five-point harness. Sadly, unsecured toddlers falling from high chairs is a common mechanism of injury within the home and it happens in the blink of an eye, so parents must ensure that harness straps are fastened for even the briefest of snacks. In addition, when not in use dining chairs should be left tucked under the table to deter climbing.

As a general rule, hot drinks should never be drunk around babies or toddlers, especially when they are being carried. If this cannot be avoided, hot coffee and the like should be drunk from an insulated spill proof mug with a screw-on lid and between sips should be placed at the back of high counters or in the centre of high tables.

Living areas are usually rife with sharp-edged coffee or lamp tables which lie at head-height to a toddler. Glass-topped tables are unsuitable for rooms with children at play as they have cut-glass edges and can shatter easily if a toddler falls onto them or climbs on top. The best solution is to store such tables until children are older and replace them with a more child-friendly option such as a wooden table with rounded edges.

Most tables possess sharp edges and corners and these pose a real and present danger to unsteady toddlers who fall frequently and may catch their face or eyes on such borders. There are a number of childproofing options which go some way to countering these edges with many different types of bumpers which aim to cover and pad table edges and/or corners. These usually consist of rubber, soft plastic or fabric, however the Achilles heel of such solutions lies in their adhesives which, if weak, sees the bumper peel away from the table under the constant grabbing of a cruising baby. Another, cheaper option is to use pipe insulators presented as long tubes with a slit along one side which can be contoured to the table edge and secured with a strong adhesive.

A more definitive option is to eliminate sharp, low tables completely from a child's play-space and replace them with an ottoman or round-edged children's table, both of which provide a flat, table-like surface without the sharp edges.

THE SAFETY BUBBLE

Avoid placing such low furniture under windows as they can be used to climb by a curious child with potentially tragic consequences.

The toppling of heavy furniture onto children is a very real risk in the living room and is often initiated by a toddler climbing or reaching for an object and pulling the furniture onto themselves. All furniture which is vulnerable to tipping, such as bookcases or televisions, must be secured. The easiest and cheapest way to achieve this is to bolt pieces to the floor or wall with a simple 'L' bracket available through hardware stores. These brackets can be hidden behind the furniture and should be screwed into wall studs for added stability

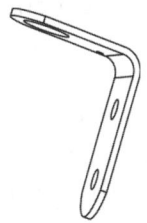

In addition, place heavier items on lower shelves so that the unit is not top heavy. Where possible, store children's toys on reachable shelves to discourage climbing and allocate a lower shelf or drawer as a child's own where they can safely play.

Keep all other drawers closed and locked with childproof latches and store sharp, breakable or poisonous contents out of reach in high cupboards or drawers. Aside from containing potentially hazardous contents, open drawers can also be used as climbing aids or toddler stairs.

Make sure *every* reachable cupboard is secured with childproof latches to stop children exploring. It is remarkable how resourceful babies can become and no typical living room cupboard is completely free of baby hazards; between glassware, cutlery, assorted small objects and the like, it is best to stop the cupboards opening altogether.

Sofas and couches are a popular attraction for children and they should be taught how to safely climb up and down as well as how to sit quietly. Discourage bouncing and climbing on couches as children can become boisterous with disastrous consequences.

Beware of reclining armchairs as they have multiple hinges in their mechanisms which can close on a child's finger, arm or head. It is advisable not to have these chairs around with young children, however, if choosing a recliner ensure it is one that has concealed or guarded hinge points and does not snap shut rapidly. Locate any children before closing the chair as the lure to creep underneath such chairs seems irresistible to them.

Any storage chests or trunks with a heavy lid should be removed from the living space as they can close suddenly onto a child's finger or head. Alternatively, install a slow-closing hinge which prevents slamming of the lid. Heavy trunks without ventilation holes can also cause suffocation if a child climbs inside and should be removed from the house or have ventilation cut-outs placed.

It is essential that flooring within the living space is safe and non-slip. Whilst carpeting has been linked with allergies and asthma, any tiled or wooden surfacing must have a high anti-slip rating. Avoid gloss finishes to tiles and floorboards as these can be treacherous to toddlers and be sure to clean all spills immediately.

Rugs should have an anti-slip backing and should be low profile and without fringing to avoid tripping.

Lamps and Ornaments

Living rooms often set the design tone for the home and so can contain an abundance of intricate decor, some of which will be inappropriate for a childproof space. And while style and childproofing are not mutually exclusive, designing a chic and childproof space does require a different approach.

As an example, expensive artwork and toddlers do not mix, and all such art and ornaments should be kept well out of reach in stable and locked cabinets or in a another room. Small artefacts present a choking risk, whilst larger ornaments may topple and injure a child. Less expensive ornaments should be kept on display and used to teach children about not touching certain things and about handling objects gently.

Table lamps must be placed well out of reach as many of these lamps are heavy and will cause serious injury if pulled over. In addition is the risk of electrocution, or shattered fittings and globes. Ensure that electrical cords are as short as possible, wound up and secured, as dangling cords will be yanked on by curious babies.

Large, heavy pictures should not be hung over children's play areas, and in particular, avoid glass-fronted pictures which will shatter and spray glass should they fall.

Decorative and aromatherapy candles are a current decorating trend but are an unacceptable fire and child hazard regardless of position. Children are attracted to naked flame and will be creative and unrelenting in their efforts to reach fire. Candles should be removed from a room if a child is present. Try light bulb scent diffusers instead.

In addition, poisoning of children by aromatherapy oils is on the rise and many essential oils which are relatively benign if applied topically to skin can cause systemic illness if ingested. A few of the more toxic oils are eucalyptus, camphor, pennyroyal, wintergreen and tansy all of which may be lethal to a child and should never be kept in the home. As a general rule, aromatic plant oils should be stored with medications or cleaning agents; in a locked, high cupboard and should not be used when children are present. For more poisons information see Chapter 10.

Handbags are a hidden living room hazard and represent a veritable microcosm of potential child hazards; from medication and makeup to any number of choking hazards, it is essential that handbags are placed thoughtfully out of reach of children. Children love to explore and unpack these bags and so be particularly vigilant with guests and their bags; great aunt Esme may have medication or breath mints atop her open handbag so make sure it is kept away from floors and low surfaces.

Fireplaces

Many modern homes feature wood-burning or more commonly, gas fireplaces. For some models, instant flame is produced at the flick of a switch making it particularly important that these fireplaces are adequately protected.

As a rule toddlers and older children should be taught to

stay away and that the fireplace is an absolute 'no-go' zone. Ideally fireplaces should not be used when babies or toddlers are loose, but if they are actively burning with children present, adults must not leave the room, or must take the child with them when they leave.

Place a fine-mesh or glass guard or a playpen around the fireplace to restrict access by babies, and when a fire is burning, the guard should be checked regularly to ensure that it remains cool to the touch. Fire guards may tip or move when pushed and may be stabilized by attachment to the walls surrounding the fireplace.

Ashes and coals should not be left in fireplaces as even the next day they can be hot enough to cause burns. Do not assume that empty and unused fireplaces are safe as children may climb and become stuck inside causing suffocation.

Fireplace tools should not be kept by the hearth as they are heavy, sharp and tempting to a mobile baby or toddler. Similarly, fire-starting briquettes, sticks, logs and coal should not be stored at floor height as they can fall on, stick into, or be ingested by, babies and toddlers. Any gas keys should also be removed from the fireplace and where possible, ignition switches should be locked or covered.

Modern, enclosed glass-fronted fireplaces look fabulous and so attract babies and toddlers, but they can also become extremely hot and should be treated with the same caution as an open fireplace.

Alternatives to fireplaces such as floor level radiators and heaters are also dangerous and should not be used around children. Floor radiators with exposed elements and an open grille are lethal and should never be used around children. Even electrically operated heaters can become extremely hot and usually contain a heating element and a fan both of which may be reached by a probing finger.

Options such as central air or hydronic heating are far safer but if radiators or heaters must be used, ensure that they are wall-mounted at a child-proof height and are switched off before leaving the house or going to bed.

Any floor level central

heating ducts must have secure, well-fitted covers which are not easily removed. Metal grill covers can become very hot and a plastic grill guard shielding the duct will help to discourage a curious baby.

Regardless of the type of heating used in a home, clothes should never be hung over a heating source to dry as this poses a significant fire risk. All heat sources must be kept clear of curtains, furniture and other flammable materials, and children should wear clothing and nightwear made from low fire risk materials.

Electricity and Appliances

Abundant electricity requirements mean that the living and dining rooms often possess a relative over-supply of power points. This in turn mandates extra vigilance in the provision of childproof outlet covers and power points containing Residual Current Devices (RCDs). Pay a little extra for power boards with surge protection and don't forget to cover every outlet on these boards with a childproof plug, and to leave empty sockets switched off.

Where possible, these power outlets and power boards should be positioned out of a child's reach and concealed within cupboards, behind furniture or at the back of benches.

All electrical cords should be hidden from a child's view rather than left to dangle tantalisingly. Contain these cords using cord organiser tubes or wind them inside cord spools and for a cheaper option, coil excess cord and secure it with duct tape. Clusters of these cables can then be run along a concealed course at the back of desks, along skirting, or behind furniture and secured using wall clips. Bring these cords through the back of desks or cabinets to appliances rather than having them reach the power outlet by cascading over the edge of a desk or the like.

Where feasible, appliances should not be left on or around floor level, as these are particularly vulnerable to an inquisitive baby. In particular, heavy floor lamps are often tall, relatively narrow based and heavy, making them an unstable beacon to toddlers who can topple them with ease.

Ornamental lamps may be

equally heavy and precariously perched atop small tables where they are often attached to a long cable lying languidly over the edge. If pulled over, the result can be serious head injuries, burns from hot globes, electrocution or lacerations from shattered glass. Place these heavy, expensive lamps in storage for a few years and replace them with light, non-breakable options which are also cheaper to replace should the worst happen. Position the lamps off the floor and out of reach and stow the cords safely.

Similarly, floor-standing fans fascinate children but may be easily pulled over or have fingers poked into the blades and should therefore be avoided. If fans are necessary, they should be wall-mounted, out of reach and have mesh covers. Ceiling fans should not be used on low ceilings and furniture should not be placed directly below the fan as children may climb to reach the rotating blades.

It is important to remember phone cords, as they too may be yanked on and a heavy phone unit pulled down onto a toddler.

Windows, Doors and Stairs

An important component of most rooms is the presence of doors and windows, the safety implications of which are discussed more extensively in Chapter 7. These structures are particularly prominent in the living and dining rooms which often form the centre of a home and so act as gateways to the outside, to stairs or to other rooms such as the kitchen.

Young children love playing with doors and with so much time spent in the living room, it is essential that all doors and windows are rendered safe with restricted access to any dangerous areas beyond.

All doors to the outside as well as other off-limits areas must be kept locked with the keys removed from the door and stored out of reach. Doors which are to be kept unlocked should be fitted with door-stopping devices which fit over a door edge and stop doors closing completely; this will avoid fingers, limbs and heads being caught. These have the advantage of being placed and removed easily as required. In addition, the use of a slow-closing spring will dissipate force and ensure that doors cannot slam, although it does not prevent the door trapping limbs.

An alternative is to remove doors completely from certain rooms and replace them temporarily with childproof gates or barriers. This allows for child containment whilst maintaining the ability to hear and see them from another area, for e.g. the kitchen.

Doorstops should be fitted behind doors to prevent children being trapped or squashed by opening doors. Ensure however, that they are moulded in one piece and do not have separate rubber tips which can be removed and swallowed by inquisitive babies.

Window apertures should not open more than 10cm to restrict a child's access and should have window guards fitted especially if above ground floor level. Flyscreens are not a substitute for window guards and are not designed to withstand the weight of a falling child.

All furniture should be moved away from under windows to prevent children climbing.

Make sure curtain and blind cords do not reach the floor and are wound and stored at height with no dangling ends to be climbed or pulled on. Be especially cautious with looped curtain cords which can cause strangulation or hanging, so tie them well out of reach or if necessary, cut the loop in half to create two single, weighted cords.

Stairs should have safety-endorsed childproof gates at top *and* bottom with mechanisms which can be opened one-handed if carrying a child. Accordion-style safety gates can pinch and trap fingers within their mesh and so are generally not recommended. They are often the cheapest option however, and even an accordion gate is better protection than no gate.

Plants

It is a surprise to many parents that the humble houseplant can turn out to be poisonous to children with most people choosing their houseplants based on aesthetics often without knowing about any poisons risk, but it is a mistake to assume that all common plants are safe plants. In this instance the most effective form of childproofing is knowledge and so it is essential that parents are as educated as possible about the plants growing in their home.

For a more comprehensive look at toxic and safe plants for home and garden see Chapter 10.

Home Office and Computer

COMPUTERS HAVE BECOME such an integral part of modern life that many homes now include some type of home office. For some, this office is a room in its own right, while for others it exists as a small study nook or even a desk within the main living area. But whichever form it takes one thing is constant; this very adult space replete with its many accessories is a serious childproofing challenge.

Between electronics, stationary and cabling, nothing about the home office is naturally child-friendly and thus children should never have unsupervised access. The office is a unique environment within the home and one to which children are naturally attracted given its interesting array of sounds, lights and gadgets. Chief amongst the many dangers for young children are the risks of choking on small objects, electrocution or strangulation from the various electrical devices, cords and power outlets, as well as injury through falls from furniture.

Remember that toddlers love gadgets as much as most adults and can't wait to mimic what they see parents do on the computer or with the shredder, and so it is vital to educate children from an appropriate age about the safe use of various objects.

With so much of our lives now intertwined with computers, childproofing the home office is as much about protecting valuable information and equipment from damage, as it is about keeping children from harm; no one wants their child to find the global delete button on an idle keyboard.

Access

The simplest way to childproof the home office is to and restrict access by ensuring that the doors are kept closed and secured at all times. This may be done physically through the use of a door lock, a childproof door handle cover and/or a high door handle and also through teaching older babies and toddlers that the office is off-limits; after all setting boundaries is an essential part of childproofing.

For some children, having a parent locked in an office is too much to bear and they will scratch and whine at the door endlessly. This is distressing for everyone and usually results in parents abandoning their work in exchange for peace. A possible solution however, is to remove the office door completely and install a childproof gate instead; this allows a child to see in whilst still restricting access. For many children, once they can see their parent they will quite happily be taken elsewhere to play.

Isolating the home office certainly fits the childproofing ideal, but the reality is that from time to time it may be necessary for a child to be within the office space, especially if this space exists as an unsecured zone of the living area or bedroom. It is important, therefore to prepare the space for this eventuality with effective childproofing.

An essential component of this childproofing is proper supervision of children in any home office environment and kids should never be left alone amongst such hazards. If the home office is in use and 'active' and a parent needs to leave the room for any amount of time, the child must also be removed; accidents happen in a moment.

For a child who wants to 'help' in the office, another option is to set up a small desk at which they can work complete with crayons, and an old keyboard or phone with the cords cut off, this will help keep them away from the real thing. Younger babies can be contained for short periods of supervised play within a playpen whilst the office is in use.

Children play on the floor, and so any childproofing should begin with a tour of the office on all fours; it is amazing how many cords, plugs and spilled stationary will be revealed with a crawl about the office.

Choking hazards are a particular concern in an office full of stationary and so regular surveillance of floors and surfaces should be performed for any small objects which may be inhaled by a baby. As a general guide, any object which fits inside a cardboard toilet roll inner is a definite choking hazard, but be mindful of larger objects which may also produce small parts. In addition, there are a number of small, sharp items in an office such as staples and drawing pins which, if ingested, may cause serious internal injury.

Cords and Outlets

Most offices contain an abundance of electrical appliances with a typically haphazard arrangement of cords, cables and power outlets. In general, power points should all be fitted with childproof guards and concealed from view where possible. Rather than having power outlets and power boards immediately next to the desk, position the desk in front of these outlets therefore keeping them hidden. This, in turn will deter babies from probing outlets or pulling on plugs. It is also important to check that power points are installed with Residual Current Devices (RCDs).

Power boards are commonly used to multiply outlet availability and may, as a consequence, also multiply the risk of electrocution to a small child. These boards must be placed out of reach and/or concealed behind furniture and should be secured to the wall or desk. All power boards should be surge protected and when not in use, individual sockets should be left covered with a childproof guard and switched off.

Electrical cords and other cables should be bundled and hidden from a child's view rather than left to dangle. Cabling may then be routed along a concealed course at the back of desks, along skirting, or behind furniture and secured using wall clips. Cables and cords should reach appliances through the back of desks or cabinets rather than being left to cascade over the front of a desk or shelf.

To contain and control cords and cables use a combination of three main techniques; spooled cord protectors which wind excess cords safely inside a cover, cord clips which group cords and hold them along a desired path, or a hollow cord control tube to conceal and control cords.

Extension cord connections which are remote to an electrical outlet should be cocooned by a childproof cover which encloses the connection and protects from direct manipulation of the plug and socket.

Appliances and Stationery

Stationery appeals to all ages, and to a curious child, opening a desk drawer full of bright, colourful stationery is akin to opening a treasure chest. Lock all stationery including staples, drawing pins and paper-clips in a drawer or high cupboard installed with a childproof lock. These items are choking hazards if inhaled and if swallowed, any sharp edges may damage or perforate the gut.

Store all pens, inks, markers, Textas and glues out of reach to avoid ingestion or office redecoration and in particular, all sharpened pencils must be locked away.

Small appliances such as faxes, photocopiers and the like should be kept in locked cabinets or at the back of desks where children cannot reach to randomly press buttons, open covers or play with plugs.

Of more immediate danger are devices such as shredders and electric pencil sharpeners which can cause untold injury to limbs or worse, should hair become entangled. Such appliances should not be stored on the floor and when not in immediate use, should be left unplugged and not merely switched off.

Furniture

Office furniture is frequently bulky and heavy as well as being heavily laden with potentially dangerous objects. To prevent tipping if climbed upon, all free-standing furniture such as bookshelves, desks and filing cabinets should be secured to the floor or wall-studs using a simple 'L' bracket.

Avoid making bookshelves top-heavy by storing heavier items on the lower shelves, with the highest shelves being reserved for valuable or breakable items. Pack books tightly on bookshelves to avoid having them emptied onto the floor. Another idea is to reserve a low shelf or drawer for child-safe items or toys which may be reached by a toddler without the need for climbing.

Use lockable filing cabinets and keep them closed and locked as these heavy drawers can crush little fingers. Open drawers may also be used as a toddler's staircase. In addition, these cabinets and drawers usually contain important documentation which, if not secure, may be damaged or lost, after all a 2 year old cannot distinguish a piece of scrap paper from a marriage certificate.

Another option is to enclose filing cabinets and drawers within a built-in closet where the closet doors are kept closed. However, any appliances, shelves or cabinets which cannot be well-secured or hidden may be fenced off behind a playpen or childproof gate.

Use corner protectors to soften any desk or cabinet corners as these are often at the same height as a toddler's head and secure all drawers and cupboards with simple childproof latches which are kept engaged.

Lock swivel/swing chairs into a desired configuration to stop babies being injured if attempting to pull up or to climb on them. The rapid spinning or tipping of such chairs can hit a toddler in the head or push them to the ground with significant force. Similarly, adjustable height or incline office chairs should be locked into a neutral position.

Attend to office waste and recycling bins and store them within childproof cupboards or well off the floor. Buy bins with tightly-fitted lids and dispose of any sharp or poisonous waste directly into outside bins.

Computer

Computers form the centre of most home offices and for many

older children they have also become a core educational (and social), tool. But for babies and toddlers not yet computer literate, there are multiple reasons to childproof the family computer; it protects children from physical harm, but it can also protect them from content which is inappropriate for their age and developmental stage. Thorough computer childproofing also goes a long way in protecting this valuable equipment from damage.

Hardware
Do not allow children to bring food or drink into the office, as this rule will neutralise any risk of spillage and possible damage to the computer hardware.

As a general rule, young children should only be able to reach and use computers with adult assistance, thus the childproofing of computers becomes largely about limiting access.

Pushing monitors to the back of the desk will prevent young children reaching them easily. Modern LCD monitors are bigger and thinner than ever are consequently are not as balanced as the older, bulkier screens. This means that they topple easily if pulled on and so must be fixed securely to the desk or the wall behind using safety straps or screws.

Floor-based equipment such as servers are a real temptation to children and should be stored in cupboards or up high where possible. An alternative is to use childproof gates or playpens to seal off these items. Computer tower guards are available to cover the façade of most servers and can prevent little hands from opening the CD drive and turning the power on or off. A cheaper alternative is a home-made guard, using adhesive Velcro and a card or cloth covering the front of the hard drive, CD drive and power button. In addition, a simple piece of duct tape over the power button can protect it from little fingers.

When not in use, store keyboards in a roll-away drawer, on top of the monitor or by hanging them using an adhesive hook on the wall behind the monitor. Never leave an optic mouse unattended as the laser light can be damaging if pointed directly into eyes.

Cables and power cords are a constant threat and temptation to children who may pull attached objects onto themselves, may electrocute themselves or may become entangled and risk suffocation. Where possible, go wireless when using the computer around children; run on battery using a wireless mouse, wireless internet access and a wireless keyboard.

Where cables and cords are necessary, check that they are properly plugged in and in good condition with no exposed wiring or breaks in the coating and teach children not to touch or unplug cables.

Software

There are a number of software downloads, many of them free, which will render a computer relatively childproof. Most are based on the use of passwords and screen lockouts as a means of neutralising a toddler attack.

Begin with the simplest measures such as liberal use of the computer's lockout codes and passwords to stop children activating the computer screen. For example, initiate a screensaver password to stop a child accessing the desktop. Another simple habit is to use win + L to lock the screen when leaving the computer temporarily.

Most importantly, back up, back up, and back up! Frequent back up of computer files and software to an external memory source will ensure that nothing is lost forever if a wayward finger presses the wrong button.

Another alternative is to download free keyboard-childproofing software which uses a password to prevent children from accessing files and programs. Software is also available to hide the desktop and all windows from view and to provide instead a child-friendly toolbar which lists only selected programs for children to access.

Education is a key part of computer childproofing as even young children will soon find ways to circumvent many of the lockouts and filters installed by parents. Therefore, it is important to teach children respect for the computer by giving them supervised access to appropriate programs and showing them the correct way to handle and care for the equipment.

The internet has become an integral part of life and from schooling to socialising children have access to a greater mass of unfiltered information than ever before. The challenge for parents is to know how best to protect their children from age-inappropriate material.

Parents' Bedroom

On any typical Sunday morning in homes around Australia there are usually 3 or 4 in the bed with the little one loudly saying more than just 'roll over'. Most children delight in climbing or bouncing all over their parent's bedroom with most accidents therefore involving falls from the bed or other furniture.

Children seem to find being in this room comforting and will often hang out while a parent dresses or showers. This makes the parental bedroom an interesting hybrid; existing as both an adult zone and as a children's space. It is an interesting challenge, therefore, to create a childproof room which also functions as an adult zone, without relegating the parental bedroom to a featureless safe-box.

Access to parental bedrooms should be limited through the use of childproof latches, handle covers or locks and children should only be in the room in the company of an adult. At all other times, this room should be secured.

Floors and Surfaces

As with all rooms, the first childproofing survey of the bedroom should be taken from the floor. By crawling around the room on all fours as a baby does, previously hidden hazards will be revealed from under furniture or in dark corners.

Be particularly alert for choking hazards such as jewellery, hairpins and coins. As a general guide, any object which fits inside a cardboard toilet roll inner is a definite choking hazard however, larger objects may also have small components which can break loose.

As the bedroom is primarily an adult area, the low surfaces and floors will inevitably fill with possible choking hazards therefore constant vigilance and regular clearing of such surfaces is required.

All power points should all be fitted with childproof guards and concealed behind furniture where possible. Power boards must not be left idly on the floor but should be concealed and secured on walls or behind furniture. All sockets should be guarded and the board should be surge protected.

Curtain cords are a strangulation risk and should be shortened if possible, wound up off the floor and stored out of reach. Looped curtain cords pose a particular threat of hanging and must be divided into two single cords, weighted at each end and then wound out of reach.

Chairs and tables must not be positioned under windows as they can be used for climbing, and window guards should be fitted to all windows, especially those above ground level. Flyscreens are not a substitute for window guards and are simply not designed to take the weight of a child.

Bedside Tables

Bedside tables can be a childproofing nightmare; they are low, easily accessible and are often filled with a treacherous collection of items; from electronics and lamps to jewellery, coins and pens. Stow all small items or valuable ornaments on high surfaces, for example on the top of a tallboy, or in secure drawers.

Ensure the drawers of the bedside table are secured with a childproof latch and in particular, do not contain any medications or sharp objects. Move any perfume, lotions, essential oils or medications to a high, locked bathroom cabinet to prevent ingestion and poisoning.

Never burn candles when children are in the room and do not leave matches or a lighter exposed. Instead of aromatherapy candles, use light bulb diffusers instead.

Bedside lamps are a particular source of entertainment for toddlers as they love flicking them on and off, consequently, children will reach and pull on any dangling cords. This in turn may topple and break a heavy or fragile lamp so replace any heavy, tall, and narrow-based or glass bedside lamps for smaller, lightweight unbreakable options. Lamps which affix to headboards are a useful option. Consider lamps which fully enclose the light bulb as this will minimise the risk of burns from touching a hot bulb.

Contain and conceal any electrical cords or power boards behind the bedside table.

Beds

An adult bed poses several risks to an infant especially from a soft mattress or bulky bedding all of which can cause smothering and suffocation. This is particularly true if it is a waterbed and these are completely unsuitable for babies. Consider switching to a firm mattress and pillow as well as tucking bedding securely to minimise movement.

Babies should never be left to nap, or left unsupervised in an adult bed as they may roll off the bed, or end up face down and unable to right themselves, or may even pull bedding over themselves.

Children just adore jumping on mum and dad's bed which superficially may seem like innocent fun. Bouncing on the bed however, not only risks violent falls especially with multiple children playing at once, but also sends the message that the bed is a playground. A simple game of bouncing on the bed may lead to serious head injury or fractures and should never be encouraged.

Co-sleeping

Co-sleeping, when babies and children sleep with their parents, is a controversial subject with some safety organisations recommending against it for children under 2 years old. This has not, however, stopped co-sleeping being embraced by many parents. Whatever your opinion of co-sleeping there are a number of safety recommendations which can be implemented to minimise risk to an infant.

Co-sleeping should never be undertaken if either parent has had any alcohol or drugs as this can impair their awareness of the infant and lead them to roll on top of the infant, to cover them with bed covers or to wedge the baby between wall and mattress; all of which may lead to suffocation. Parents who sleep particularly soundly and do not wake readily to noise should reconsider the use of co-sleeping.

Mattresses should be firm and flat with no depressions into which a baby may roll and bedding must be tucked securely to minimise movement over the baby's face.

Babies may roll during the night and either fall off the bed or wedge themselves between the bed and a wall. Use infant guardrails made of mesh to prevent baby rolling off and check nightly to ensure there is no gap between the bed and wall where a baby may become lodged. Similarly, check that there are no gaps between the mattress and any head or footboard.

Use common sense to assess whether there is enough room in the bed to safely sleep everyone and do not allow pets to sleep on the bed with the baby. Excess weight has been shown to add to the risk of co-sleeping as babies will roll into a larger depression in the mattress and potentially suffocate.

Babies should be dressed appropriately and not allowed to overheat as this will add to the risk of SIDS.

Wardrobes and Drawers

Children love to hide in wardrobes which may lead to trapping and suffocation. All wardrobes should be kept closed with childproof latches on the doors and if the robe is also free-standing they must be secured to the wall stud using an 'L' bracket to prevent toppling if pulled on.

Similarly any chest of drawers, bureaus or tallboy dressers should also be bolted to the wall. Consider childproof latches on the chest of drawers to prevent toddlers climbing up the open drawers.

Coat hangers invariably seem to find their way onto the floor and parents should be careful to place them back onto hanging racks immediately after use.

Be wary about using moth balls, insect strips and the like inside the wardrobe; the smell will attract children who may place these items in their mouth risking choking or poisoning.

The copious plastic wrap over returned dry-cleaning should be removed before replacing it into the wardrobe as it attracts a child's attention. These sheets are large and sticky which may cause a child to become entangled and suffocate. Place a knot in the plastic to prevent children from placing it over their heads and dispose of the plastic immediately in a secure bin.

Ensuite

Many master bedrooms now have an ensuite attached which must be treated with the same caution as any other household bathroom. Fit a childproof latch to the door to ensure that children do not have free access to the ensuite and childproof the remainder of the bathroom as detailed in Chapter 2.

Windows, Doors and Stairs

Most modern homes are blessed with an abundance of windows and doors all of which pose a number of serious threats to young children if not properly guarded or secured. Most accidents involving doors and windows involve falling from height or digital crush injuries.

Windows, doors and stairs are also portals which, if not secured, can give babies and children undesirable access to other rooms or to the outside. The key to effective childproofing of such home infrastructure is to choose simple, easy-to-use childproof methods and to stay consistent throughout the house.

As always, the basis of any childproofing lies in adequate child supervision, as well as preparing the home for those unforseen, unsupervised moments. Children should never be left alone near open windows or unguarded stairs.

Windows

Increasing urbanisation has meant that living spaces are moving upwards, with more high-rise living and more multi-storey homes. Add to that, the modern design aesthetic for light-bathed rooms and we are faced with homes filled with enticingly large windows.

These windows may breathe light into a home, but they are also a very real lure to children

THE SAFETY BUBBLE

and so a challenge for parents. The main risk of windows leading to the outside, and in particular of those above the first floor, is the potential for children to fall out. In addition, opening and closing of doors and windows may lead to finger or limb trapping and amputation. Rarely, a small child may be caught in a heavy window by the torso or head, risking suffocation or head injury.

So serious is this issue becoming in large cities, that the New York City Board of Health adopted legislation requiring owners of multistorey buildings to provide proper window guards for all dwellings where children under the age of 10 years reside. The pilot programme resulted in a 35% reduction in deaths attributable to falls from windows and a 50% reduction in incidents, with no child falling from a window that had a window-guard fitted.

Window guards are of steel construction and have bars across the windows which are spaced less than 10cm apart to prevent young children squeezing through. They are mounted over the window and are designed to

resist the weight of a falling child. This allows parents to safely leave windows open for ventilation as desired. Window guards should also be fitted with an emergency release button which may be activated by adults in the unlikely event that the house must be rapidly evacuated.

More recently available in Australia, is a polyethylene netting system, long used in South America to secure high-rise windows and balconies. The clear netting can withstand 500kg per square metre, is quick to install and does not interfere with views. There have been reported problems with strata management bodies in some buildings worried about the aesthetics of such nets and all tenants of such buildings should seek advice.

Many people make the dangerous assumption that flyscreens fitted over a window will suffice in protecting children from falling. This is completely erroneous as flyscreens were never designed to withstand the weight of a child and there are a growing number of cases where children have fallen through flyscreens and out of the window leading to serious injury or even death.

Window guards may not be as aesthetically appealing as transparent flyscreens, but their use is temporary and they can be easily removed as children grow; it seems a small price to pay to keep children from toppling out of the window.

There is detailed building legislation governing the type of glass to be installed at various heights and locations, but as a general childproofing rule, windows likely to be subjected to human impact should be fitted with toughened safety glass. This glass resists breaking, but if broken does not produce long shards of glass, but breaks into many small pebbles.

Older single-paned glass shatters easily but a less-expensive alternative to replacing non-safety glass is to apply a transparent safety film. These products are available from glass retailers and hardware stores and while they will not stop the glass from breaking, they will keep it from shattering into jagged shards. Ensure that the film meets the Australian Standards specification AS/NZS 2208 which will bring the glass rating up to the required level.

Unguarded windows and doors, including sliding doors to outside areas should be secured with childproof locks and the keys should not be stored in the lock but secured in a childproof box, cupboard or drawer. However, equally given recent occurrences of children being trapped during fires, the keys to designated emergency exits should be easily accessible to adults in case of an urgent evacuation.

Alternatively, windows may be fitted with a childproof latch with an emergency quick-release mechanism.

Another simple way to secure windows is to limit the opening aperture to less than 10 centimetres, either through window design or through the retro-fitting of approved devices. The so-called 'tilt and lock' mechanisms are excellent for this purpose as they allow the window to be tilted vertically to form a limited opening at the top, and can then be locked in this position. The opening slit should not allow anyone to squeeze through.

Sash windows should open from the top rather than from the bottom and any winding windows should be limited by removing the winding crank from the window and storing for adult use.

As a general precaution, chairs and other furniture should be removed from under windows to prevent children climbing. Any tempting objects that children love to swing around or throw, such as golf clubs or baseball bats should also be stored away from windows.

Windows should not be covered by heavy drapes which reach the floor and may be climbed but should have window coverings that reflect and fit the window size. If drapes are particularly thick and heavy, children may wind themselves up and become trapped, risking suffocation. Install blinds or curtains so that a loose cord cannot form a loop over 220mm long at a height under 1600mm from the floor.

In addition, ensure that all curtain and blind cords are wound up and stowed over 1600mm from the floor and out of reach. There are some simple cord-winding spools available, or the cord may simply be tied out of the way. Be especially cautious with looped curtain cords which can cause strangulation or hanging. These loops may be cut in half, weighted on the ends and then stowed out of reach.

Doors

Doors are a double jeopardy to children as they can be inherently dangerous in the form of entrapment, but may also function as an entrance to an unsafe environment. Childproofing, therefore must involve both securing the door mechanism as well as the consideration of what lies beyond.

Heavy doors should be mounted with spring-loaded, slow-closing devices to avoid slamming. While many doors are manufactured with this equipment, it is not difficult to install them later.

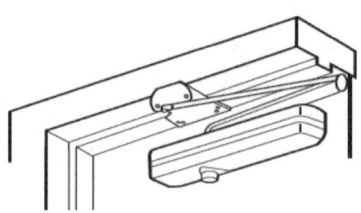

Various door-stopping devices are available to place at the top or on the side edge of the door, providing a buffer to stop the door closing completely. Another, more temporary solution is to hang a rolled-up towel over the top of the door. The disadvantage of these stops is that the door cannot be closed until they are removed which means that they must be taken off to secure a room on leaving.

Floor-level door stops which prevent the door hitting the wall behind are often constructed from a spring capped with an easily-removed rubber tip. This small rubber tip is a choking

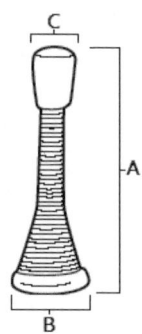

risk and must be removed from the door-stops. A better option is to install moulded one-piece doorstops.

Doors are themselves an effective childproofing tool and can be used to restrict access to hazardous areas. The use of locks, childproof latches and high door handles are useful ways to control door access.

Doorknob covers may be installed to prevent a child opening a closed door. Lever-type door handles are harder to childproof although there are a number of purpose designed latches available. A cheaper option is to simply fit door knobs and handles out of reach.

As a rule, any doors to the outside, including sliding doors must be secured with childproof locks. Any door keys should be removed from the lock and stored securely close to emergency exits but out of reach of children.

Glass doors are a popular part of many homes, but can also be source of great confusion to young children, and to many they are completely invisible. A disturbing number of children are seriously injured each year by running into, or through, glass doors. All glass doors must be made of toughened safety glass and have decorative markers placed at child height alerting them to a closed door.

If present, all cat and dog flaps should be sealed shut or completely removed from the door, as they are not only portals to the outside but children may also get their head or chest stuck, causing suffocation.

Stairs

Stairs seem universally adored by children as they climb up and down with endless amusement, and so it is crucial part of home childproofing to make sure that all stairs are rendered safe.

Stairways should always be kept clear of tripping hazards such as loose carpeting or toys and should also be well lit, or instead be fitted with wall-mounted night lights along the staircase.

Properly secured safety gates should be installed at the *top and bottom* of all stairs and should not be taken down until children are old enough to reach hand railings. Stair gates should be made of solid, durable materials such as steel or heavy duty plastic with softer gate materials such as a fine mesh are not suitable.

There are childproof gates which screw directly into the wall (hardware mounted) and there are others which use a spring-loaded horizontal banner to secure the gate between two points (pressure mounted). These sprung gates are not suitable for use as stair gates as they are vulnerable to collapse if leant on by a child. It is essential, therefore, that gates guarding stairs are secured directly into the wall (hardware mounted), after all, plaster can be patched much easier than a child.

Folding accordion-style safety gates with collapsible lattice can be finger traps and so are generally not recommended. They are however, often the cheapest gate option and so if it is a choice between an accordion gate and no gate, then any gate is better.

Stair railings and balustrades should be at least 90cms high and should reach the entire length of the stairs. Parallel, lower handrails may be installed under the full-size railings to better suit children. Make a strict house rule to outlaw sliding down the banister.

If staircase balustrades are greater than 10cms apart then your child's head or body may fit through and risk becoming caught, or worse, risk the child falling through completely. Entrapment of a child's head, neck or chest may also cause suffocation. If the balustrades of an established staircase are too far apart, a clear Perspex guard should be installed to cover the balustrades and eliminate dangerous gaps, this will also prevent children throwing objects through the balustrades onto unsuspecting siblings below! All glass balustrades must be manufactured from toughened safety glass.

The combination of wooden stairs and socks risks slipping and serious injury, and so to avoid this all wooden stairs should have rubber grips or 'nosings' installed at the leading edge. Carpeted stairs are safer, but make sure they have no raised metal edges which may cause tripping. Be aware that spiral staircases are more difficult for young children to navigate, so ensure that they hold the handrails and take their time.

As children become more mobile, they should be taught how to climb and descend stairs; for crawlers this means coming down the stairs backwards, while for walkers, they should be taught to walk slowly and to use the handrails.

Dogs and Cats

MANY COUPLES HAVE FURRY children long before they consider having the human kind and the transition to becoming a blended family may be tricky if not considered in advance. Dogs and cats get used to being the centre of the household, and like any older sibling, they may not appreciate being deposed by the newer, cuter baby.

Every pet will react differently to the introduction of children into the household and many parents do not adequately prepare their dog or cat for the change because they are so 'gentle' or they 'wouldn't hurt a fly'. This is a dangerous assumption as pet personalities may change if they perceive a threat to their world, and many a child has been hurt by a pet that had unrealistic and unfair expectations placed upon their behaviour. Given the right set of circumstances any dog can bite and it is essential to create a safe environment for both pet and baby.

Childproofing your pet and pet-proofing your child involves three key points; preparation of home and pet, education of both child and pet and supervision of any child less than seven years old when in the room with an animal.

Dogs

In Australia each year, over 10,000 dog bites need hospital attention with over three quarters of dog bites occurring in children under five. The height of a toddler means that approximately 80 percent of bites are to a child's face.

Most dog attacks take place either at home or at the homes of neighbours or friends and by a dog that is known to the child. Further, dog bites are far more likely to occur on a dog's home turf than out in the street.

Modern dogs enjoy a position within households which has evolved from the backyard kennel to the master bedroom. With this transition has come a humanisation of dogs with owners attributing their dogs with emotions and so treating them like a human child.

While this may work well for some families, in those families with new babies or young children, this humanising of dogs can lead to a loss of dominance for the human family members. This in turn may lead to dangerous dog behaviour to any child or baby they see as weaker than them.

So while suddenly kicking the dog out of the house to make way for baby is not appropriate, it is important to take steps to educate both dog and child about their relative places within the family.

Reasons Dogs Bite

There is so much dicusssion between dog owners and some experts as to whether dogs feel jealous of a new baby or child. It is likely that they can certainly feel displaced which may lead to conflict. There are three main reasons why dogs bite.

1. Misunderstood communication

Commonly, incidents may stem from the baby using something that the dog wants or usually has; such as a favourite chair. The dog may attempt to communicate his displeasure to baby as he would another dog (see warning signs below). When this fails to work, the dog will give a little snap as a warning, or to see baby off. To another dog, this snap would be the equivalent to a light slap, but to a baby with soft skin it can mean a significant injury.

It is also important to understand the basics of how dogs relate and communicate to each other as not understanding the pack ways and language of dogs and assuming they think and behave as humans can lead to dangerous miscommunications. For example, something as simple as staring at a dog may spark an unanticipated outburst.

2. Defensive reaction

The time when a baby becomes mobile coincides with a peak in their curiosity and a need to explore their environment. This often leads to a fascination with the family dog and a mobile baby may seek out the dog repeatedly.

If baby is doing something that the dog doesn't like or is scared by; for example being cornered by a toddler or having their tail repeatedly pulled, they will react defensively. The dog will give body language warnings that mean: 'Don't poke me in the eye' or 'Don't pull my tail' but if the baby ignores these signs, the dog may lash out.

3. Hunting instinct

In some situations, dogs can see a small baby as prey; a baby squeaks and gurgles, waves its arms around and stares with big eyes, all of which can trigger the hunting instinct in dogs, causing them to harm the baby. This reaction is more common in some of the hunting breeds and in dogs such as terriers.

Dogs May Bite When:
- approached while eating
- startled by sudden movements
- awoken suddenly
- cooped up in a car
- cornered
- stared at from close range
- jumped on
- climbed on
- tugged or poked at
- Looking after puppies.

Behavioural Warning Signs

Very few dogs bite without warning and children should be taught the warning signs dogs give when they are unhappy. This can allow them to back off and avoid the dog lashing out. Some of the commonest signs are:
- ears back
- body tense
- tail up (not wagging)
- growling
- backing away
- staring
- bearing teeth
- hackles up

Guidelines for Parents

General Guidelines

Many people put an unfair expectation on the family dog

to 'be nice' and to tolerate anything a baby/toddler may dish out which undoubtedly is unfair and unrealistic. Both children and dogs must be educated from a young age not only to respect each other, but also how to behave around each other.

Dogs are pack animals and pecking order within that pack, aka your family, must be established early to set the groundwork for pet safety. Parents must work with the dog and child to clearly establish the dominance of a child. In addition, all puppies and dogs should be obedience trained and socialised from an early age and where possible children should be involved in this training

If pregnant, start preparing the family dog for a baby early on with behaviour modification and training and establish any boundary changes as soon as possible. It is best to keep dogs out of the nursery and young children's bedrooms completely, and these areas should be well-established as 'no-go' zones prior to delivery.

How children perceive and interact with dogs depends on their age and developmental age. For instance, a toddler may see a dog as a plaything, whereas a baby will see them the same as a stuffed toy. In general, children younger than seven years are not developmentally equipped to make the complex judgements required to safely interact with a dog.

Supervision of babies and pets must be constant, and when this is not possible the two should be separated by physical barriers such as child safety gates or closed doors. If in a single room, playpens can be an effective way of separating dog and child temporarily.

When supervising young children with dogs, standing in the kitchen and keeping an eye on dogs and children from 10 metres away is not enough. The interaction must have your undivided attention and you should stay within arms length of the dog so as to be able to intervene quickly if required. Young babies should have limited contact in short bursts and it is important to positively reinforce good dog behaviour with rewards.

If choosing a new family dog, research breeds which are appropriate to your needs and are recommended as family dogs. (See section below).

Behavioural Training

Dogs must not be treated like human children and this differentiation must be made clear to both the dog and the child. Dogs have different needs to children and live by a pack hierarchy. The family becomes the dog's pack and all humans must establish themselves, children included, as more dominant members of the pack, otherwise the dog will assume leadership and run the pack with behaviours which may put children in particular, at risk. Dogs must always take a submissive role when playing with children.

Set house rules (such as no jumping up on people, no sleeping on beds etc.) and involve children in making these rules. All family members must know and enforce the rules at all times, as any inconsistency from person to person will only confuse the dog.

Dogs should be taught the rules by firmly but gently disciplining him for breaking them and generously rewarding appropriate behaviour with praise, patting, food rewards or a favourite toy.

Accordingly, be quick to stop any bad behaviour as letting it slide even once or twice sends dangerous mixed messages about who is in charge.

Other behaviours which may be used to establish dominance are to greet the dog last and always after the children on arriving home. Feed the dog after the family and children have eaten as this mimics pack behaviour where the dominant dogs eat first; do not allow the children to feed the dog from the table.

Part of establishing leadership may be done by taking your dog to obedience school or having a dog trainer work with you at home. It is essential that dogs are safely and easily controlled around children. Older children can become involved in the training so as to learn how to establish control with firm commands and rewards for good behaviour.

It is important to note that the techniques used to train a puppy and those for training an older dog are quite different and in particular, the methods used for puppy training should not be applied to older dogs as they may lead to biting.

Build positive associations for the dog by rewarding him (i.e. doggy treats) when the children are in the room. Sending him away or yelling at him every time the children are around will only foster negative associations. Bear in mind that the excessive noise of children can unsettle and even distress a dog who is not used to it. Even before a baby arrives, dogs can be acclimatised to loud noises with the use of food rewards to reinforce a positive association.

If your dog is taught, encouraged or bred to be a guard dog, there is no room for training; keep it away from children.

What to Teach Your Dog

No dog is completely childproof and no amount of training will make him so. Every dog has its breaking point if treated inappropriately and it is unfair to expect the family dog to tolerate unlimited provocations. Parents should be mindful of protecting a dog from a curious and playful child as much as they are protecting a child from the dog.

Many dogs and cats are afraid of children and will run away from them and this fear may undermine an interaction and lead to dangerous and defensive behaviour. Patient and calm familiarisation is the key to building confidence and obliterating fear between dog and child.

Whilst a detailed guide to dog-training is outside the scope of this book, there are a few basic guidelines which will encourage pet safety. Much of the training and behavioural guidelines can and should be enforced during pregnancy so as not to associate sudden discipline with the arrival of a baby.

Dogs must never be allowed to jump up on anyone, especially children. Not only can this injure a small child, but it also asserts a dog's dominance over the child. Similarly, rough-housing, and allowing dogs to roll around with children or place their teeth around arms or legs is unacceptable and can easily spiral out of control. Dogs may see a young child as a littermate and so rough house as he would a sibling, children must be established as clearly dominant to the dog to avoid such confusion.

Once a baby becomes mobile

this may awaken predatory behaviour in dogs that was not present when the baby had to be carried from place to place. Practice keeping the dog in the sit/stay position next to you while the baby moves about and reward him calmly and generously.

Dogs may be gradually desensitised to the idiosyncratic physical handling they may receive from young children by gently grabbing their ears or their tail and then praising them and rewarding them for their tolerance. When he accepts this level of stimulation happily, grab more quickly and firmly, but never harshly. Soon your dog will associate this type of grabbing with positive feedback.

In general, hugging between child and dog is not a good idea but, just in case, prepare your dog. While your dog is relaxed, give a quick, gentle hug then release and reward.

If at any time a dog growls, stiffens or bites during training then stop and find a qualified dog trainer. If not performed correctly, training techniques can be mis-interpreted by dogs and lead to worsening of behaviour.

Puppies

All puppies should be taken to formal obedience and socialisation classes from an early stage to establish acceptable behaviour. Puppies must learn about their new pack, and their place in it and they must grow up understanding that children are not littermates but are dominant to them.

Dominance can be established by gently pushing a puppy to the ground and by feeding them after the children have eaten as would happen in the pack. When feeding a puppy, stroke their face and head as this helps to avoid them becoming food-aggressive.

Puppies should always be submissive in their play with children and must not jump up or nip them. Rough house play is normal between littermates but must not be allowed between children and dogs; what begins as seemingly harmless fun can turn to disaster in the space of a few seconds and allowing this type of play sends the wrong message to both child and dog.

Puppies should be desensitised to physical stimulus

by gently and quietly tugging at ears, tails and legs and rewarding them with treats to establish positive associations but if a puppy does do something wrong make a deep, growling sound to establish disapproval from a pack leader. Rules and rewards must be reinforced constantly and must also be consistent across all family members, mixed messages will confuse a puppy and may lead to erratic behaviour.

It is best to perform training sessions out of sight of young children as they may not understand the context of your actions and may try to imitate you.

What to Teach Your Child

Toddlers and infants are too young to learn detailed rules for pet interaction and so at this young age, separation is still the best strategy. But it is never too soon to begin teaching children the difference between pets and toys and that animals can feel pain and fear and should be treated with gentle respect.

Avoid scolding children for inappropriate treatment of pets, but instead teach them an alternative behaviour for interaction. Children will primarily watch and model others' behaviours and so leading by example is a very effective strategy.

Children will take more chances with dogs they know, consequently, most children are bitten by dogs they know and on the dog's home turf. Children must understand that the family dog, no matter how placid and non-threatening, should still be treated with the same gentle respect as other dogs.

It can be fine balance to have children respect dogs without instilling a fear of them, but it is important that kids understand the difference as fear will only make children more likely to behave in ways which endanger them. Instead they must be given the knowledge and the confidence to interact safely with dogs.

Children must first be taught to avoid the behaviours which may put them at risk. Toddlers cannot understand the difference between a dog and their other toys, and are unaware that they may cause pain by pulling, biting or jumping on dogs, or that chasing a dog unrelentingly will eventually result in the dog objecting.

It is not enough to simply chide a toddler for pulling the dog's tail, they must instead be given alternatives and should be shown how to interact appropriately with dogs. Firstly, children should be taught to be calm, confident and gently dominant whenever they are around a dog, so if, for example, a dog jumps on them or nips at them, they should be taught to say a firm 'no' and to push or poke it away whilst moving to an adult for help.

Babies should always be taught to play calmly with dogs without the rough physical contact which may encourage aggression from a dog. Rough play such as tug-o-war or wrestling, can quickly become dangerous and result in serious injury to a small child. Instead use more appropriate games with the dog such as 'fetch'.

Guidelines for Children

- If you see a dog you don't know and he's with someone, ask if it's okay to pat the dog. If the answer is yes, then approach the dog calmly and quietly.
- Never approach or pat a dog on it's own without an owner, even if it looks friendly.
- Before patting, always let a dog sniff your open hand.
- Never reach suddenly over a dog's head without letting her sniff it may frighten the dog.
- Don't tease dogs, even if they are tied or inside a fence or car. Teasing is mean. Besides, the dog could get loose and bite you.
- Don't shout at dogs and don't pretend to bark or growl at them, even the family dog.
- Dogs don't like it if you pull their tail, grab their fur or try to sit on them.
- Don't hug a dog.
- Do not place your head or face next to or at the same level as the dogs.
- Pat a dog gently on the back, not on the head or the nose.
- Don't grab food, toys, bones, or other things away from a dog.
- Don't approach an eating dog.
- Don't wake a sleeping dog suddenly.
- Don't go near a mother dog looking after puppies.
- Never stare at a dog's eyes, especially if you don't know the dog, they see this as a sign of aggression.

- Never run away from a dog screaming—it'll most likely give chase.
- If a dog barks, growls, or shows you her teeth, puts her ears back against her neck, and walks on stiff legs with her hair sticking out, she's telling you she's angry and she'll bite if you come closer. If you see a dog acting like that, look away from the dog's face and walk very slowly sideways until the dog relaxes or you're out of sight.
- If a dog comes close to you, 'be a tree'—stay still, look at the ground and cross your arms with your hands on your shoulders.
- If a dog attacks or knocks you over, 'be a ball'—curl up on the ground on your knees with your face tucked onto your legs and your arms around your head. Lie still and don't scream.
- If you get bitten, tell an adult right away. Try to remember where you were when you got bitten, where the dog lives if you know or which way he went if he was loose, who else was around when he bit you, and what the dog looked like.
- If you see a dogfight, don't try to break it up! Stay away from the dogs, and find an adult to help.

Outside the Home

Children cannot be allowed to walk the family dog alone in the street until they are both physically able to control the dog and cognitively able to understand its behaviours. This will vary depending on dog size and child maturity but in general, the necessary strength and judgement will not be present until the early to mid-teens.

When visiting other people's homes where dogs are present, it is important to locate the dog on arrival and to ask friends and relatives to keep their dogs away from your children. You may be very comfortable around your friends but you have no way of knowing their dogs' level of comfort with children. Most people with children will understand the request, or will already have secured the dog before you arrived.

Similarly, if children are visiting your home, confine your dog in another room or outside, away from the crowd. When large groups socialise, there is usually too much noise and chaos for proper supervision of any dog-child interactions and many dogs will be overwhelmed by so many children. Further, the visiting children may not be familiar with dogs or how they should behave.

Do not hesitate to call the local animal control if there is a dog loose in the street, especially if it threatens you or your child. Loose dogs are a potential threat to local children and they should be taught never to approach a dog without an owner nearby.

Hygiene

It is essential that all dogs are de-fleaed, de-wormed and fully vaccinated. Transmission of disease from dog to human is unusual and the main risk comes from intestinal worms. Flea infestation of carpets and bedding can occur and result in flea bites to children.

Dogs should be well groomed and have their claws trimmed regularly to reduce the risk of any nasty scratches. It is widely suggested that decreasing the amount of dog hair lying around a house can decrease the incidence and symptoms of childhood asthma and allergy.

Dog toys often resemble baby toys and are often found by babies lying around on the floor. Children should not be allowed to handle or suck on dog toys as they harbour saliva, dirt and germs and may also have dangerous small parts.

A dog's food and water bowls must be kept in a room not accessible by young children. Dogs are protective of their food bowls and will guard them from small intruders, whilst water bowls pose a serious drowning threat to an infant as they can drown in as little as 3cm of water.

Bringing Home Baby

The introduction of a new baby creates great change for all family members, including the family dog, who for many has been the only child in the house … until now. Planning for the baby during pregnancy should therefore include the gradual preparation of your dog for the inevitable changes he faces, rather than simply putting him outside the minute the baby arrives home.

Like many of us, dogs are creatures of habit and the arrival of a newborn is sure to bring more unpredictability to everyone's routines. While pregnant gradually acclimatise the dog to a certain degree of chaos such as walking at a different time, or spending more time alone in the garden or in a laundry room.

A house filled with new noises can be unsettling for a dog. Get her used to the sound of a crying baby by playing recordings while pregnant and by simultaneously patting or feeding him to form positive associations.

Scent plays a very powerful part in the pack life of a dog and can be a useful way to introduce a baby into the home. Once the baby is born, have someone bring home a blanket or piece of clothing the baby has worn and give it to the dog to sniff and snuggle with.

A newborn tends to dominate the house and it is easy to neglect other things, especially when feeling tired and overwhelmed yourself. When sleep deprived and grumpy, resist the temptation to yell at the dog or to throw him out and instead remove yourself and the baby to another room.

Try giving the dog a treat while you're feeding or changing the baby, as this will teach the dog positive associations and they may come to enjoy these times rather than to resent your focus on the baby.

It is important not to relegate the dog permanently to the backyard as he will eventually react to the lack of attention. When the baby is napping or with another adult, bring the dog back inside for a play or a pat, even if it is only for 10 minutes.

It can also be nice to walk the dog as a new family complete with the newest addition. Do not, however, be tempted to tie the dog lead to the pram or to have one hand on the pram and one on the dog lead, as both scenarios may lead to a runaway pram and disastrous outcomes. Instead, use two adults on the family walk, one for the baby and another responsible for the dog.

Another strategy to ease dogs through the baby transition is to create a safe place away from the baby zone, where the dog can escape should he want to. This may take the form of an indoor kennel or a dog bed, and should be placed in a quiet room away from the baby activities.

Buying a New Dog

Informed research is the key to purchasing a new family dog and is most easily done through the local vet, RSPCA, or kennel clubs. It is important to buy a dog appropriate to the age, size and maturity of your children and to identify the features your family wants and needs from a dog.

It has been suggested that it is safer and easier to wait until your children are over five years old before adding a dog to the family mix as they are far better than toddlers at learning safe dog behaviour.

But if you really can't wait to purchase your dog, services such as The Petcare Information and Advisory Service and Petnet.com.au offer a Selectapet survey to help identify the right dog for your family.

Breeds

It must first be clearly stated that there is no perfectly child-proof breed of dog and that relying on breed stereotypes alone can be dangerous. While it is true that there are general breed characteristics, it all comes down to the temperament of the individual dog.

Despite the media hype about "dangerous dog breeds", a survey of dog bites in Britain showed that Golden Retrievers were actually the most common attackers in part perhaps as they are one of the most popular pets. Thus, there are docile Rottweilers and aggressive Labradors.

Toy breeds (e.g. the Chihuahua) – often selected for children because of their small size – can be nervous and snappy whilst many of the giant breeds can be surprisingly gentle despite their huge size.

Breed Selection
Know your children
Do you have quiet, gentle children or noisy, boisterous kids? Are they naughty toddlers or moody teenagers? These characteristics are important in finding a compatible family dog. An athletic sporting breed such as the German Short-Haired Pointer might be the ideal companion for an active teenager whilst a more placid

breed, such as the Bassett Hound, might be more suitable for a shy, quiet child.

Find a reputable breeder or adopt a dog

If you have a particular breed in mind, look for a registered breeder and stay away from suburban 'puppy farms' often advertised in local classifieds. These dogs are often inbred, poorly treated and not socialised and this will predispose dogs to behavioural problems no matter the breed. In addition, such cruel and criminal businesses should never be supported.

If considering buying from a local breeder, check their status with the Australian National Kennel Council. Better yet, adopt a needy dog from a shelter as they have already been temperament and health tested, as well as wormed and vaccinated; these dogs can make the finest family pets.

Study the litter

Regardless of the breed, there will be a range of personalities in each litter. For families, it has been suggested that the 'middle' puppy will be best suited; i.e. not the one who charges forward first to greet you (this will be the confident, dominant puppy who may be too much for a busy family to handle), nor the one hanging back and cowering in the corner (this puppy may be too shy or nervous and might not deal with a busy household). Pick the puppy that approaches you but does not climb or mouth at you too aggressively. Other reassuring traits are if the puppy does not panic at an unexpected loud noise (e.g. clapped hands) and does not struggle too much if held firmly.

Family Favourite Breeds

There are universally agreed breeds with family-friendly reputations of all different shapes and sizes, and these characteristics can be a starting point for choosing a family dog.

While the following is not a comprehensive list, it is an introduction to a few of the more popular family breeds.

Shih-Tzu – full of infectious, extrovert enthusiasm, these intelligent little dogs are fun companions although they can be independent and wilful

Pug – friendly, affectionate

character but may cost more to run due to possible medical problems associated with their short face and bulging eyes. Despite their small size tend not to be snappy or nervous like many toy breeds.

Cavalier King Charles Spaniel – A cute dog with a rounded face and soft floppy ears, the Cavalier King Charles Spaniel was deliberately bred as a companion. They are sweet and affectionate family dogs, and energetic playmates with a loving nature who will adapt to any lifestyle but needs regular exercise and grooming of its long, silky coat. Heart disease is a problem in this breed.

Border Terrier – a compact, robust, short-coated dog that's great for families with active children. Good watchdogs although terrier characteristics such as digging and chewing may have to curbed.

Beagle – happy, sociable, ideal family dogs with placid temperaments. They can be a little stubborn in training, but they adore their food and will usually perform well if food is offered as a reward. They are also inclined to wander.

Staffordshire Bull Terrier – a powerful, muscular dog which is nevertheless tolerant and affectionate with children and devoted to its family. Highly intelligent and fearless, they must be well-socialised when young.

Cocker Spaniel – sensitive, affectionate and intelligent little dog which required some grooming and a fair amount of exercise. They have keen hunting instincts and can be strong-willed.

Labrador – The popular Labrador Retriever is intelligent, obedient, faithful and easy-care due to its short coat. They love food and need lots of exercise to offset their predisposition to obesity. They can be great for families and couples, but there are some aggressive Labradors around, which is why the Golden Retriever is often recommended for families.

Golden Retriever– The Golden Retriever makes an ideal family pet. It is sound, even-tempered, good with children, loyal, eager to please and easy to train. Golden Retrievers are happiest when indoors with the family. They are prone to weight gain so require daily exercise.

Designer Mongrels-These include the Cavoodle (Cavalier King Charles Spaniel x Poodle), Maltalier (Maltese x Cavalier King Charles Spaniel) and the Maltese x Shih Tzu. They are all fabulous little family dogs, which tend to demonstrate fewer veterinary problems than their purebred parents.

German Shorthaired Pointer – These dogs love people and they're safe with children. They are also large enough to be good watchdogs, but not aggressive enough to attack people. They are a little slow to mature and they have boundless energy, so require a lot of exercise.

NOTE: Many of the giant breeds such as the Newfoundland, St Bernard and Great Dane are renowned for their placid natures and gentle tolerance of children, but they also have a lengthy period as huge, clumsy, boisterous puppies and as such, are generally unsuitable for households with young children.

Cats

As many owners know, cats are creatures of habit and so are sensitive to changes in their surrounds. When a baby is introduced into their world, rather than mounting an aggressive response, cats are more likely to display mood change. If suddenly not allowed into certain rooms and in a house full of new sounds and smells, some cats will simply retreat into a quiet corner or under a bed, while others will re-assert themselves by urine spraying. A few will manifest anxiety by obsessively over-grooming.

As with dogs, it is best to begin preparing a cat for change whilst pregnant and to be mindful of their behaviour and anxiety levels after the baby arrives.

Pregnancy

Whilst pregnant begin excluding the cat completely from the room designated as the nursery and do not allow them to sleep on baby equipment, blankets or cots which may be lying around the house.

Contrary to popular belief, cats can be trained and they should be taught to obey a few simple voice commands such as 'get down' or 'stay'. This voice control can really help a new parent with few free hands.

Acclimatise the cat to as many baby smells and sounds as possible by using baby powders and lotions in advance. Similarly, play recordings of crying babies whilst petting and rewarding the cat. As with dogs, the establishment of positive associations for the cat with baby smells and noises can go a long way to easing the transition for everyone.

Prior to delivery, establish a safe place for the cat to which they can escape if feeling threatened or overwhelmed. This is best to be a high place such as a climbing pole with a perching platform or a secure box as cats will always prefer this to hiding under a bed or couch.

Bringing Baby Home

Once baby comes home, maintain the cat's daily routine as much as possible and introduce the cat gradually to the baby, allowing him to sniff around the baby and associated equipment. Otherwise, for the first few days, isolate baby from the cat until familiarity creeps in.

Do not allow the cat to lick the baby as this can lead to skin rashes. In particular, keep the cat out of the nursery and cot completely as there is a potential suffocation/SIDS risk if babies sleep with cats. If the cot cannot be isolated completely from the cat, invest in a purpose-made net which covers the cot and acts as a barrier.

It is important never to leave a baby or toddler alone in a room together with the cat as it only takes a minute for a misunderstanding or injury to occur. Use doors or childproof barriers to separate cats from children.

During the initial period of having baby at home, allocate someone within the household, perhaps a husband or partner, to monitor the cat's behaviour and to give daily attention and rewards. Do not simply banish the cat to a laundry or outside every time the baby is awake, as this will set up negative associations for the cat. Instead, when possible try to lavish attention and rewards on your cat at times when the baby is being fussed over to set up positive associations i.e. when the baby is around the cat gets attention and food.

When baby is sleeping, try to spend a few minutes of quality time talking to and petting the cat but do not let these sessions go on too long or the cat will associate attention only with the absence of the baby.

In extreme cases cats may respond to the new arrival by urinating or defaecating on baby clothes or on your bed. This is not jealousy but territorial marking by covering other scents with its own. Do not scold the cat as this will only raise tensions, but block access to certain rooms and try to spend more time reassuring the cat.

Older Children

As babies become toddlers, education becomes the key to a harmonious family, and it is important to teach babies from early on about treating cats and other animals with respect.

During supervised interaction, teach children that cats are not toys, but living creatures. Show them gentle petting with emphasis on not pulling fur, ears or tails.

Teach them about not scaring the cat with loud noises and not chasing the cat into corners or under beds. In addition, they should be instructed never to disturb sleeping or eating cats.

Instead, children can be shown safe games to play with cats such as chasing string, or rolling balls, so as to encourage positive interactions.

Separation of cats and toddlers is still a mainstay when supervision is not available and be aware that mobile babies and toddlers will find exposed cat toys and litter boxes and mouth them indiscriminately. Make sure these items are in a room which is not accessed by toddlers, or are behind childproof safety barriers or in covered boxes. Water bowls are a baby favourite and should also be kept out of reach as babies can drown in as little as 3cm of water.

Do not allow cats to sleep in cots or on the beds of young children. While the health risks are small, external parasites including fleas and ticks, as well as the ringworm fungus, can be transmitted from cats to people. This is especially important if children have asthma or allergies, as dander and fur can trigger both conditions.

It is also recommended that parents rather than children are responsible for cleaning litter boxes.

Cats and Disease

Many health concerns regarding cats and children are over-exaggerated and are fed by urban myth. More than one pregnant woman has been advised by friends or strangers to dispose of their cat but in fact, there are few diseases that can be transmitted from cat to human, and most are related to handling of cat faeces.

Toxoplasmosis

Toxoplasmosis is caused by a parasite called *Toxoplasma gondii* with parasitic cysts shed in cat faeces which in turn may infect humans.

In healthy adults, Toxoplasmosis causes only mild symptoms but if a woman becomes infected during her pregnancy it can have devastating affects on the unborn foetus. Pregnant cat owners should ask their doctor to do a blood test for antibodies to Toxoplasmosis, which would indicate a past exposure to the parasite.

If infected with Toxoplasmosis in the past, there is little to no risk of passing it on to an unborn baby but without prior exposure it is advisable to have someone else clean litter trays during the pregnancy. If this is not possible, use rubber gloves and a mask and avoid inhaling the dust from litter trays.

It takes between 24–48 hours for the cysts to become infective, so daily cleaning of the litter tray will almost entirely eliminate the risk of infection. It is perfectly safe for pregnant women to co-exist with their family cat as long as these precautions are taken.

Keep all sandpits or sandboxes covered as these can be another contact source of cat faeces for children.

Ringworm

This disease is caused by a fungus carried by some cats, and not by a worm as the name suggests. If your cat is indoors and has had the all clear from your vet, there is little chance of you or your baby catching ringworm.

Ringworm are more an unsightly nuisance than a serious

health danger to children and can be treated with topical creams.

Cat Scratch Disease

Bacterial infection of cat scratches and bites can be very serious, and can lead to the dangerous Cat Scratch Disease caused by the bacteria *Bartonella henselae* which must be treated with antibiotics. This most serious infection is rare in people with normal immune systems but young children may be vulnerable.

All cat bites and scratches should be thoroughly cleaned and disinfected and medical attention sought at the first sign of increasing pain, redness or fever.

Rabies

Rabies is not a concern in Australia, but in other countries cats should be current with rabies vaccination at all times

Disease Prevention Guidelines
- Do not let children or pregnant women handle the cat litter box
- Keep cat fully vaccinated and wormed
- Use regular topical solutions for flea and tick control and though many are proven safe for children, it is best to discourage handling of the cat for 24 hours after application.
- Groom cats regularly and trim claws short
- Teach children how to treat cats appropriately to minimise risk cat scratches or bites

Cat Breeds

There are many cat breeds that make excellent pets, but before choosing a cat simply based on its appearance, it is a good idea to do a little bit of research. Just like dogs, certain cat breeds are ideal for certain people.

Don't forget the humble moggy and consider adopting a cat from the local shelter where they have been vet-checked, temperament checked, vaccinated, de-wormed and in some cases de-sexed.

Here are a few cat breeds which have been dubbed family-friendly.
- **Norwegian Forest Cats** – Known as fluffy and friendly, and often calico or striped, these cats are known to be very affectionate. While Norwegian Forest cats get along very well with children, they

tend to be the most well-mannered when they are the only pet in the house.
- **Maine Coon Cats** – These cats are unbelievably friendly and outgoing, and are considered great companions for young children. Although they tend to fare better with other cats, most of these kitties get along with other dogs as well. One of the only downfalls to Maine Coon cats is that they do shed a lot, so you will need to groom frequently.
- **Birman Cats** – These cats are known to be incredibly gentle animals that are very loyal to their owners. Instead of roughhousing like other cats, Birman cats show their non-aggressive side by lounging around the house most of the time. Keep in mind that these cats do shed a decent amount, so grooming is required.
- **Persian Cats** – The Persian cat breed is one of the most popular breeds and they are generally friendly and well natured. Persians make great companions for children, but often tend to fare better as the only pet in the house. They are however, very hairy cats that require extensive grooming and can be expensive to purchase.
- **Russian Blue Cats** – These short-haired cats are incredibly affectionate and loyal and love being held which is not a common cat trait. Russian Blue cats fit nicely into a household that has several other cats or dogs, and are known to be one of the best companions for children.

Television

Most parents feel a little guilty about propping their children in front of the television and letting quiet descend on the house. It is the guilt that they are somehow doing their children harm by turning on the dreaded box.

As with most things, television can be helpful or harmful and the difference comes down to a variety of factors such as, the child's age and personality, as well as program content and absolute time spent in front of the TV.

The influence of television varies greatly across different age groups and demographics and so guidelines for TV viewing should continue to evolve as children grow. Parents are the key to childproofing the television area as well as the content.

Television Screen Time Recommendations

'Screen time' is defined as time spent viewing television, DVDs, computer screens, handheld electronic games or video games. Long screen times have been shown to correlate with decreased physical activity and are considered a strong risk factor for childhood obesity.

The Australian government published recommendations in February 2010 which can be found in their report *Get Up & Grow: Healthy Eating and Physical Activity Guidelines for Early*

Childhood. This report suggests that children under two should have zero screen time i.e. no TV or computer time at all. Further, it suggests that TV in this age group may stunt language and physical development.

The two to five year old age group should have screen time limited to less than one hour per day as more can reduce their amount of active and social time. This can lead to obesity, poorer social skills, slow language development and long term sedentary behaviour.

Television Content

Violence

It is estimated that a U.S. child will witness 200,000 acts on violence on TV by age 18. These take the form of cartoons, crime shows and increasingly via current affairs programming. The influence of television violence on children has become a hot topic for debate in recent years with hundreds of studies on the subject reaching varying conclusions. Establishing a direct cause/effect is difficult as some children are more vulnerable to violent images than others.

What is clear is that pre-school children are far more likely to exhibit aggressive behaviour after witnessing violent TV. Importantly, kids this young are unable to distinguish between fantasy and reality and therefore cartoon violence can be as detrimental as adult-based violent content. Further, cartoon violence is often portrayed as humorous or as having no consequences to the victim.

Children aged 2–7 years are particularly disturbed by scary images such as grotesque monsters and cannot be comforted by simply telling them that the images are not real.

Older children are better able to distinguish between reality and fantasy and are more disturbed by the threat of violence in current affairs and news coverage. This can lead to an increased fear of the 'mean world' and anxiety regarding the welfare of their friends and family. Constant exposure to violent images can also desensitize children to real life aggression.

As children age, they can be reasoned with and reassured by discussion of what they have seen and any anxieties they may have.

Ethnic and Gender Stereotypes

A 1996 Children Now Survey found that children want to see people like themselves on television and that those from ethnic minorities feel left out and have lower self-esteem if that is not the case.

Many shows feature characters which reinforce ethnic and gender stereotypes and can act as powerful role-models in influencing children's behaviour.

Sexual Themes

While it is true that television can be educational, it is also true that sexual issues are rarely dealt with by TV programming in a responsible and meaningful manner. In addition, sexual behaviour is often linked to other risk-taking behaviours such as alcohol-drinking and there are rarely discussions about consequences.

A 2001 Kaiser Family Foundation study 'Sex On TV' found that 75% of primetime programs contained sexual references with sitcoms being the most prominent of these. In particular, only 17% of shows portraying teens in sexual situations had any safe sex messages written into the scenes.

It has been suggested that teens who watch a lot of sexual content on TV are more likely to initiate intercourse or participate in other sexual activities earlier than peers who don't watch sexually explicit shows.

Developmental Impact

Television can impact on childhood development in a number of ways, primarily by taking time away from other activities needed for mental, physical and social development.

One of the commonest parental battles is over television and homework and according to the Canadian Paediatric Society, as little as 1–2 hours of TV per day can detract from academic performance.

The alarming rate of childhood obesity has been linked, in part, to children's viewing habits, both in terms of promoting a sedentary lifestyle and from the relentless marketing of junk food to children through television advertising.

Benefits

Letting your children watch television should prompt feelings of responsibility from parents rather than guilt. TV can be used as a tool of entertainment and education and can expose a child to an entire world of experiences and cultures far outside their own. Parents should watch television with children, not only to police content, but also to promote family togetherness and discussion; this can also be used as a catalyst to promote reading and activity.

By using a few simple guidelines parents can transform television from a passive babysitter into a valuable part of family life.

Parental Controls

Currently in Australia, televisions are not fitted with any software to allow content blocking as is seen in the U.S. with the v-chip; which is installed in all new televisions over 13 inches and which allows parents to block inappropriate content. In Australia, the Senate Standing Committee on Environment, Communication and the Arts recommended that parental controls be fitted on all new digital TVs and set-top boxes, but so far, it has not been adopted. In any event studies have shown that despite 60–70% of U.S. parents being concerned about television content, only 15% with the v-chip device actually use it.

As a guide to program content, parents should familiarise themselves with the television classifications given to all programs before screening. In addition, the best way to regulate cable or pay television programming is to simply choose to receive only channels you are happy for your children to see.

Television and Entertainment System

The simple TV set has morphed into the 'home theatre' and for many has become a complex array of technology with requirements for multiple power outlets, power boards as well as entwining cables as thick as tree trunks. These entertainment units often take pride of place in the living room and are as tantalising to babies and toddlers as they are to adults; only far more dangerous.

Storing all entertainment appliances within a childproof entertainment cabinet is essential as it acts as a barrier and deterrent against having sandwiches shoved in the DVD player or buttons pressed indiscriminately. Ensure the doors of such a cabinet are lockable or, if not, fit the doors with childproof latches. Doors are often left open whilst watching programs to facilitate the use of infra-red remote controls, to counter this, consider buying a cabinet with slotted doors to allow the use of remote controls while the doors remain closed.

Floor-level glass doors are a sharp and dangerous choice for an entertainment cabinet and are not recommended. Try replacing them with a fine mesh or slatted wood door which will still allow infrared signals through.

One of the main challenges when childproofing entertainment equipment is managing the vast array of cords and cables and ensuring that they are organized, shortened, concealed and not left dangling. Many entertainment areas end up with a morass of cords tangled on the floor which act as a fatal temptation for an infant as they become entangled and risk strangulation. Other risks include biting the cords, finding the power source or pulling equipment on top of themselves.

Cords should be wound within cord spools, shortened as much as possible and then run within cord organiser tubes or wall clips along a path concealed behind furniture or at height. A cheaper option is to wind and secure excess cords and secure with duct tape. Appliance cables should be taken through spaces created in the back of the cabinet, rather than bought in through the doors at the front. The overall aim is to keep all cables, plugs and power boards out of sight, out of reach and out of mind to a baby.

All unused power outlets including those on power boards should be covered with childproof plug and switched to the 'off' position.

The current trend for large flat-screen televisions is a worrying one in homes with small children and there have been serious head injuries and even deaths, from small children being crushed by unsecured flat-screens. Such televisions are relatively narrow-based, top heavy and are far less stable than their older, bulkier counterparts. The safest option for flat-screens TVs is to wall-mount them preferably using a steel mount kit appropriate to their size. Otherwise these televisions should be pushed to the back of the bench and anchored to the wall or table using purpose made screw anchors.

Commercially available television, DVD and VCR guards may be purchased to cover the facade of any exposed units. These inexpensive guards are designed to protect buttons and slots whilst still allowing for the use of remote controls.

Remotes controls should be kept out of reach of children as obscure buttons will be pressed randomly and may take months to unscramble.

Poisoning

THE INTRODUCTION OF CHILD resistant packaging has made significant inroads into childhood poisoning prevention in Australia, however, unintentional poisoning of children under 5 remains the second leading cause of hospital admission. Despite poisoning being relatively common however, death is thankfully rare.

The Victorian Injury Surveillance Unit (VISU) state that most poisonings occur at home with 84% due to improper storage of substances. Parents are often surprised at the sheer number of potentially harmful substances within the home, however, 70% of childhood poisonings still involve medication. Any disruptions to daily routine increase the risk of poisoning e.g. visitors, travelling or moving house.

Poisoning is a function of developmental age, with the 1–3 year old group being most at risk; they mouth objects, imitate adults and have little ability to assess danger. In addition, their small body mass means that only small aliquots of toxins can be poisonous. Contrary to popular myth, young children will ingest even foul or bitter-tasting substances as easily as sweet ones.

Prevention of poisoning is about knowing the poisons in your home, ensuring they are stored securely and then knowing what to do in the event of a poisoning. Most children who are accidentally poisoned have attentive, caring parents or guardians, but with the best will in the world it is impossible to watch children every minute of the day.

> ## *Australia-wide Poisons Information Line*
> # **131126**

Poison Types

Types Poison	Common Substances
Medicines	• Paracetamol • Ibuprofen • Anti-depressants • Over-the-counter cold medications • Heart and blood pressure medications • Anti-histamine • Anti-convulsants • Antibiotics • Sedatives, anti-anxiety • Iron tablets • Vitamins • Narcotic painkillers
Essential Oils / rubs	• Camphor; chest rubs • Eucalyptus • Teatree • Pennyroyal • Wintergreen • Tansy

Types Poison	Common Substances
Recreational	• Alcohol • Stimulants; caffeine, guarana • Narcotics • Amphetamine
Household Chemicals	• Bleaches • Detergents • Dishwasher tablets or powder • Drain and oven cleaners • Turpentine • Batteries • Airfresheners
Pesticides	• Insect sprays and repellants • Mothballs • Rodent bait or pellets
Health and Beauty	• Nail polish and remover • Hair dye • Mouthwash • Toothpaste • Deodorant • Perfume • Vaporiser solutions • Cosmetics
Outside	• Fertiliser • Pool chemicals • Building products • Paint and thinners • Petrol and hydrocarbons • Anti-freeze • Glues • solvents

Medicines

Ingestion of medications is a common cause of poisoning in children. Common scenarios include swallowing adult dose tablets, or giving the wrong dosage of children's medications.

One of commonest substances involved in child poisoning is paracetamol, seen by many as a fairly safe medication. Whilst the introduction of child-resistant packaging such as blister packs has slowed a child's ability to rapidly access large numbers of tablets, the liquid forms used to treat children are far easier to ingest. Particular risk occurs when an open bottle is left out during use.

Paracetamol toxicity causes liver failure and renal failure a few days after ingestion and hospital admission is required to monitor organ function.

Ibuprofen, another common medication used to treat childhood fever causes drowsiness and breathing difficulties in overdose.

The commonest adult medications involved in child poisonings were medications prescribed for depression, anxiety, heart or blood pressure problems, sleep disturbance or allergy. Many of these cause life-threatening illness in young children, and a significant proportion require admission to the intensive care unit for treatment. It is important to not to dismiss over-the-counter medications or vitamins as less harmful to children simply because they are easier to obtain, these too can cause serious illness in overdose.

All medication should be bought and stored in child-resistant bottles or blister packs which will slow children down, making it more harder for them to access large numbers of tablets quickly. But be aware that such childproof containers only slow kids down and are no match for a determined child with enough time to work the mechanism.

Medications must be stored out of reach and out of sight, in a childproof, locked cupboard at least 1.5m off the ground or in a high cupboard within a locked container. Similarly, if medications need to be refrigerated, do not store them in the door, but in a locked container at the back of the top shelf.

When giving medicine,

double-check the recommended dosage as it will change depending on the weight and age of a child. Do not be tempted to get creative with dosing; parents may know their child but most will not understand the pharmacology of drugs. Similarly, whilst medications are in use, it is critical that open containers are not left out, even for a second; curious children are always faster, taller and more agile than we think. Return medications to storage immediately after use.

Children learn behaviour through imitation so when possible, avoid taking medication in front of children. Do not refer to tablets as lollies as many are the same colour or size and avoid using old medicine cups or containers as toys; this will only confuse safety messages.

Never stockpile old medication and dispose of all expired or unwanted medications by taking them to the pharmacy rather than tipping them down the sink, or putting them in domestic garbage bins.

Beware of leaving handbags on the ground or low surfaces, especially when entertaining visitors, or when visiting someone else. Some bags contain dangerous medications and which can be ingested while adults are distracted.

Essential Oils and Rubs

One of the most toxic substances comes from the most apparently benign of sources; chest or muscle rubs and inhalers. These old favourites contain camphor, which has a characteristic smell, but which swallowed in small amounts can cause convulsions, muscle twitching, gastrointestinal burning, confusion and respiratory depression,

The use of essential oils within the home is increasingly common, however so too is child poisoning from ingestion of such oils which can cause respiratory distress, coma, convulsions and low blood pressure. A few of the more toxic oils are eucalyptus, camphor, teatree oil, pennyroyal, wintergreen and tansy small doses of which may be lethal to a child and should never be kept in the home. As a general rule, aromatic plant oils should be stored with medications or cleaning agents; in a locked, high cupboard and should not be used when children are present.

Recreational

Alcohol poisoning in young children can occur from relatively small amounts, such as those found in unfinished drinks, and can lead to seizures, coma or even death. When drinking alcohol, ensure all glasses are placed to the back of high benches, between sips and are out of reach of young children. Similarly, children must be closely supervised by a non-drinking adult at parties involving alcohol and all unfinished beverages must be poured immediately down the drain.

Stimulants such as guarana and caffeine are not recommended for children or adolescents and can cause agitation, tremor, palpitations and at high doses, hallucinations, seizures or heart arrhythmias.

Household Poisoning Prevention

Although poisons can be found all over the house and garden, they are concentrated in the bathroom, laundry and garage and it is critical that these areas are inaccessible to young children. This can be achieved using high door handles, knob covers, and effective locks.

Store all cleaning products and chemicals in cupboards over 1.5m above the ground and fit them with childproof locks. It is critical then that these locks are engaged at all times.

Choose hazardous solutions contained in child-resistant containers. All substances must be stored in the original, childproof packaging, which not only protects against exposure but also contains important product ingredient information required by doctors if poisoning does occur. Never store chemicals, solvents, paints or cleaning fluids in old food jars or drink bottles; this sends confusing messages to young children and only encourages ingestion.

It is essential that chemicals and cleaners are stored separate to food to make a clear distinction between the two.

Do not leave spray bottles of cleaning chemicals on low surfaces or on the floor, and turn the spray nozzle to "off" when not in use. Children love these bottles and will instinctively point the nozzles at their faces before squeezing the trigger. In fact, if you are called away whilst using cleaning products or chemicals, remember to take it with you or return it to its childproof home.

Consider switching from hazardous cleaning products such as chorine bleach and lye products to less toxic, greener alternatives such as vinegar/water or bicarbonate as a glass and surface cleaner. This is not only safer but also saves money and 'recipes' for making such cleaning solutions are freely available online.

Dishwashing detergent is extremely alkali and can cause extensive burns to the mouth and gastrointestinal tract if ingested, so fill the detergent dispenser immediately before starting the cycle and do not leave a dishwasher sitting dormant with detergent loaded. Further, keep children away when adding detergent.

When emptying a load, check for any leftover or undissolved powder.

Choose a dishwasher with a built-in childproof lock, or buy an adhesive lock to ensure it cannot be opened by children.

Any dishwasher powder or tablets should be stored in high, secure cabinets. Look for non-caustic detergents which are becoming increasingly available and which minimise the risk of serious injury if accidentally ingested. White vinegar may be used as a non-toxic alternative to commercial rinsing aids.

Plants

Ingestion of household and garden plant parts by children under five is the leading cause of calls to US poisons, although actual poisoning and death from plants is relatively rare. Apart from the risk of poisoning, however, plant leaves also pose a risk from inhalation and choking.

In general, children are attracted to succulents as well as brightly coloured petals, berries and leaves, and so what looks best in the home may not be best for children.

Unfortunately, there are no absolute characteristics which identify plants as poisonous, but in general, plants with a bitter taste, milky sap, red seeds and berries or a strange odour may be poisonous. Chemicals tend to be concentrated in the cells of roots, leaves, bark and seeds and serve as the plant's defence against insect or animal attack. It is these compounds which can also be most toxic to humans.

If a child swallows a potentially poisonous substance, time is of the essence so ensure that the phone number for the local **Poisons information Centre** on **131126** is clearly displayed by the phone.

Childproofing Plants

Plants are a beautiful and creative part of every home and garden, to be enjoyed by children and adults alike. But it is important within this beauty to identify any potentially harmful plantings. There are many plants which are perfectly safe to grow, but there are also a number of benign-looking plants which are toxic or dangerous in other ways. It is important to be as knowledgeable as possible about what is growing in your garden.

It is important to realise that because something is a common plant, does not mean it is safe plant. In fact most people choose plants based on aesthetics often without knowing about any poisons risk.

Start by identifying all plants in the house and garden and labelling them for future reference and if any plants remain a mystery, take a representative leaf to the local garden centre for identification. Similarly, before buying a new plant any possible poisons risks should be researched.

Young children should be taught never to eat anything straight from a plant without checking first with an adult, however children under three years old cannot reliably be taught this lesson and must always be supervised within the garden. Placing hazardous plants out of reach or behind fences is not enough, as dropped petals or leaves can be ingested by babies or children.

As a general precaution, all houseplants should be kept out of reach of small children or babies even if they are not directly poisonous as the leaves can pose an inhalation and choking risk. Clear any dropped petals or leaves immediately as these may be ingested by babies or children. In addition, dangling vines and branches may be used to pull a heavy pot plant onto a child resulting in significant injury.

Insecticides are extremely toxic to children and should

never be used on houseplants. Similarly, fertilisers are quite noxious and fertiliser pellets or powders must not be left on the surface of potted plants as they can prove irresistible to children

Pebbles have become a popular garden accessory but may also pose a choking risk to young children and should not be used to surround pot plants.

Any flower arrangements bought into the home should be vetted for poisonous content as they may contain toxic elements such as the florist's favourite Dieffenbachia, a beautiful but poisonous leaf.

What follows is a detailed, though not exhaustive, list of some common poisonous plants as well as a list of safe alternatives. If in doubt about always ask the local nurseryman.

Poisonous Plants Guide

The potential danger of various plants depends on the amount ingested and the size of the child. Some plants are toxic from only the slightest amount while others need large doses for even mild reactions. Further, some plants cause only skin or eye irritation.

In general, plant families to be wary of include:
- The Poinsettia family (*Euphorbiaceae*)
- The Philodendron family (*Araceae*),
- The Cactus family (*Cactaceae*)
- The Tomato family (*Solanaceae*)
- Many forms of lilies are also hazardous, so check with your local nursery before buying

Below are tables detailing a number of poisonous plants, however it is by no means an exhaustive list, so if you are unsure of the potential harm of a particular plant in your garden, you should enquire at your local nursery.

The list below has been divided into 3 categories;
- Highly toxic plants which should be removed from gardens
- Plants which can cause problems and should be avoided
- Common plants which are safe to plant

Table 1: Highly toxic plants which should be removed

Common Name	Scientific Name	Toxic Parts	Adverse Reaction
Angel's trumpet	*Datura* sp. *Brugmansia* sp.	All parts, especially flowers, seeds	Dilated pupils, delirium, gastroenteritis, fever, confusion, convulsions
Apple of Sodom (devil's apple)	*Solanum sodomaeum*	Fruit	Gastroenteritis, dizziness, confusion, hallucinations
Arum lily	*Zantedeschia aethiopica*	All parts, especially flower	Mouth swelling, acute gastritis and diarrhoea, shock. Dermatitis.
Autumn Crocus	*Colchicum autumnale*	All parts	Burning mouth, abdominal pain, vomiting, diarrhoea, neurological symptoms, May have delayed onset symptoms >48 hours.
Azalea		All parts	Fatal. Nausea & vomiting Respiratory distress Coma
Cape tulip	*Moraea flaccida* *Moraea miniata*	All parts	Acute vomiting & diarrhoea. Possible paralysis.
Castor oil plant	*Ricinus communis*	Colourful seeds, flowers. Deadly ricin poison – just 1 milligram can kill.	Burning mouth, abdominal pain, bloody diarrhoea, fever, convulsions, respiratory and cardiac arrest
Coral tree, bat's wing coral tree	*Erythrina vespertilio*	Leaves, bark, seeds	Nausea, coma, respiratory distress

Common Name	Scientific Name	Toxic Parts	Adverse Reaction
Cunjevoi (elephant's ears)	*Alocasia macrorrhizos*, *Alocasia brisbanesis*	All parts.	Skin & eye irritation. Burning & swelling throat and tongue. Severe gastric irritation and vomiting.
Daphne	*Daphne cneorum*	Berries	Fatal. A few berries can kill a child
Deadly nightshade (belladonna)	*Atropa belladonna*	All parts	Nausea, dilated pupils, loss of coordination, heart rhythm disturbance, respiratory distress, death
Delphinium	*Delphinium* x *cultorum*	All parts, especially seeds. Leaves can be irritant	Nausea & vomiting, diarrhoea, weakness, convulsions, paralysis
Foxglove	*Digitalis*	Flowers, leaves, seeds	Confusion, Blurred vision, Cardiac rhythm disturbance, Nausea, vomiting Weakness, Fainting
Glory/gloriosa lily (climbing lily)	*Gloriosa superba*, *Gloriosa rothchildiana*	All parts, especially roots.	Tingling, numb lips, throat, skin. Dizziness, nausea & vomiting, respiratory distress. Irregular heartbeat.
Golden dewdrop (sky flower, pigeon berry)	*Duranta erecta*	Leaves and berries	Insomnia, fever, rapid pulse, vomiting, convulsions
Lantana	*Lantana species*	All parts, especially green berries	Vomiting, diarrhoea, muscle weakness, respiratory distress. Dermatitis

Common Name	Scientific Name	Toxic Parts	Adverse Reaction
Lily of the valley	*Convallaria majalis*	All parts, especially berries	Mouth irritation, nausea, vomiting, dizziness, slow pulse, respiratory distress, cardiac arrest
Oleander	*Nerium oleander*	All parts contain glycosides	One leaf is fatal. Disrupts heart function.
Rhus or wax tree	*Toxicodendron succedaneum, Toxicodendron vernicifluum*	All parts cause intense skin irritation especially sap. Smoke from burning causes allergic results	Dermatitis of varying severity from rashes to blistering. Swelling. Chronic systemic illness.

Table 2: Toxic plants which should be avoided but are not life-threatening

Common Name	Scientific Name	Toxic Parts	Adverse Reaction
Agapanthus (African lily)	*Agapanthus praecox*, subsp. Orientalis	Leaves roots and saps	Severe mouth ulceration, skin rash and burning sensation
Aloe Vera	*Aloe* species	Glycosides in the latex sap	Nausea, vomiting Cramping Diarrhoea
Australian Umbrella Tree	*Scheffiera* syn. *Brassaia*	All parts contain oxalic acid and saponins	Vomiting Loss coordination
Scotch or English Broom	*Cytisus scoparius*	Seeds and leaves	High blood pressure, nausea, high doses affect heart
Bulbs	Examples; daffodils, jonquils, lilies, bluebells, tulips	Mostly bulbs and saps. Taste unpleasant so unlikely for much to be eaten.	Dermatitis, nausea, vomiting.
Cacti and succulents		Spikes on contact	Local skin injury. Eye penetration.
Chillies	*Capsicum* sp.	Juice and seeds	Intense skin and eye irritation on contact
Devil's Ivy	*Epipremnum* syn. *Scindapsus*	All parts contain calcium oxalate	Intense irritation of mucous membranes. Swelling of tongue, lips and palate
Dwarf Sago plants (cycads)	*Cycas revoluta*	Fruits, seed and young leaves	Nausea & vomiting
Dumb Cane	*Dieffenbachia*	All parts contain calcium oxalate	Intense irritation of mucous membranes. Swelling of tongue, lips and palate

THE SAFETY BUBBLE

Common Name	Scientific Name	Toxic Parts	Adverse Reaction
False acacia (black locust)	*Robinaia psuedoacacia*	All parts	Dizziness, nausea, vomiting, diarrhoea, convulsions, drowsiness
Golden chain tree	*Laburnum anagyroides*	All parts especially seeds	Burning mouth, nausea, vomiting, diarrhoea, convulsions, respiratory distress
Hemlock	*Conium maculatum*	All parts	Nervous symptoms, trembling, respiratory distress
Holly	*Ilex aquifolium*	Leaves and berries	Nausea, vomiting, weakness and collapse
Hydrangea	*Hydrangea macrophylla*	All parts	Dermatitis. Nausea, vomiting
Heart-Leaf Philodendron	*Philodendron scandens*	Leaves contain calcium oxalate	Intense irritation of mucous membranes. Swelling of tongue, lips and palate
Jerusalem Cherry	*Solanum pseudocapsicum*	Fruit contains highly toxic solanine	Burning mouth and throat. Gastric irritation. Fever. Diarrhoea
Lupins	*Lupinus* sp.	Dried and fresh leaves and stems	Vomiting, dizziness, headache. Extreme case may have respiratory and cardiac distress.
Morning glory (creeper)	*Ipomoea indicia*	Seeds	Visual distortion, restlessness, nausea
Mushrooms/ toadstools	Assume all wild growing mushrooms are toxic. Remove from garden	All parts	Dizziness, drowsiness, vomiting, irregular pulse, hallucinations

Common Name	Scientific Name	Toxic Parts	Adverse Reaction
Pencil Plant	*Euphorbia tirucalli*	Milky sap	Sap in eyes causes severe irritation and temporary blindness. Blistering in mouth and other soft skin areas
Poinsettia; A Christmas favourite	*Euphorbia pulcherrima*	Milky latex sap contains terpenes and diterpenes	Nausea, diarrhoea, vomiting. Severe skin irritation
Rhubarb	*Rheum x cultorum*	Leaves, (stalks edible once cooked)	Nausea, vomiting, diarrhoea
Sweet pea	*Lathyrus odoratus*	All parts especially seeds	Slow pulse, respiratory distress, convulsions

Safe plants guide

So as not to give the impression that all plants are evil, here a number of the many safe, non-toxic plants which are suitable to be grown outdoors.

Common Name	Scientific Name
African Violet	*Santpaulia ionatha*
Spider plant	*Chlorophytum comosum*
Wandering Jew	*Zebrina pendula*
Peperomias	
Jade plant	*Crassula ovata*
Christmas Cactus	*Schlumbregera species*
Herbs	Basil, oregano, mint, rosemary
Coleus	*Coleus*
Camellia	*Camellia sinensis*
Maidenhair fern	*Adiantum species*
Impatiens	*Impatiens wallerana*

Common Name	Scientific Name
Golden Bamboo	*Phyllostachys aurea*
Baby's tears	*Soleiria soleirolii*
Bungalow palms, most other palms	
Kangaroo paws	*Anigozanthos* sp. *Macropidia* sp.
Ajuga	*Ajuga reptans*
Fig tree	*Ficus benjamina*
Olive tree	
Roses	
Norfolk island pine	*Araucaria excelsa*

Poisons Information Centre
131126 Australia Wide

Poisoning First Aid

Undoubtedly, the best treatment for poisoning is to stop it from ever happening but given the unpredictable nature of life, being prepared in the event of a poisoning is the next best thing.

The type and severity of poisoning symptoms will vary according to the type and amount of plant ingested and the size of the child. Parents should have a high index of suspicion for poisoning if a child suddenly develops unexplained symptoms.

Symptoms of poisoning can include;
- Skin irritation or rash
- Stinging or burning in and around mouth
- Vomiting
- Stomach cramps
- Confusion
- Convulsions

It is critical that families have a plan for if poisoning does occur and that the phone number of the local poisons information centre is clearly displayed near the telephone. This should form part of a list of emergency numbers.

First aid for Poisoning

If the child is unconscious, fitting, has mouth swelling or is having difficulty breathing, call local emergency number.

000 in Australia

Identify the ingested substance or take some of it to the hospital for identification.

If the child is conscious and stable, take the poison to the phone and call the poisons information line. Don't wait for symptoms to develop, call as soon as you become aware of an accidental poisoning. Try to note the amount taken and the time of ingestion.

Swallowed poison

- DO NOT induce vomiting as in some cases this may worsen injury to the throat and mouth.
- Don not use Ipecac Syrup unless recommended by the Poisons information line or a doctor
- Wash out child's mouth and hands
- Give a sip or two of water
- Identify plant and call poisons information

Skin Contact

- Remove contaminated clothing, avoiding contact with chemical
- Flood area with clean running water, then wash gently with soap and water
- Call local poisons information centre

Eye Contact

- Hold eyelids opens and irrigate the eye with clear running water for 20 minutes. If not from a tap then use jug or cup.
- Call local poisons information centre

Inhaled poison

- Immediately take the child to fresh air where possible and/or open doors or windows wide
- Avoid breathing fumes yourself
- Call local poisons information centre

PART 2

Outdoors

Backyard and Playgrounds

One of the great childhood joys is the hours spent in the backyard being transported on all manner of adventures. It is important, therefore, that the backyard and outdoor play areas are adequately childproofed to create a safe zone for childhood exploration.

The number one cause of injury in a backyard or playground is falls, often due to young children playing on equipment meant for an older age group. A child who falls from greater than 1.5 metres is four times as likely to injure themselves as a child falling from a lower height.

Surface type is also a factor to be considered, as a child falling onto asphalt or concrete is twice as likely to be injured as one falling onto an impact-absorbing surface such as rubber.

Consideration should also be given to safe landscaping and planting throughout the garden, with minimisation of steep drops, climbing opportunities and tight crevices. In addition, thoughtful fencing and gating is a critical part of designing a childproof garden.

Actual poisoning and death from plants is relatively rare as most poisonous plants taste horrible and deter children from ingestion, however, children are attracted to succulent and brightly coloured petals, berries and leaves. What looks best in the garden may not be best for child safety. It is essential therefore, that all plants in and around the house are identified and checked against lists of potentially poisonous flora.

As with most childproofing, the key to creating and policing a safe garden is to change your perspective. By getting on the ground and looking into every dark and cobweb-infested corner, you will see what your child sees and spot potential hazards you never knew existed.

Supervision of young children under 5 years in the garden must be vigilant and is inadequate if undertaken from inside the house. This is especially true if there is a playground area or trampoline as few people can see their entire garden from a window no matter its size.

The ubiquitous garden shed can be the wildcard in garden safety as it is often a mysterious and multi-functional space. Childproofing strategies will therefore depend on how the space is used; for chemical and tool storage, as a workshop, as a junk room or as a combination of all these.

Any playground equipment must be carefully researched prior to purchase and should be age-appropriate, well-built and properly installed.

The Playground

Playgrounds are incredible wonderlands for children to exercise and play in and they can help children to grow socially and creatively. But poorly thought-out or poorly constructed playgrounds can also become one of the most serious child hazards.

First and foremost, all playgrounds must be adequately fenced off from roads and driveways and this is especially relevant when equipment is placed in the front yard. Strict separation of play areas from moving vehicles will go a long way to preventing driveway accidents.

All playground equipment should be made from durable materials and should be age appropriate. If equipment is too high or too large for children it greatly increases the risk of injury.

All supervision of children under 5 on play equipment should be from arms length where quick action is possible if required and for this age group, all equipment should be less than 1.5m high. As a general guide, if a child cannot reach or navigate a piece of equipment themselves or with minimal help, it is probably not appropriate for their age and size.

For families with a spread of ages using the playground, it is best to cater for the lowest age group. If older children are using bigger equipment, explain to the young ones which equipment is out of bounds and supervise them closely.

Surfacing

With falls the number one cause of playground injury, the surface placed underneath equipment is a vital part of injury prevention. In general, surfacing should be between 23–30cms deep depending on the maximum height of equipment and the higher the equipment from the ground, the deeper the surfacing should be. As a guide, 30cm of surface depth will comfortably service equipment at the recommended 1.5 metres high.

Any surfacing should extend for a minimum of 1.8 metres around playground equipment, whilst for swings, surfacing must extend in the front and back for a distance equal to twice the height of the suspending bar.

All surfaces and surrounds should be regularly inspected for animal faeces, embedded foreign bodies, dangerous objects and tripping hazards (e.g. divets). Remember, children in playgrounds are usually running and distracted and can readily come to grief on uneven surfaces.

There are a number of materials recommended for child play areas (Table 1), but ultimately the choice between these will depend on cost, availability and personal preference. When considering the right ground cover for your playground area, remember that surface properties can change in different weather conditions.

Surfaces <u>not recommended</u> for playgrounds include sharp gravel, concrete, hard-packed dirt which can be eroded and grass which does not cushion well.

<u>Recommended</u> surfaces include soft sand, woodchips, pea gravel (rounded) and rubber.

Table 1: Playground Surfaces

	Advantages	Disadvantages
Pea gravel	• Drains well • Durable • Doesn't blow around • Effective in rain	• Can be put in mouth, ears, nose etc. • Scatters • Can be thrown • No good for wheelchairs or pram • Can hide foreign objects
Wood chips	• Durable • Drains well • Children tend not to play with it	• Can lead to splinters • Compacts • Can scatter • Can hide foreign objects
Soft sand	• Drains well • Cost effective • Durable	• Can get into clothes, shoes, mouths etc. • Pets and animals attracted as litter box • Scatters • Can be thrown • Can become difficult in wet conditions • Can hide foreign objects
Rubber	• Drains well • Often made from recycled material • Durable • Good with wheelchairs and prams • Good in rainy conditions • Easy to clean • Can see foreign objects easily	• Can become hard/degenerate over time • Can be flammable and become tacky at high temperatures • More expensive

Equipment

In general, playground equipment should be age-appropriate as younger children's playing on over-sized equipment is a leading cause of injury. In particular, the under 5's may not have the upper body strength for some of the bigger climbing equipment

As a general guide, equipment for children under 5 should

be less than 1.5 metres. It is tempting to raise this height for older children, however, research shows that injuries, limb fractures and fracture complications increase exponentially over this height. If there is a mixture of age groups, safety choices must be made. You may choose to install equipment for all levels and fence off the larger equipment, limiting access to younger equipment, or you may choose to cater for the lowest age group and install suitable equipment.

Some equipment may be modified to limit access for young children, for example, by removing the bottom rung of a ladder, but this should not replace diligent supervision. No one is more resourceful and determined than a 2 year old with a mission!

Leave as much space as possible around equipment, ideally more than 1.8 metres; this is especially important between equipment and fences. Be aware that extra space is needed at the bottom of slides and in front and behind swings.

Equipment over 75cms high should ideally be spaced more than 2.75 metres apart and swings should be over 60cms apart and over 75cms from the frame.

Think carefully about the location of play areas within a garden and do not locate playgrounds next to roads, buildings, large trees or water. Even a well-fenced pool may be accessed from adjacent elevated play equipment and young children in particular can quickly drown in as little as 3cms of water.

There is a dazzling array of play equipment available in all price ranges and so it is important that parents know what to look for and what features to avoid. All playground equipment should be of solid construction, made from durable, non-toxic materials and should have no sharp edges, cracks or splinters. If considering a piece of equipment, imagine how it will weather and be aware of such factors as metal slides becoming hot or wooden climbers giving splinters.

Swing seats should be made of a soft material such as rubber in case it hits a child in the head and moving part equipment should have no exposed hinges or 'pinch' points to protect little digits from being crushed.

Think about the gaps within

equipment, as children can entrap their heads or limbs. All openings should be under 9cms or over 23cms based on the head and torso measurements of young children. In addition, any platforms for the under 5's or those which sit over 1.2 metres high should have ramps and guardrails which are a minimum of 75cm high.

The correct installation of play equipment is central to its ongoing safety profile and should always be done according to the manufacturer's instructions. Many stores will offer an installation service which may be of value for more complex equipment. All equipment should be firmly anchored to the ground, and for bigger equipment, this can often include sinking part of the base underground for added stability.

It is essential however, that safety does not stop with installation and that all equipment is well-maintained and inspected regularly for sharp protrusions, splinters, cracks, rust, missing screws and broken parts. Remove and fix any broken equipment, as children will continue to use it regardless.

Sandpits are a popular part of many playgrounds and should be kept well-covered when not in use as they attract animals as a litter box and can harbour bacteria, waste and rocks. Check the sand regularly for sharp or foreign objects and sharp and change the sand every year.

Arsenic Treated Woods

One of the commonly used chemical wood preservatives is Chromated Copper Aresnate (CCA), which includes arsenic as a fungiside. This has been found to leach into surrounding soils and concerns have been raised, though not proven, about the dangers of CCA-treated woods to humans. Consequently, in 2006 the Australian Pesticides and Veterinary Medicines Authority (APVMA), banned the use of CCA to treat woods used in "intimate human contact" applications such as children's play equipment, furniture, decking and handrailing.

As CCA timber is still widely available for other uses, it is critical to check that all backyard fencing, furniture and play equipment are made from arsenic-free wood.

Playground Use

Before allowing them into the playground, children should be dressed in snug clothing and proper footwear with no bare feet. Remove anything from children which may choke them if caught on equipment e.g. drawstrings, necklaces, scarves and even big, baggy 'hoodies'.

Bike helmets should also be removed as not only can the strap catch on equipment, but they may cause the child's head to become stuck in a space through which it would normally fit.

Never attach clotheslines, ropes or pet leashes to equipment as they can be used to swing on which in turn risks falling from or colliding with equipment. In addition, such hazards can garrotte or strangle a child.

Make sure all that objects such as bags, scooters, skateboards and bikes are placed away from equipment and that wet equipment has been adequately dried before use to avoid slipping.

Teaching children how to use playground equipment properly is a critical part of childproofing and this should involve clear and consistent guidelines for all age-groups. Outline specific behaviours which are not acceptable and enforce them reliably. This should include when guests are using the equipment, and it can be helpful to clearly display a list of rules near the equipment to avoid confusion.

Children should be taught not to push or wrestle on the equipment and to look for other children before jumping off or sliding down equipment. No standing on swings should be permitted and children should be shown a clear exclusion zone around swings to avoid being struck.

Only the stairs should be used to climb to the top of the slide as one of the commoner playground accidents results from climbing up the slide itself and falling over the edge.

Backyard Garden and Plants

Gardens represent a wonderland of colours, textures and smells to children, but a poorly considered and badly maintained garden can become a child's nightmare.

Childproofing the garden involves a few simple measures

in the planning as well as solid upkeep along the way.

Hard and soft landscaping, as well as fences and gates must all be considered in the creation of a child-safe garden. This includes the minimisation of steep drops, climbing opportunities and tight crevices, as well as the avoidance of toxic vegetation and pesticides. Any high drop-offs in the garden should be fenced or heavily planted to stop children falling

Maintain pathways by fixing or replacing any loose bricks or stones and check lawns for potholes and hidden objects such as tree stumps which can be tripped on.

Garden borders should not be made of sharp rocks as this risks serious injury if tripped over. Choose instead wooden or other smooth materials and as an interesting alternative, remember that old car tyres are often free, are soft and using them helps the environment.

Keep grass short for adequate vision and to discourage snakes and other critters from visiting. In addition, clean doggy waste regularly and encourage them to use a specified corner of the garden away from play areas. If a dog has not been recently wormed, their poop can be added to compost bins or worm farms.

If spraying lawns or working with garden fertilisers and chemicals, remove shoes or boots before entering the house as babies will crawl over walking tracks and this risks ingestion of the chemicals. Do not allow children into freshly sprayed backyards and use liquid fertilisers in preference to pellets which are left in garden beds and can be mistaken for food by children. Consider using non-toxic, natural pesticides as a safer alternative.

Young children will pick up and/or taste anything found on the ground, so when mowing grass, check regularly for discarded rubbish and hazardous objects. The current trend for pebbles on paths and around plants may be dangerous, as small pebbles in particular can pose a choking risk to a small child.

Rake and throw leaves into green recycling or compost bins as they can create a slippery surface and may lead to serious falls. Curious children rustling through a pile of leaves can risk contact with any number of bees, spiders and assorted bugs nestling inside.

The backyard clothesline can be seen by children as another piece of play equipment and those with an adjustable height should always be stored in a high position greater than 1.8 metres to avoid garrotting. Keeping it out of reach will also discourage swinging or the attachment of toys (or siblings) to the clothesline.

Water

Water, in many forms tends to be a feature of most gardens and may take the form of pools, ponds, puddles or hoses. Whatever its guise, water is both an attraction and a danger to children and extra though must be given to securing water sources within a garden.

Check the yard for anything which may fill with water in the rain, e.g. wading pools, buckets etc. They should be stored in a shed and in an inverted position as young children can drown in less than 3cm of water and are usually unable to right themselves.

Similarly, secure all hose pipes and tighten all taps to minimise the risk of children accessing water.

Ponds should be netted with a heavy net which if fixed properly, can provide some protection for children while still allowing the pond to be seen. The pond water level should be kept as low as is feasible if children are under 5 as they are attracted to water and to any fish they can see and may fall in.

Swimming pools are an Australian backyard staple and it is mandatory under law in all states that pools are properly fenced off from the house and garden. Drowning is a leading backyard killer and can happen silently and in matter of seconds. A detailed account of childproofing pools and ponds can be found in Chapter 12.

Barbeque Areas

As a general rule, backyard barbeque areas must be complete 'no-go' zones for young children and the grill and any gas bottles should be secured. For a comprehensive guide to the BBQ area and safe grilling refer to Chapter 15.

Decking and Balconies

Modern gardens often contain an entertaining area consisting of decking or a balcony and a detailed guide to childproofing this area can be found in Chapter 14.

In general however, all raised decking and balconies must be protected by railings and balustrades which are at least 90cms high and which reach the entire length of the railings. Horizontal palings should be on the outside and there should be no other gaps or protrusions which could be used as a foothold for climbing.

If balustrades are more than 10cms apart then your child's head or body may fit through and so risks entrapment.

All outdoor furniture should be in good condition and free from splinters, sharp protrusions and exposed hinges. Do not place furniture near balcony railings as they can be used to climb over barriers and choose heavy quality outdoor furniture which is not easily moved by children. Replace or remove broken furniture items as children will climb on them regardless and risk serious injury.

Fences, Gates and Doors

Gates

All gates should open towards the garden from outside not outwards from it. In this case, if the gate does not close properly, a child trying to push out of the yard will push the gate closed rather than open.

Gates should also be self-closing and self-latching and should never be propped open, for any reason or for any period of time; children are opportunists.

Garden Access from House

Many homes have a door opening directly onto the garden area from the house, and this door is commonly made of glass. Garden doors should be kept locked and have decals or markings at the eye-level of a child to ensure that they do not run into or through the door thinking it is open. All glass doors must be made of toughened, safety glass.

Fence

Childproof fences and gates are the cornerstone of any child-safe garden and a more detailed account is found in Chapter 14.

A curious child can scale any fence if it is too low or if there are footholds and handhold to facilitate climbing. The top of the fence, therefore should be more than 120cms above ground and palings should be less than 100mm apart to avoid entrapment of body parts and a possible foothold through the gaps. These measurements are based on the average width of a toddler's foot.

Fences should also be regularly maintained and there should be no missing or rusted screws, and no holes in the fence.

Garden Shed

Garden sheds come in many forms, from the small potting shed, to the grand garden workshop and these spaces usually present a concentration of hazards for children. Quite simply, one of the best ways to childproof the garden shed is through adequate security, organisation and storage of contents.

First and foremost, the garden shed must be established as a 'no-go zone', and children must be taught from a young age that it is not a play area. Childproofing the shed is about keeping them out with childproof locks, but is also about preparing the space in the event of an invasion.

Sheds are often a multifunction space, and childproofing strategies therefore will depend on how the space is used; for garden storage for tools, mowers and power tools, general household junk, as a workshop or as a combination of all these and more.

Ensure that any power points within the shed are certified for outdoor use and are fitted with childproof guards and concealed from view where possible; out of sight out of mind.

Be on constant lookout for choking hazards which may have been left on low surfaces or have fallen on the floor. Sweep floors regularly for nails, chips and other small debris. As a general guide, any object which fits inside a cardboard toilet roll inner is a definite choking hazard but larger objects may also have small components which can come loose.

All garden tools pose a threat to children, and all children want to play with tools; this means that tool storage must be impeccable. Sharp tools and garden equipment must be stored in a locked cage or box, which, optimally is fixed out of reach. Tools must also be stored so they cannot fall on a child below. Long-handled tools should be stored high and horizontal in a cage, or fixed to the wall with handles resting on the ground, so they cannot be pulled down by children.

Nails, wire twists and all other little garden doo-dads should be stored in sealed containers, in a locked box, out of reach. Don't leave any strays on benches or floors as when swallowed or inhaled these sharp objects can cause serious damage to a child's airway and gut.

Power garden tools are a particular attraction and a real threat and they should *never* be left on a bench or plugged in. They should be stored unplugged, switched off, and in a high, locked cabinet. In addition, wind all electrical cords up and do not let them dangle when stored or when in use.

If taking a break, unplug the tool, and return it to the shed, then lock the door.

Safety guards should never be removed from power tools; this is good safety practice for adults and children.

Do not let young children 'watch' you use power tools, as you are distracted and they have short attention spans. Children may wander into the line of a moving blade or flying debris. They may also wander off into other parts of the shed or garden without you noticing. Make sure you know they are in the house under supervision. If older children are watching, ensure that they have safety goggles, masks and ear protection as appropriate.

Any outdoor garbage bins should be covered with a lid which can be locked in place. Alternatively, a childproof guard can be installed to stop the lid being opened as easily, this will prevent children from foraging through potentially dangerous trash. Where possible, keep all bins out of view and stored in a locked shed or garage or in a fenced off area.

Mowers

According to the Victorian Injury Surveillance System (VISS), 80% of lawn mower injuries occur in boys aged 0–14, and relate to them either playing in the vicinity of an active mower, or to them assisting with mowing itself. In addition, over 800 children are run over by ride-on mowers in the U.S.A. every year and their popularity is only increasing in Australia. The commonest mower injuries to children are more severe and primarily involve laceration or amputation to the lower extremities. In short, children should not be in the yard when mowing is in progress and should never be allowed to ride on or push a lawn-mower. Children should not even be allowed to watch the mowing as they risk injury from flying debris and may wander into harm's way. Double-check the location of a child before moving the mower and ensure that they are under the direct control of another adult. In addition, do not leave mowers running to attend to another task, even for a second, as children will see this as an opportunity to play.

Lawn mowers and any other motorised vehicles stored in the shed must be well-secured and keys should *never* be left in the ignition or stored in the vehicle. Instead they should be kept in a high, secure and even secret location, preferably outside the shed. If children gain access to these engines they may set the vehicle in motion or run the engine in a confined space risking carbon monoxide poisoning. Where possible, the mower should be locked or disabled from starting by other methods.

Be aware that exhausts and engines remain hot for up to an hour after use, and can cause serious burns within seconds. Children should be kept out of the shed completely during this time.

Engines should not be started whilst in the shed, but if they must be started in order to move, the main door should be opened before starting the engine as they produce carbon monoxide (CO), an odourless, tasteless gas which is lethal.

Chemicals and Cleaning

Garden chemicals exist in many forms, from cleaning products, to painting, and gardening substances. All must be stored in high cupboards, fitted with childproof locks and importantly must be kept locked at all times;

childproofing is completely undermined when locks are not engaged.

Keep all substances stored in the original, childproof packaging, which not only protects against exposure but is also important for product ingredient information if poisoning does occur.

Do not store chemicals, solvents, paints or cleaning fluids in old food jars or drink bottles as this sends confusing messages to young children and encourages ingestion. Ensure spray bottles of cleaning chemicals or insecticides have the nozzle turned to the 'off' position when not in use; children love these bottles and instinctively point the nozzles at their faces before squeezing the trigger.

Vermin control substances pose a particular threat as they are formulated to be lethal to other animals, and can, in larger doses be similarly lethal to children. Prime examples include snail pellets and rat poison where tablets or pellets are left in low areas. These are extremely attractive to pets and children and must not be left in traps or on the ground for children to eat.

Switch from pellets to liquid fertilisers and pesticides and keep children away from freshly sprayed areas. Or perhaps it is time to consider a switch from hazardous gardening products to safer, greener options which may be less toxic to everyone.

Store all buckets and other large containers upside down to ensure that they are empty and to prevent fluid collection which will pose a drowning risk. Do not place these items next to benches or under cupboards as children may use them to climb.

Pools and Ponds

In Australia drowning is the number one cause of death for children under five and is an unfortunate Australian reality largely due to our love affair with water and the abundance of backyard pools. For every drowning, there are estimated to be three children treated in hospital for a near-drowning, with some of these resulting in brain damage and permanent disability.

Toddlers are inquisitive and impulsive and are attracted to water and without a realistic sense of danger they are vulnerable to drowning. Babies and toddlers are top heavy and can drown in as little as 5cm of water especially if unable to right themselves.

One of the most unique and disturbing hallmarks of drowning is that they are silent deaths; it is unlikely that splashing or screaming will occur to alert parent to trouble, and many children are found already submerged.

Whilst teaching children about water safety is critical, the most vulnerable group to drowning are children under 5, who have limited cognitive capacity to learn extensive swimming skills. In fact, 80% of child drowning deaths in Australia were of children under 5 years, with most having fallen into the water, most commonly a swimming pool. Toddlers in particular are top heavy and can topple into water easily and find it difficult to right themselves.

For 62% of infants under 1 year, the bath was the commonest location for drowning. The U.S. Consumer Product Safety Commission (CSPC) studied pool drowning and near-drowning and found that it was the leading cause of death around the home for children under 5. In fact, 75% of the children involved in pool submersions were between 1 and 3 years old.

Adult supervision of children forms the central tenet of water safety, but what is deemed adequate supervision varies greatly between parents; from keeping an eye on them from the kitchen window, to being in the water with them. In a group situation, in addition to distraction, there may also be a confusion as to which adult is supervising children in the water. Alarmingly most of the drowning victims in the CSPC study were being supervised by a parent when the accident occurred.

In most cases, children were noted to be missing before being found in the pool with 77% of them only missing for 5 minutes or less. Nearly half of the children were last seen in the house rather than the backyard prior to the pool accident with only 23% sighted in the backyard prior. So 69% of the children involved in pool accidents were not supposed or expected to be in the pool.

Two thirds of pool accidents occurred in a pool owned by the victim's immediate family and another third occurred in friends' or relatives' pools. Less than 2% were a result of a child trespassing onto a neighbour's property.

Mandatory childproof pool gates and fences are now in force Australia-wide and according to a 1996 Kidsafe study caused a dramatic reduction in drowning incidents. When children do drown in a pool, barriers are usually found to be incomplete, non-compliant, faulty, or the gate has been popped open.

Source: *Safety Barrier Guidelines for Home Pools.* U.S. Consumer Product Commission. Publication no. 362 2004

Childproofing Pools & Ponds

All States and Territories throughout Australia have their own laws and exacting specifications for the construction of pools and pool barriers. This chapter is meant as a general guide and cannot be used as a substitute for local government requirements. Always check local laws by accessing government websites or by ringing your local council directly.

In general, any pool over 300mm or 30cm in depth must be effectively isolated from the rest of the backyard and creating an effective childproof barrier between the pool and the rest of the house is the best way to stop unsupervised access. This is obtained through a combination of a self-closing, self latching gate with a childproof latch out of reach of children, as well as suitable pool fencing.

For a pool barrier to be effective children should not be able to:
- Climb over or under
- Establish a foothold or handhold to climb
- Squeeze through gaps
- Open gates or doors to access pool

In effect, the pool must be made a 'no-go zone' both physically, and by teaching children from a young age that it is off-limits and not a part of their play area. In addition, children should be taught about water safety from a young age, and should be taught to swim as soon as they are old enough; many swimming schools are offering infant and toddler programs. Such water familiarisation programmes however, do not make a child drown-proof as many children under 5 who drowned had attended swimming lessons; this may not adequate preparation for the sudden immersion of a fully-clothed child.

No matter the effectiveness of barriers and gates, there is still no substitute for vigilant adult supervision as there is no more determined force than a resourceful child. If possible ensure a clear view of the pool from the house by removing vegetation or other obstacles in line of sight.

Pool Gates

Pool gates are the lynch pin of pool safety and should always open outwards from the pool and not towards it. This means that if the gate does not close properly, a child trying to push from the outside into the pool will instead only push the gate closed, and may even activate the latch.

The keys to an effective pool gate are the latch and

closing mechanisms. All pool gates should be self-closing and self-latching and must not be able to be pulled open once closed and latched, even if bounced on.

In addition, the release mechanism of the self-latching device should be placed over 150cms above ground at a height inaccessible to most young children. If under this height, the latch should be placed on the pool side of the gate over 7.5cm from the top of gate; this stops a child reaching over the top of the gate and releasing the latch.

The gap between the gate and the adjacent fence should be less than 10cm to prevent children's hands squeezing through. This is particularly important within 45cm of the latch release, as children squeezing their hand

through at this distance may be able to reach the latch.

Of utmost importance is that the gate is kept closed at latched at all times, even when the pool is in use and must **never** be propped open, for any reason and of for any length of time; it only takes a few seconds of distraction for a child to sneak through.

Access From The House

Many homes now have doors, often large glass doors, which open directly onto the pool area. This effectively means that this wall of the house forms part of the pool barrier.

It is essential therefore, that the access door must be kept locked and the keys must not be left in the lock; instead, these should be stored in a locked drawer or cupboard, away from the door and out of reach of children.

If this door is the only barrier before the pool, it is advisable to install an audible alarm which sounds when the door is opened unexpectedly and is loud and distinct from any other alarm. It should have an automatic reset and a temporary deactivation mechanism (for up to 15 seconds) which is located over 165cms off the ground.

For a completely indoor pool, all walls and doors should be equipped to serve as pool safety barriers.

Pool Fence

Pool fences must be made impenetrable to a determined, climbing child. A child may be able to scale a pool fence if it is too low or if there are footholds and handhold to facilitate climbing.

The top of the fence should be more than 120cms above ground and the horizontal rails should be on the pool side of the fence and over 115cms apart; this minimises the risk of footholds and climbing from outside the enclosure. The maximum distance from the ground to the bottom of a pool fence or gate should be lower than 10cm to prevent a child squeezing under.

Vertical palings should be less than 100mm apart to avoid entrapment of body parts and a possible foothold through the gaps; this is based on the average width of a toddler's foot. Any decorative cut-outs should also be under 100mm diameter to stop hand or footholds.

Any lattice or mesh fences must have opening sizes of less than 30mms across. In general, all openings on or around a pool fence should not allow passage of a 100mm sphere (a cricket ball is approximately 72mm). Children can force their whole body through gaps as small as this, as this is based on the chest depth and head breadth of a young child.

Inspect solid walls and barriers for any indentations or protrusions which could be used as traction for climbing. In general, pool fencing should be well maintained and must be checked regularly for broken palings, missing or rusted screws, or holes in the fence.

In recent times glass, and even frameless glass pool fences have become popular. The same strict criteria must apply to gaps and openings in these barriers, and they have the additional concerns of potential sharp corners and shattering. Ensure that all glass meets Australian safety standards so it is the correct form of thickened, toughened safety glass for the job.

One of the commonest ways children break through pool barriers is by utilising climbable objects such as outdoor furniture, pool filters, toys, or pot plants. Such items should not be left within a metre of the pool fence and any easily moveable objects such as toy cars, should be secured when not in use. Similarly, trim all overhanging trees and bushes so that they cannot be used to access the pool area.

Pools and Pond

Water familiarisation is an important weapon in helping children play safely in pools. This can be started as young as 6 months old and becomes more sophisticated as appropriate, look for suitable programs in your local area. Although it is never too early to start teaching water safety, children are usually ready to commence more formal swimming lessons after the age of 3.

Supervision

Proper adult supervision in the pool means being within arms reach of a child under 5 at all times, this will ensure that a submerged child can be immediately retrieved. This, of course will require parents to be *in* the pool with your children.

Supervision of children in a pool must be formalised,

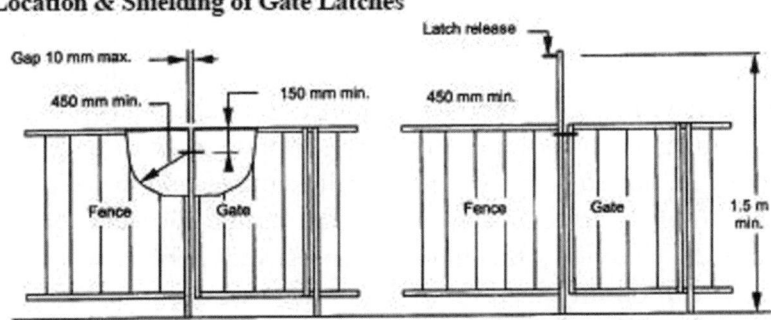

Location & Shielding of Gate Latches

Shield not required for latch or release located at 1.5 m or higher

especially if there are a group of children and adults. Allocate a parent or adult who is in charge of monitoring the children at all times and be aware of how many children are in the pool at one time, to ensure none are unaccounted for. If the supervising adult needs to go inside or do something else for a while, they should formally hand supervision responsibilities to another adult. Relying on a group of distracted adults to keep a vague eye on the children is not enough and can set the stage for tragedy. It is important that the supervising adult not be drinking alcohol and is alert.

It is neither fair nor safe to leave older children to supervise a younger child.

Covers

For added safety pools may be covered when not in use. This can also have thermal and cleaning advantages, but choose covers carefully as not all are designed to give a safety element. Covers should be heavier and have sturdy, multipoint fixation to stop children lifting an edge and becoming trapped underneath.

No matter how sturdy the cover is however, it should never be treated as a substitute for a proper pool barrier.

Backyard ponds can be covered with a heavy net which if fixed properly, can provide some protection for children while still allowing the pool or pond to be seen. If ponds or dams are too big to fence in or cover, fence off a child's play area to maintain separation of the two areas.

Pool Surrounds

Some States now require that a poster with paediatric CPR and drowning first aid guidelines is displayed clearly at the poolside (see Appendix 1). All parents and in particular those with a pool on their property should be trained in paediatric CPR.

In addition, a resuscitation and first aid kit with child attachments should be kept poolside, and a phone should always be present in case of an emergency.

Pool decks must have a non-slip surface and be kept clear of tripping obstacles including hoses and pool toys. Remove pool cleaning devices from the pool whilst children are swimming as they can become entangled or trip over the hoses at the poolside

All poolside electrical outlets should have childproof covers and be fitted with residual current circuit breakers. Check with your electrician that the power outlets are suitable for a poolside location. Keep all electrical appliances such as audio and video equipment well away from the pool as they may be knocked into the water resulting in electric shock.

Pool Toys

Wearable or free flotation devices should not be used as safety devices and are not a substitute for adult supervision. Be aware that some of these inflatable and floating toys can tip a child upside down and can also make it difficult for them to right themselves, leaving them trapped and submerged.

All pool toys and float aids should be deflated and stored in a childproof cupboard or a locked shed as they attract children to the pool and can lead to children reaching for them and over balancing.

Paddle pools should be emptied after each use and must be stored upside down and away from children.

Pool Chemicals

Pool chemicals are highly toxic and can cause poisoning and sever internal burns if ingested. All pool chemicals especially chlorine should be kept in a high, childproof cabinet remote from other chemicals especially turpentine or ammonia; if mixed, these compounds become explosive. The storage area must also be well ventilated as inhalation of chlorine causes severe breathing difficulties and may be life-threatening.

Pool testing and addition of pool chemicals should not occur while children are in the pool or pool area. Use liquid products and avoid the use of granules or tablets particularly when placed in feeder containers which float in the pool and can be accessed directly by children.

All chemicals should be kept in original, childproof packaging and be easily identifiable. Never place chemicals in old food or drink containers as this can only confuse children and makes accidental ingestion far more likely.

Spa Pools

Spa pools should be treated with the same safety precautions and barriers as larger pools but these pools have the added hazard of suction intake nozzles which are responsible for injuries in children every year. Drowning can occur if hair is sucked into these intakes, trapping children underwater.

Spas should have at least two suction outlets for each pump thereby distributing the force of suction and reducing the risk of hair, finger or toe entrapment. There should also be an emergency shut-off switch for the spa and its location must be within reach of the spa and clearly labelled.

Children should be kept away from the spa, which should be fitted with a solid, lockable cover. Indoor bathtub/spas should be secured by a lockable door and must not be used without adult supervision.

Children must be taught not to place their head underwater in a spa as this will only increase the risk of entrapment and drowning.

Public Pools

Public pools pose no less a threat for children than backyard pools and in some ways are potentially more dangerous as there are many people of varying age and maturity and it is easy to lose sight of a child.

Choose a pool which is appropriate to your child's age in terms of maximum depth and age of other children present. For children under 5 years, the supervising adult must be in the pool with the child and not just watching from the side.

Parents cannot rely on life guards to look after their child as they are watching hundreds of other children and cannot constantly monitor yours; lifeguards are not baby sitters.

Garage

MOST GARAGES ARE USED AS a multi-purpose space, playing several different roles within the household. Consequently, the childproofing strategies employed within the garage will depend on how the area is being used, i.e. to park cars, for general storage, as a workshop or as a combination of all these and more. Childproofing the garage takes a bit of thought and planning to ensure that it exists as more than just a dangerous family junk room.

The garage represents a unique environment for a child, one full of secrets and adventures, but it also contains a high concentration of child hazards such as tools and chemicals and most garage accidents result from children obtaining unsupervised access.

In many cases, the garage is directly accessible from the home and can act as an indoor/outdoor threshold. The garage therefore, must be enforced as a strict 'no-go zone' for children using childproof doors and locks and children must be taught from a young age that it is off-limits and not a play area. In short, childproofing the garage is about keeping children out, but is equally about preparing the space for possible invasion.

It is especially important when inspecting the garage for hazards that you change your perspective and crawl around on the floor; it is amazing how much is revealed. In particular, look for nails, screws, wood chips or any other small debris which may pose a threat to children. As a general guide, any object which fits inside a cardboard toilet roll inner is a definite choking hazard. Be aware that some larger objects may also produce small components.

Garage Doors

Garage doors are the key to restricting a child's access to the space There are usually one or two doors to a garage; a main, large door to the outside, and in some cases, a smaller door to the main house.

Most modern garage doors are fitted with automatic opening and closing mechanisms, often using a remote control. The older, manual doors however, have dangling ropes as well as old, often rusted and stiff hinge or spring mechanisms. All of these features pose a risk to children for strangulation, pulling the door down on themselves, and limb entrapment. In addition, these doors do not have the sensor functions of the automated doors which stop an object or person being crushed by the door. In short, these manual doors cannot be effectively childproofed and so if you have young children then it's probably time for a new door.

Automated garage doors offer better safety features, but must be properly maintained well to ensure safe functioning. In the USA there has been regulatory demand since 1982 for all automated garage doors to have an auto-reverse function. That is, if the door comes into contact with an obstruction such as a person whilst closing, it senses resistance and reverses direction. Many remote opening units also have the option of an in-built laser sensor system that stops door closure if the laser is broken. To ensure that this sensor includes toddlers and babies, it should be placed less than 15cm off the ground.

The door should be checked monthly for smooth opening and closing. To test the auto-reverse function, a cardboard box should be placed under the door as it closes; if the box is crushed, it is time to call the repairman, or to buy a new door.

Note that a slow-closing door offers extra safety time.

The remote control for the garage door should be kept locked in the car, out of reach of children, and should not be given to them in fun. Watching the door go up a down may amuse them, but it will also allow them to see the door as a toy to be played with. Equally, wall-mounted door controls within the garage should be placed well out of reach of children; over 1.5 metres off the ground.

Any electric door should have an emergency manual release in the event of a power failure, especially if the garage has no other access point.

Beware of any hinge, spring, roll or pulley mechanism and teach children not to touch. These moving parts should preferably be out of reach at over 1.5m off the ground.

Never walk away while the garage door is still closing, but watch it close to completion to ensure a child does not dart underneath at the last minute. Similarly, adults should never run underneath the closing door, not only is it dangerous, but inevitably children will copy such behaviour.

Any internal garage door into the main house should be kept closed and locked at all times as curious kids will gravitate to such spaces, full as it is of interesting things. Further, the key should not be left in the door but must be stored out of sight and out of reach. Alternatively, consider fitting a combination lock. Utilise a high door handle fitted over 1.5 metres off the ground to further restrict access for young children.

Tools and Equipment

All tools pose a threat to children, and all children want to play with tools; an incompatible combination and one which requires therefore, impeccable tool storage.

Sharp tools and garden equipment must be kept in a locked cage or toolbox, which optimally is fixed on a wall and out of reach. In addition, tools must also be stored so that they cannot fall on a child below.

Long handled tools should be stored high and horizontal in a cage, or fixed to the wall with handles resting on the ground so that they cannot be pulled down by children.

Nails, screws and all other little hardware doo-dads should be stored in sealed containers, in a locked box, and well out of reach. Be sure not to leave any strays on benches or floors as when swallowed or inhaled these sharp objects can cause serious damage to a child's airway and gut.

Power points should all be fitted with childproof guards and concealed from view where possible and avoid overloaded power boards left haphazardly on benches and floors.

Power tools should *never* be left on a bench or left plugged in. They should be stored unplugged, switched off, and in a high, locked cabinet. Wind all electrical cords and secure them and never have cords dangling from the bench either while the tools are in use or when they are stored. If taking a break from using power tools, unplug the tool, and move it to the back of the bench or to a higher, safer place.

Safety guards should never be removed from power tools as they protect fingers being exposed to blades and other hazards; this is good safety practice for adults and children.

It is not recommended that young children be allowed to watch adults use power tools. The adults are concentrating and distracted potentially leaving children to wander into the line of a moving blade or flying debris. They may also wander off into other parts of the garage without being noticed. Instead, before beginning ensure that children are accounted for and are in the house under supervision.

If older children are watching, they should be fitted with safety goggles, masks and ear protection as appropriate.

Motorised Vehicles

Cars, motorbikes, lawn mowers and any other motorised vehicles stored in the garage must be carefully secured. All vehicles should be kept locked and keys should *never* be left in the ignition or stored in a vehicle but must be kept in a high, secure and even secret location, preferably outside of the garage. In particular, car doors and boots should be locked at all times to stop children climbing inside and becoming trapped.

If children are able to start the engine they may set the vehicle in motion, become trapped in the boot or run the engine in a confined space risking carbon monoxide poisoning. It is sometimes possible for mowers and the like to be locked or disabled via other mechanisms to prevent them from being started.

Motorbikes should also be stored so that they cannot be pulled over on top of a small child.

Be aware that exhausts and engines remain hot for up to an hour after use, and can cause serious burns within seconds. Children should not be allowed in the garage during this time as many of these hot engine parts are at a child's height.

If possible, engines should not be started in the garage, but if they must be in order to move the vehicle, the main garage door should be opened before starting the engine. This is especially important if the garage is connected to the main house, and the internal connecting door should be closed when an engine is running. Engines produce carbon monoxide (CO), an odourless, tasteless gas which is lethal. (See below)

Never move any vehicle if children are not in view or their location is not known. They must be under the direct control of another adult, and preferably should be inside the house or in a secure backyard until the car is clear of the garage and driveway.

For more detailed car childproofing information see Chapter 16.

Garage Contents

Garbage bins are the repository for any number of child hazards and all bins should be stored out of view, preferably in a locked room or fenced area, but at the very least should be covered with a lid which can be secured. Alternatively, it is possible to install a childproof guard to restrict lid opening which will prevent children from foraging through potentially dangerous trash.

Dispose immediately of any broken glass, sharp off cuts or poisonous substances rather than placing them into the regular bin to await emptying. Similarly, wrap recyclables such as glass and opened tins and place them in an off-limits recycling bin immediately after use.

Bikes and trikes should only be accessible when adults are present and so should be chained up and unrideable when stored. Ensure that bicycles cannot be toppled onto a small child. For more information on bikes see Chapter 20.

Do not leave furniture or boxes under work benches or cabinets as they can be used to climb. In addition, any shelves, benches and cabinets should be fixed to the floor or wall to avoid toppling if climbed on; a simple 'L' bracket into the wall studs will suffice.

Large cabinets should have childproof latches or locks and should be kept locked as children love to hide in such places, risking suffocation.

If the garage houses a chest freezer or a large cooler or esky, it should have a childproof latch fitted to the lid and can even be stored behind a playpen to limit access. If a child opens the lid, they can risk falling in and shutting themselves inside, and as these freezers are sealed, children will be subject not only to hypothermia, but also to suffocation. These units are also relatively soundproofed and so any calls for help may go unheard.

Any exercise equipment should be left unplugged and switched off to prevent children being thrown or becoming entrapped. The electrical cord must also be safely wound and not left hanging, as this has been known to cause strangulation.

Whilst every garage is different, other commonly found hazards include, ropes, extension cords, batteries, wire and others.

Chemicals and Cleaning

The garage is a hub for toxic cleaning, painting and gardening solutions, any of which are potentially poisonous to a child. It is mandatory, therefore that each chemical substance is accounted for and thoughtfully stored rather than left haphazardly around the garage.

Store all cleaning products in high cupboards or cabinets, fitted with childproof locks and then keep them locked. All substances must be stored in the original, childproof packaging, which not only protects against exposure but also contains important product ingredient information if poisoning does occur. Never store chemicals, solvents, paints or cleaning fluids in old food jars or drink bottles; this sends confusing messages to young children and only encourages ingestion.

Do not leave spray bottles of cleaning chemicals on low surfaces or on the floor, and turn the spray nozzle to 'off' when not in use. Children love these bottles and will instinctively point the nozzles at their faces before squeezing the trigger.

Consider switching from hazardous cleaning products such as chorine bleach and lye products to less toxic, greener alternatives such as vinegar/water as a glass and surface cleaner. This is not only safer but also saves money and 'recipes' for making such cleaning solutions are freely available online.

Never leave a bucket of water or other cleaning liquid around as toddlers can drown in as little as 3cm of water especially if they become stuck in a bucket head first. If the water is hot it can also pose a burns risk, and as most will also contain cleaning solutions, they are also a poisons risk. Further, all buckets should be stored upside down to ensure that they are empty and so as to avoid collecting fluids.

Carbon Monoxide

Carbon monoxide (CO) is a colourless, odourless and highly poisonous gas which is produced by the incomplete burning of fuels. Any appliance fuelled by petrol, natural gas, coal, charcoal, LP gas, oil, kerosene or wood may produce CO; car engines are an important source of CO.

CO replaces oxygen in the blood and the symptoms of CO poisoning are flu-like and include headache, fatigue, shortness of breath, nausea and dizziness. Eventually, coma and death follow.

If you suspect CO poisoning, turn off the appliance, get to fresh air immediately, and call 000.

Do not run fuel-burning/CO producing appliances such as cars, mowers, furnaces, ranges and water heaters in contained, non-ventilated areas such as the house, garage, tents or an RV, especially if people are asleep. Similarly, avoid using petrol-powered tools inside, and if necessary ventilate the area well and exhaust the engine outside.

It is important not to run a car engine in the garage especially if it is in communication with the house, instead, start the engine only once the garage door is open, and move the car outside quickly.

A CO detector should be installed in all garages and homes as this will alarm when harmful levels of CO are detected. If the CO detector does alarm, open all windows and doors, call the fire department and move outdoors to fresh air. Be aware that some local authorities require installation of CO detectors in all new homes. It is also worth considering the installation of CO detectors in boats and motor homes.

Fire Safety

The garage contains many potential fire hazards and requires regular maintenance to minimise the risk of fire. Make sure all surfaces are free from fuel build-up such as sawdust, wood chips, and flammable chemicals; this is especially important if using power tools which may spark and ignite such materials. It is also unsafe to smoke in the garage and all lighters and matches must be kept well out of reach and locked away.

Ensure all electrical cords are in good condition and do not overload power points or power boards. Using heaters or radiators within a garage or workshop may ignite flammable chemical fumes or debris.

Install a smoke detector within the garage and check the battery every month. Some detectors come with lithium batteries which have a 10 year life-span, but should still be checked monthly.

All garages must have a fire extinguisher mounted in a readily-accessed area. It should be an all-purpose extinguisher which can be used on electrical and chemical fires and most importantly, make sure you read the instructions for use *before* you need it. Have a fire blanket wall-mounted for extinguishing any fires or wrapping around a person if alight. Teach children to *stop, drop and roll* if clothing catches on fire.

Have family fire drills to instil in children an action plan should a fire occur. This should include discussion of escaping from a fire, by staying low to the ground under the smoke, covering their mouth and nose with a moist towel or piece of clothing, and touching doors before opening to check they are not hot indicating fire on the other side.

Fences, Gates and Balconies

CHILDREN LOVE TO CLIMB, open, close and squeeze through just about anything they can; after all, there might be something exciting on the other side! But just how good at climbing are our children? Very good it would seem.

A study of 500 Australian toddlers has revealed that 80% of 2 year olds can climb a 60cm fence and 20% of 3 year olds can climb a 1.2m barrier; 5 year olds can scale it in an average time of 12 seconds! The median age for being able to climb a 1.4m safety fence is 4 years old and 5 year olds can climb it in approximately 17 seconds.

In short, underestimate your children at their peril, and pay close attention to the fences and gates protecting your children for they may not be as child-proof as you thought.

In fact, predictions are that if it was compulsory for a child hazard to be protected by a barrier with a minimum height of 90cm, childhood trauma could be reduced by 65%. If this barrier height was increased to 1.4m, the reduction could be as much as 75%.

Source: Nixon, J. W., Pearn, J. H. and Petrie, G. M. (1979). *Aust. Paediatr. J.*, 15, 260–262 Childproof safety barriers. An ergonomic study to reduce child trauma due to environmental hazards.

Childproofing Fences, Gates and Balconies

First and foremost it is important never to doubt a toddler or child's resourcefulness and determination to reach an object, especially a forbidden one. It is a parent's job therefore, to carefully identify any child hazard within the yard and ensure it is effectively fenced and gated.

In particular pools and ponds attract children like bees to honey and can rapidly result in drowning unless impeccably fenced and gated. For more detailed information about the particular requirements of pool barriers see Chapter 10.

To build an effective childproof barrier it is necessary that children:
- Cannot climb over or under
- Cannot get a foothold or handhold to climb
- Cannot squeeze through gaps
- Cannot open gates or doors

But no barrier is truly impenetrable and there is no fence or gate big enough to replace vigilant adult supervision; in particular of children under five. Parents can also reinforce the roles of fences and gates by setting a good example in their use. If children see an adult standing on fences or hanging over the balcony rails, they will copy.

Always check local building regulations as many states have specific local requirements for barriers, gates and balconies.

Gates

As a general rule, all gates should open inwards towards the yard, not outwards from it. In the event that the gate does not close properly, a child trying to push from inside the yard will therefore push the gate closed, and may even activate the latch.

Gates should also be self-closing and self-latching, with a sturdy childproof mechanism which once closed and latched, cannot be pulled open, even if bounced on. The release mechanism of the self-latching device should be placed 140cms above ground. If below this height, it should be placed on the outside of the gate more than 7.5cm from the top of gate, as this prevents a child reaching over the top of the gate and releasing the latch.

The gate to fence gap should be less than 100mm to stop children's hands squeezing through. This interval is particularly important within 45cm of the latch release, as a child reaching through from this point could access the opening latch.

Of great importance is that gates should *never* be propped open, for any reason and not even for a minute; children will seize any opportunity to sneak through, perhaps unnoticed.

Access From House

Most homes have some sort of door which opens directly onto the garden area and not uncommonly, this door is a large sliding glass door. In effect, this also means that the wall of house forms part of the garden barrier.

This door must be a well-constructed and sturdy one, not easily opened by young children, and should be fitted with a door latch which is childproof; young children will learn quickly how to open many standard latches. Further, any access door to the garden should be kept locked and the keys removed from it. These should then be stored in a locked drawer or cupboard out of reach of children.

In addition, large, sliding glass doors should have decals or markers at the height of a child's eyes so they do not run into the door thinking it is open; this is a common source of impact with children running around the house and garden, and has lead to children running through shattered glass resulting in severe injury. All glass doors must be made from toughened safety glass to prevent dangerous shards being created if broken.

If the main back door is not a sliding door, it is helpful to install a self-closing mechanism to ensure the door is not inadvertently left open. Ensure however, that it is a slow-closing mechanism to minimise the risk of entrapment of fingers or limbs from a slamming door.

Fence

The proper placement and construction of fences around the home is essential to effective childproofing and requires careful thought and planning for each individual yard.

Fences should be used, in particular to divide and segregate areas of the garden which are incompatible with child safety; e.g. the play area from the driveway

Children are eternally climbing and exploring and fences

must be made to ensure difficult climbing. A child can climb over a fence if it is too low or if there are footholds and handholds to facilitate climbing.

Therefore, the top of the fence should be over 120cms above ground with the horizontal rails on the outside of the fence and over 120cms apart; this will minimise the risk of foothold and climbing. Vertical palings should be placed less than 100mm apart to avoid entrapment of body parts and possible a foothold through the gaps; this is based on the average width of a toddler's foot.

Any decorative cut-outs in the fence should be under 100mm in diameter to stop hand or footholds and it is essential that solid walls and barriers have no indentations or protrusions which could be used as footholds. Lattice or mesh fences should also have opening sizes less than 30mm.

In general, all openings on or around a fence should not allow passage of a 100mm sphere, which is slightly larger than a cricket ball or baseball (which are approximately 72mm in diameter). Children can squeeze their whole body through gaps as small as this, as this is based on the chest depth and head breadth of a young child.

Similarly, to prevent a child squeezing under a fence, the maximum distance from the ground to the bottom of the fence or gate should be less than 100mm.

To further restrict access over fences and gates, remove all furniture, toys or other climbable objects which could be used to scale the fence; there should be a clear zone around the fence of greater than 1 metre. Be sure to look up as well, and similarly prune any overhanging trees or bushes which may be used to clear the fence.

Fences must be regularly inspected and maintained, and there should be no broken or missing palings, no rusted screws, and no gaps in the fence. Importantly, ensure that fences are not made using arsenic-treated wood as a fungicide.

Balconies and Decks

Balconies and decking areas are adult zones, and young children should never be allowed access without adult supervision and they must never be left there alone, even for a minute; if you need to go inside, take them with you. Kids should also be taught repeatedly and from a young age that the balcony is a 'no-go' zone unless with an adult and even then, that it is not an area for running, riding or overly-energetic play.

Childproofing a balcony, therefore, is primarily about preventing access to children, but must also be about preparing as safe a space as possible if access occurs.

Balcony doors must have high, childproof locks which are kept engaged at all times and the keys should not be kept in the door but placed in out of reach of children.

Opening limiters for doors can be bought to limit any door opening to less than 100mms and can be used as a backup should a child unlock the door.

Stairs leading from and decking to the wider garden should be blocked with a childproof gate, as this will restrict access to both the stairs and to the wider garden area.

More recently available in Australia, is a polyethylene netting system, long used in South America to secure high-rise windows and balconies. The clear netting can withstand 500kg per square metre, is quick to install and does not interfere with views. There have been reported problems with strata management bodies in some buildings worried about the aesthetics of such nets and all tenants of such buildings should seek advice.

Under the Building Code of Australia (BCA) a balustrade or barrier is required where people could fall over 1 metre in height, but in the case of young children, injury may occur if falling from a height much less than this. It is advisable therefore that all decking and balconies should be fitted with barrier no matter their height.

Barrier guidelines for balconies are as described above for fences; in particular that for any decks or balconies over a metre off the ground, the barrier must be over 120mm in height, with no gaps over 100–125mm. Further, for heights greater than 4 metres off the ground, there must be no climbable elements to the barrier between 150mm – 760mm off the ground.

In particular, barriers and

railings should not allow any foothold or handhold for climbing. If railings are too far apart, or allow for some foothold, balcony shields are available and consist of netting, lattice or Perspex sheeting to cover the barrier and stop children squeezing through or climbing up. Any support poles on verandas should be wrapped with padding to minimise injury from any impact.

Minimise decking furniture and other climbable objects such as air conditioning units and remove any clutter. Any outdoor furniture should be heavy and not easily moved by children, and/or anchored to the deck. Additionally, all furniture and other objects should be placed over a metre away from balcony railings and edges to prevent them being used for climbing. Similarly, remove pot plants from around edge of a balcony, as they can be used to climb on and check that any plants on or around the balcony are not poisonous.

To minimise the risk of balcony collapse, it is essential to regularly inspect decking and balconies for signs of degradation or wear, paying particular attention to rusted or broken screws, nuts or bolts or rotting wood. Any repairs should be performed by professional tradesmen who will also organise safety checks of balcony integrity. Think about weight loading on balconies and avoid overloading it with people (13 people weigh as much as a small car) or heavy furniture and spas.

Similarly inspect any furniture for splinters, broken struts, sharp protrusions or missing screws as children will continue to use furniture even if it is broken, and so risk entrapment or lacerations.

CHAPTER 15 — 148

Barbeque

Every summer, backyards are filled with the rich aromas of the great Australian barbeque, often to the accompanying squeals of delight from the assembled children. But at the centre of such events is the barbeque grill, complete with temperatures well over 100 degrees Celsius and naked flame, it is both a great attraction for young children and a great danger.

Most barbeque accidents involve burns from unsupervised access to the hot grill, fire or to matches and firelighters. Contact with barbeque surfaces will cause full thickness burns within seconds, whilst children playing close to an open flame can have their clothing set alight.

There are a lot of distractions at a large family barbeque and it is easy to lose track of children, but one moment of inattentiveness to the barbeque area may be enough to cause tragedy.

As fire and children do not mix, BBQ childproofing is all about restricting access to the area as well as providing vigilant supervision.

First and foremost, it must be clear that the barbeque area is a 'no-go zone' for all children with clear boundaries shown to children, especially those who are visiting. Matches and firelighters must be kept out of reach and not left around the barbeque area.

At least one adult should be designated not to drink alcohol so children can be safely supervised, preferably with a few adults taking it in turns to watch the children whilst the others enjoy the barbeque.

Barbeque Grill

Fire attracts children, and wanting to 'help' or mimic parents at the BBQ is a dangerous starting point. In short, there is no safe way to integrate young children and a barbeque grill and childproofing this area is all about keeping the two apart.

Make the grill area a 'no go zone', preferably through the use of a fence and childproof gate. If this is not possible consider temporarily placing a playpen around the area when grilling.

If there is no physical fencing or barrier around the grill, mark a clear exclusion zone around it with chalk. This gives young children a visual cue and allows for clearer communication with them. Recruit other adults and parents to police the boundaries and reinforce the exclusion zone.

No two barbeques are quite the same, so before use read the instruction manual or refer to the assembly and use guidelines found on the manufacturers' website.

The barbeque structure itself must be stable and resist tipping or spilling of contents. If the grill is on wheels make sure that they are lockable.

In addition, ensure that any electrical cords or gas lines are not dangling but are wound up and secured to the barbeque using cord clips.

Install childproof stove guards around the grill to stop little hands reaching the hot surface, and similarly, install childproof knob covers where possible to stop activation of the heat or gas by children.

Beware of heavy lids or grill covers which can crush little fingers and look for slow-closing lids, or fit a spring system yourself. At the very least, find a way to wedge the lid open when the grill is in use or fix it temporarily to a wall or post to prevent it slamming shut.

Remember that the dangers of barbequing do not end with completion of cooking as barbeque grills may remain hot for over an hour after use. So make sure the lid is closed and clipped or locked and that the barbeque area is secured after use. Maintain supervision of the BBQ area even after the cooking is finished.

As a general tip, the grill should be cleaned thoroughly as the build up of grease occurs quickly and can cause grease fires and sudden flare-ups.

Storage of a BBQ is critical to its safety as children will want to 'play barbequing' and imitate behaviours. The grill should be covered with lids which are secured with childproof latches or locks and all knobs should be in the 'off' position and fitted with childproof covers.

Many barbeques come with solid all-weather covers which stretch over the entire structure and are of some additional value as safety protectors.

Gas barbeques should also be stored with the gas turned off and completely disconnected to minimise the risk of gas leak or flame activation.

Tools and Accessories

Barbeque tools are traditionally long, heavy duty and have many sharp, jagged edges and if in use, they will also be hot. These tools should be kept out of reach of children at all times and should not be left hanging over the edge of the grill as they can be pulled down by children.

Supervision

It is important, even for the simplest of gatherings, to formalise supervision of any children. Allocate a parent or adult who is not drinking alcohol to be in charge of monitoring the children at all times. If this adult needs to go inside or do something else, they should formally hand supervision responsibilities to another adult. Relying on a group of distracted adults to keep a vague eye on the children is not enough and can set the stage for tragedy.

A helpful idea is to create a supervised, enclosed play area filled with toys and distractions away from the BBQ area. Older children may want to be involved in the cooking process, however should not be allowed to help at the grill, but can be included instead by making salads or buttering bread away from the grill area.

A Table Full of Food

Do not have tablecloths hanging over the edges of the table as these can be yanked on and the contents of the table pulled down on top of children. Placemats are a safer option, but if a tablecloth is preferred, then use table edge clips to secure the cloth to the table.

Place all hot food and drinks, knives and other sharp objects towards the centre of the table and away from the edges where they can be reached by little hands; never underestimate the reach of a determined child.

All food, especially meats and creamy salads should be kept refrigerated before cooking and should equally be cleared away immediately rather than being left out for hours afterwards; this is to lessen the risk of food poisoning. Children have a smaller bodyweight and so even a small amount of ingested bacteria can render a small child very ill.

Keep all alcohol well out of reach of children including leaving glasses and bottles unattended as alcohol poisoning can occur in kids from relatively small amounts.

Fire & Fuel

If a fire lighter is used, it should have a childproof button which locks the trigger and prevents it being fired. This and any matches should not be kept with the barbeque but should be removed as soon as the BBQ is lit, and taken into a high childproof cupboard inside.

Never use fire accelerants such as kerosene, lighter fluid or petrol as they are dangerous and unpredictable. The solutions become a heavy gas at lower temperatures and can explode causing serious injury to all, and in addition they also pose a serious poisoning threat to children. Instead, coal and wood burning grills can be started using briquettes; dense bricks of fuel which are designed to safely start fires.

Be aware that coal fires are bigger and more unpredictable than gas fires and should never be left unattended. Watch for wind-blown ash, smoke and sparks and keep children upwind of the barbeque.

The main cause of gas grill fires is an unrecognised obstruction in the fuel line and gas lines should be regularly checked for blockages and other damage. All fuel tanks should be disconnected and control valves turned off when not in use.

BBQ Fire Safety
1. Make sure all surfaces around the barbeque are free from fuel build-up such as leaves, twigs, wood chips, and flammable chemicals and never smoke in close proximity to the barbeque.
2. Keep all lighters and matches out of reach and locked away and
3. Ensure all electrical cords and gas lines are in good condition
4. Install a smoke detector within the garage and check the battery every month. Some detectors come with lithium batteries which have a 10 year life-span, but should still be checked monthly.
5. Install a fire extinguisher near the BBQ area in a readily-accessible area. It should be an all-purpose extinguisher which can be used on electrical and chemical fires. Make sure you read the instructions for use *before* you need it.
6. Other ways to smother a fire are with water, or a bucket of sand for grease fires.
7. Have a fire blanket wall-mounted for extinguishing any fires or wrapping around a person if alight. Teach children to ***stop, drop and roll*** if clothing catches on fire.
8. To control a gas fire, the gas must be disconnected immediately. Make sure you know where the emergency gas shut-off valve is in case of a gas fire.
9. Display fire first-aid clearly in BBQ area.

Burns First Aid
- If clothing is on fire: **STOP, DROP AND ROLL**
- Wrap person in blanket and roll until flames are extinguished
- Hold burnt area under running water, or if too large place wet, cool sheets over burned area. Do not use ice, it can cause further damage to skin.
- Remove any constricting clothes or jewellery from burned area unless they are stuck
- Prevent heat loss by covering non-burnt area with blanket

- Minor burns can be managed with non-stick dressings and painkillers
- Major burns (>20% of body) should be treated by immediately calling 000 for ambulance
- If unsure as to depth and severity of burn, seek medical attention.

Do not:
- Do not apply ointments, fats or lotions to burn unless directed by doctor. They can impair healing.
- Do not touch burnt area or burst any blisters, it can invite infection.
- Do not remove anything stuck to the burn.

Cars and Car Seats

CARS ARE A NECESSARY PART of modern life and no more so than for parents who spend seemingly endless hours on the road. It is essential, therefore that parents understand how to childproof both their driving and their cars to minimise any risk to their precious cargo.

Surprisingly, many vehicle-related injuries involving children occur on private property or in car parks and not on public roads as might be assumed. In fact, many deaths are due to children being backed over in driveways. Tests have shown that for some cars, in particular 4-wheel drives (4WD) and sports utility vehicles (SUV), the rear blind spot can range from 5–15 metres in size depending on the height of the driver, the car and the child.

Other causes of non-traffic injury and death in children relate to hyperthermia from being left in a hot car, power window strangulation and setting the car in motion when left unsupervised.

When children do become involved in traffic accidents, the commonest causes of injury are inappropriate or inadequate restraint, driver distraction and flying objects within the vehicle.

At the core of safe car travel is choosing and then properly installing, the correct restraint for a child of any size or age. The correct use of an appropriate child restraint and car seat reduces the chance of fatal injury in an accident by 71% in the less than one year old age group and by 54% for toddlers (ages 1–4). Alarmingly, a 2005 report by the Motor Accident Authority of NSW found that 82% of children admitted to hospital following a motor vehicle accident (MVA) had not been restrained properly. Further, the U.S. National Highway Traffic Safety Administration (NHTSA) studied over 5000 children and car seats and found non-use of restraints increased in the afternoons, and on weekends, or if the child was wearing sporting equipment or padding. Interestingly, child restraint use also appears to reflect seat belt use by the accompanying adults with 40% of children riding with unbelted drivers also being unrestrained.

With the vast array of child restraints available, as well as recent legislative changes in all Australian states and territories, the choice, installation and correct usage of an appropriate child restraint can be confusing. It is essential, therefore, that parents familiarise themselves with child restraint regulations as well as car seat and individual car specifications prior to purchase of any device.

General Childproofing Guidelines

- Whilst it is essential to childproof your car, it is no less important to car-proof your child. This involves educating them from a young age about the dangers of cars both on the road and while parked.
- Don't assume that because a product is on the market, that it has safety standard approval. Look for an Australian safety standard sticker and check websites such as the Australian Consumer and Competition Commission, (ACCC) at www.recalls.gov.au for any product recall notices.
- Always read and follow equipment manufacturer's height and weight recommendations. Many injuries are caused by placing children in equipment for which they are either too large or too small.
- Purchase the best quality equipment your budget will allow, and prioritise safety

above convenience or 'gadget' features. Sturdy, well-designed equipment is priceless.
- Never leave a child of any age unsupervised in a car; even for a minute. They can rapidly overheat, set the car in motion, be abducted or injure themselves climbing about the car.
- Read all instructions before using car seats and restraints as many safety features may not be obvious. A major cause of equipment-related injury is improper use.
- It is not generally recommended that car seats be bought second-hand as they may come with an uncertain history and potentially have been involved in an impact.
- As an exercise, imagine someone else driving with your child and consider the sort of driver conduct you might expect of them. Hold yourself to these same behavioural standards. For example, would you be happy if you saw them leave your child unrestrained, or locked in the car while they ducked into a shop? Would it be acceptable for them to be texting on their mobile phone whilst driving? When it comes to their children, parents can be too close to see objectively.
- Mobile phones should only be used hands free, Bluetooth or using an earpiece; no exceptions.

Buying a Child-Safe Car

A good start to keeping your children safe around cars is to research available safety features and buy the best your budget will allow. Many modern cars come with standard safety features not found on older models. So look at consumer safety sites such as Choice.com.au, local road traffic authorities such as Vicroads, and independent car websites and choose the right car for your family.

Safety features to research include:
- Anti-lock Braking System (ABS) for faster and safer stopping.
- Electronic Stability Control (ESC) which helps to keep control of the car when skidding, swerving or in poor road conditions.

- Tyres are the only contact between road and car, and good tyres grip and handle better.
- Airbags; front and side curtain which are effective in rollovers and side impacts. If buying SUVs, look for rear airbags also.
- Reversing camera to improve rear vision and decrease blind spots.
- Cargo barrier to separate passenger area from boot in SUV/wagon/4WD.
- Automatic daytime running lights improving visibility to other drivers.
- Lap sash seatbelts are safest and should be installed in the middle rear position also. Lap belts alone are not recommended. Seat belt warning devices are also useful.
- Built in anchor points for child restraints.

Creating a Childproof Car

After buying the safest car your budget will allow, the next most important childproofing tool is regular car maintenance with safety checks of the engine, brakes and tyres. The best seatbelts in the world will not compensate for worn brakes and bald tyres.

Next, it is important to educate and 'car proof' children from a young age, by teaching them proper car behaviour. These points should be repeated frequently and rewarded with positive reinforcement when children behave well.

It is legislated in most Australian jurisdictions that children should travel in the backseat until they are seven years old and large enough to safely use an adult seatbelt and sit comfortably in an adult seat. Most agencies recommend that children less than twelve years old travel in the rear seat, but the child's size, rather than their age, should be the primary consideration.

Busy parents have an endless amount of errands to perform within an ever-diminishing window of time, so it is understandably tempting to leave children alone in a parked car, 'just for a minute'. But in only a few minutes this places babies and children at risk of overheating, abduction or other injury. It is astounding that most people would consider it naively unsafe to leave their wallet on view in a parked car and yet seem to consider it safe to leave babies and children in that same vulnerable situation.

Cars should always be locked when parked in the driveway or garage to guard against unauthorised access by children. Children have died from locking themselves in hot cars or in boots or by setting a car in motion.

Children quickly learn the power of car keys and from a young age will seek them with purpose. Keys must be stored in a childproof secure cupboard or box, out of reach and out of sight of children. A resourceful child will climb to retrieve keys from benches or hooks.

Unfortunately, many car-related injuries to children occur at home when moving cars in driveways and garages. All children must be accounted for and secured before moving a car and the safest way to do this is to ensure that they are all inside the car or inside the house when reversing from driveways or car park spaces. Check and check again that when not in the car all children are with another adult and secured. If leaving the house, children should be formally transferred to another adult before moving the car. Do not assume that children are where you think they are; be sure, as children will often rush after a parent.

The logistics of loading children in and out of cars can be daunting but as a general rule, children should get in and out of cars on the kerbside wherever possible. Things become a little more complex when dealing with multiple children of varying ages. When loading a car, start by ensuring the older, more mobile children are inside the car first and when your hands are free, buckle them in. Equally, when removing multiple children from cars, take the least mobile child first to minimise the risk of an older child darting into traffic. It can be difficult attending to a younger child whilst keeping track of an older one.

In days past, it was not uncommon for children to ride unsecured in the back of station wagons and sadly then, it was also not unusual for injuries and even deaths to occur when cars were forced to brake suddenly. Do not let children ride unsecured in the luggage space of a

4WD, SUV, or station wagon, even for a 'quick trip'. They can be thrown about the car or hit by flying objects. It is also important to ensure any fold-down back seats are locked in the upright position. This will prevent children climbing into the boot and risking rapid overheating and suffocation.

With the car in motion, young children should not be able to reach the door handle or lock, and the childproof lockout should be activated to neutralise rear door locks. Power windows are a source of serious injury if activated by children and can similarly be controlled centrally by activating the childproof lockout.

Overheating is a serious risk to children travelling in cars, but a simple way to ameliorate this is to place safety-approved sunscreens on children's windows. These must also allow for adequate driver visibility and therefore total block-out with nappies, towels or blankets should not be used.

The buttons and levers in cars are irresistible to kids and one of the most accessible and dangerous is the cigarette lighter. These hot pokers should be removed from the car as they are too easy to depress and heat. This can result in serious burns or the ignition of an internal car fire with potentially disastrous consequences.

Driver behaviour is another key to child safety, with the main risks to child passengers stemming from drink driving, driver distraction and driver fatigue. Being a sensible and responsible driver is one of the most effective childproofing instruments parents have.

Hot Cars

For busy parents, it is always tempting to duck out for that quick errand and to leave a child 'safely' locked in the car. The extra time and effort of disembarking children, prams and paraphernalia can turn even the simplest tasks into unwelcome odysseys.

The commonest reasons children are left in hot cars are:
- Parents leave them for 'just a minute' to run an errand and think it is not hot enough weather for it to be dangerous
- Children are simply forgotten in their car seat

- Miscommunication between carers means that each think that the other has removed the child from the car
- Preschoolers or older children sneak into the car to play and cannot get out
- Kids becoming trapped in the car boot

Put simply, hot cars are death traps and children should never be left alone in a car, not even for a minute. Fatal temperatures inside vehicles are reached quickly and in relatively mild weather. On a typical summer's day, temperatures inside a parked car can climb to 20–30°C hotter than the outside temperature, with 75% of the temperature increase occurring in the first 5 minutes.

For example, in one demonstration performed on a 29°C day, the air conditioning was left to cool the car interior to 19°C and then the engine was turned off. Within 1.5 minutes the interior temperature was equal to outside at 30°C and within 6.5 minutes it was 40.5°C. More dramatic still, is the finding that on a 36°C day, the interior reaches 60°C in 5 minutes and 65°C after 15 minutes, temperatures which are rapidly fatal especially to babies and children.

Due to their smaller body size and immature nervous systems young children have less effective cooling mechanisms and so are far more vulnerable to external temperatures. Consequently, children's body temperatures can rise 3–5 times faster than adults. Babies in particular cannot efficiently regulate their own

temperature and will overheat and dehydrate quickly.

There are a number of misconceptions people have about heat in cars which make them more likely to risk leaving their child. One of the biggest and most dangerous is that an open window cools the car adequately. This is a myth and there is, in fact, no lessening of interior heating by opening a window, or with lighter coloured interiors or with window tinting. In addition, large cars heat up at the same rate as smaller cars. In short, there are no weather conditions or other measures which make it safe to leave a child in a parked car.

It is essential to ensure all children are accounted for before locking the car, as children have been inadvertently left in a car when one parent assumes the other parent has removed the child. This is more common with a sleeping child as they are quiet and can be forgotten. A useful trick is to leave your bag, wallet or another essential object on the backseat whilst driving so that you must access this area before locking the car.

To avoid returning to a car full of burning hot metal, hide and protect metal latches and buckles from direct sunlight. If necessary cover the entire back seat with a reflective cover or towel.

Hyperthermia

Hyperthermia, also known as overheating or heat stroke can occur within minutes of leaving a child in a hot car and rapidly causes irreparable muscle, kidney, heart and brain damage which can all lead to sudden death. The early signs of hyperthermia include sweating, flushed face and listlessness and as hyperthermia progresses, signs may include; agitation, confusion, dizziness, rapid heartbeat, pale and clammy skin, and eventually unconsciousness, seizures and death.

Hypothermia, or low body temperature, is less common in an Australian climate however can still occur especially in small babies with their immature temperature regulation.

Travelling in Hot Weather

Driving with children over the hot summer months is unavoidable, but with a few precautions, it can be done comfortably and safely. If a car has been sitting in the heat, open up the doors and sunroof and allow it to air prior to travelling. Check the temperature of the seats and especially any metal, such as buckles, to avoid burns.

Where possible, travel in the cooler times of day, and avoid travelling in the middle of the day when direct sunlight is unavoidable. Install automotive window shades on the rear windows and do not be tempted to use towels or blankets hanging from the windows. These home remedies reduce driver visibility whilst also impairing airflow and increasing temperatures around adjacent passengers. As a preference, choose fitted window shades specific to your vehicle as these have the advantage of allowing window opening whilst in place.

Avoid the use of any hoods or bonnets fitted directly over a baby capsule as this can decrease air circulation and so increase heat around the infant. Do not drape any sort of fabric over a baby capsule as this risks not only overheating but also smothering and suffocation. The rear seat should have adequate airflow by directing ventilation and air-conditioning specifically towards children.

Children should be dressed for a hot weather trip in light clothing to promote airflow around them especially if the car does not have air conditioning. Pack plenty of cool fluids, especially water, as children dehydrate quicker the younger they are. Stop regularly to feed infants and offer drinks to children frequently as thirst is not a reliable indicator of fluid status.

As the trip progresses, stop and take breaks every 2 hours to allow children to get out of the car and walk around. This promotes cooling evaporation and is a good time to offer a drink. With young babies, remove them from the car seat and place them on the some shaded ground.

Driver Distraction

The world today provides no end of gadgets and gizmos all vying to distract a driver. Between phones, pads and pods, not to mention boring old radio and CD changers, who wouldn't be tempted to multi-task while driving? Anything which takes your eyes or your concentration away from driving is inherently dangerous.

Driving whilst holding a mobile phone and talking is not only illegal in Australia, it has also been shown to quadruple the chance of accident and is akin to driving with a blood alcohol of up to 0.10. In the U.S.A. some insurance companies have begun checking the mobile phone records of drivers involved in accidents before paying out on claims. Whilst the use of hands-free technology undoubtedly tempers some of the risks, it does not negate them completely as concentration and attention are still divided. How often have you missed a turn whilst on the phone? If a conversation is particularly heated or intense the risks increase further.

Texting while driving is an increasingly dangerous problem. A study from the University of Utah showed that texting drivers had a 30% increase in reaction times and a 6-fold increase in the risk of crash.

So the simple choice is: ignore the phone call/text or pull over and lose a couple of minutes travel time to keep you and your children safe. If you must speak on the phone organise some type of hands-free device, either an in-car kit, or Bluetooth or a wired earpiece; there is a solution for every phone and every budget.

For parents, some of the main distractors are found in the backseat, where checking on children and their behaviour, or refereeing fights can have them constantly twisting around. Instead, parents should pull over to ensure that the children are safe and unhurt and then simply try to ignore any noise out and concentrate on the road. Never adjust the rear-vision mirror to see the children rather than the road and if you must monitor back seat activity, buy a wide-angled mirror which can be mounted above the rear-vision mirror. Occupy the children, especially on long trips, with music, audio books, DVDs and toys. If particular children are troublesome together, space car seats away from each other.

Flying Objects

Flying objects within vehicles are a major cause of injury, especially with sudden braking and impact. Even light items kept on the rear shelf can become a projectile force 20 times its own weight, with a simple book becoming a 10kg missile. The rear shelf should be kept clean of any objects.

Luggage and boot space must also be managed correctly. In particular SUV, 4WD, and station wagons with cargo areas opening directly onto passenger areas can be dangerous as goods can become free flying missiles within the cabin. Have a licensed fitter install a cargo barrier with approved safety standards, and always pack luggage evenly across the cargo area. Do not stack objects higher than the back seats, and ensure that the rear window and rear-vision mirror are not obstructed.

Any folding rear seats must be locked securely into position so there is no sudden movement which may trap or injure passengers in a crash. Unrestrained baggage or parcels moving forwards at speed can also cause unsecured split seats to collapse.

Power Windows

Power windows are an unexpected but very real source of childhood injury and even death. Each year over 1000 children are injured in the U.S. after being caught in power windows. The commonest cause of injury is crush of a body part, which can range from crushed fingers, or broken limbs, to suffocation and strangulation if the chest or neck are caught in the window. Closed head injuries have also been described.

Power windows generate a significant upward force of 14–36kgs, more than enough to crush an infant. It has been estimated that is takes only 10kgs of crushing force to seriously injure or suffocate an infant. In contrast, some of the lever or toggle switches take only 900grams of force to activate a window.

Rocker switches are designed to pivot on a centre hinge, effectively operating like a see-saw, whereas toggle switches operate using small levers that push back and forth to open and close a window. Lever or push-down/pull-up switches function by pressing down on the switch to open the window, but the switch must be actively pulled up to close the window.

With rocker and toggle switches, commonly located on door armrests, downward pressure (e.g., a child kneeling or leaning) on the switch can result in windows opening or closing. These are not recommended.

With lever switches, which also are commonly located on door armrests, windows cannot be closed due to unintentional pressure. Many new car manufacturers are now forced by law to install lever switches.

Look for windows which also have an automatic reversing system (ARS); this will reverse direction when it encounters an obstacle such as an arm or torso. Most cars are now fitted with childproof central locks to inactivate door-mounted rear window buttons; these should be engaged at all times, even with older children. Accidents can still occur when using the central window control however, so always look when closing a child's window from the front seat. If you cannot see the child, do not close the window as children will often grab for a closing window.

Driveways

One in four child pedestrian hospitalisations results from injuries sustained on home driveways, and the majority of these children are under 4 years old, they are mobile but too small to be easily visible. Accidents predominantly occur with vehicles reversing at low speed out of the driveway and usually it is a parent driving. Four-wheel drives, commercial utilities and SUVs are over-represented in these incidents, and given their size, also lead to more severe injuries and subsequent fatalities.

The prevention of driveway accidents must involve addressing the driveway, the car, the driver and child supervision.

Children should be provided with fenced-off play areas away from driveways and streets. Ideally children playing should be visible from the main living area. Unfenced front yards pose a particular danger and children should not be left unsupervised. Two New Zealand studies have observed that the majority of driveway injuries occurred at homes where there was no physical separation between driveway and play areas. Still other studies have shown a 3-fold increase in the likelihood of driveway accidents in the absence of physical barriers between play area and driveways.

For higher risk vehicles such as 4WDs, install and adjust

extended mirrors and reversing cameras where possible to increase driver visibility.

All drivers should be made aware of the risks of driveway injuries and should use extra vigilance when moving vehicles on private property. Drivers must walk around the car before backing out and ensure that they can account for the whereabouts of *all* children on the property. Ideally all children should be inside the car or inside the house, or standing with a second adult who can give the all clear before setting the car in motion. If this is not possible, the child should be placed, temporarily, in their car seat before backing out.

Garages

Garages pose a specific group of childproofing challenges as they contain not only immobile cars, but also tools, chemicals and other unique contents. Chapter 13 is devoted to childproofing the garage.

Seatbelts and Restraints

It may sound obvious to state that all children must be properly restrained in a correctly installed, age-appropriate car seat; however a 1998 RACV report found that 62% of child car seat restraints were fitted incorrectly. In fairness, that vast array of child restraints and car seats on the market today has made choosing an appropriate seat quite confusing, especially for first-time parents. But using a few simple guidelines, choosing the type of seat can be simplified and from there it is all about budget and personal preference.

In Australia there have been recent changes to laws governing child restraints and car seats which have standardised laws across states and territories. These evidence-based directives, detailed below, mandate the use of child restraints until the age of 7 years, as contrary to popular belief, young children are not safe in an adult seatbelt alone.

As a general rule a child should never be carried on an adult lap as it is impossible to hold onto a child in an accident; it is also illegal. Sharing seatbelts is also against the law, either around multiple children or between adult and child. In the event of an impact, a child may be crushed against the seatbelt by the weight of an adult. The simple equation is one person per seatbelt.

Setting a good example to children is a powerful safety tool and all adults travelling in a car should set a good example by always wearing a seatbelt, even on short trips. Research shows that children will mimic this behaviour.

Teaching children safe car behaviour is essential as is positively reinforcing good behaviour with praise. Let them know that the engine will not be started until all children are buckled in and instruct children not to undo their seatbelt until the engine is turned off and an adult tells them they may. If children remove their arms from restraints, or unbuckle their own or a siblings seatbelt, stop the car and re-fasten the straps. Tell the child that this will not be tolerated and do it as many times as necessary. It can be hard to take the time during a busy day to properly manage such behaviours, but if ignored or not properly dealt with, the behaviour will continue, escalate and/or be copied, with potentially disastrous consequences. It is far safer and more efficient to set firm ground rules, be consistent and nip such conduct in the bud.

Australian Child Restraint Law Changes

In November 2009, all Australian states and territories adopted a national reform of child restraint laws.

- Children < 4 year old must be restrained in the rear of a vehicle in an approved child seat
- If the child is 4–7 years old they may be restrained on a booster in the front seat *if* all of the rear seats are occupied by children under 7.
- All children under seven years of age must use a child restraint or booster seat when travelling in a car
- Children under 6 months must use an approved, properly fastened and adjusted rearward facing restraint
- Children aged between 6 months and less than 4 years must use an approved, properly fastened and adjusted rearward or forward-facing child restraint.

- Children aged between 4 years and under 7 years must use an approved, properly fastened and adjusted forward facing restraint or an approved booster seat which is properly positioned and fastened
- In Queensland, the penalty for drivers incorrectly securing a child is AUD$300 and three demerit points. In Victoria, the penalty is $234 and three demerit points. Similar fines are served throughout other Australian states.
- For more information on the new laws visit the National Transport Commission at www.ntc.gov.au

Car Seats

Choosing the right child restraint or car seat is critical to a child's safety but it can also be confusing. Car seats must be matched to a child's age and size and must be correctly installed and adjusted to be effective. It is vital to check the individual height and weight recommendations for each individual car seat model as they may differ with different designs.

All restraints should carry the Standards Australia AS/NZS 1754 sticker denoting safety approval and it should not be assumed that just because they are on the shelves being sold that they meet all recommended safety standards.

Research the local car seat anchoring system and make sure that the car seat you buy complies with this fitting system. It is illegal in Australia to use child restraints purchased overseas. This is partially due to the fact that different countries have different anchoring systems and if you buy a car seat from another country they may not be compatible with local cars. In Australia the top tether system is used to anchor car seats, while in the U.S.A. it is the LATCH system and the ISOFIX system in Europe.

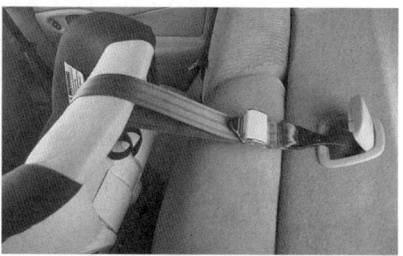

It is best to buy and fit the car seat well ahead of time as some cars do not have the correct anchor points and will require modification. If in doubt, it is always best to seek professional advice from authorised restraint installers or the Road Traffic Authority (RTA).

All children should travel in the backseat as it offers 40% more protection in the event of an accident, with the rear centre position offering greatest protection especially from side impacts. The rear centre position may not be available in some cars with fold-down rear seating if they are configured in a 50:50 split or in those cars with no centre anchoring point, and so rear left is the second choice position. Children should travel in the backseat until large enough to use an adult seatbelt (see guidelines following).

In general, young children travelling in the front seat are at increased risk of injury in an accident especially where airbags are fitted for adult height passengers. Explosive deployment of such airbags poses a serious threat to children and has proven fatal in some instances. If the child must travel in the front seat, slide the seat back as far as possible and ensure the seatbelt fits snugly.

Rearward facing travel is the safest option for any infant and should be used as long as possible, i.e. until the child outgrows the car seat. This varies but should be until the baby weighs 9–12kg and is too large to be placed in the seat, or is approximately 6–12 months old. Many car seats are 'convertible' and can be used as a rear-facing seat initially and then turned to a forward-facing car seat.

Forward-facing car seats can be suitable for babies from 9kg and 6 months of age, as long as they have good head control, but as rear-facing is the safest position for baby in case of an impact, it is suggested that rear-facing seats are used for as long as possible. Forward facing seats can be used until outgrown at approximately 18kg or up to 4 years of age.

All harness straps must be adjusted to any individual child and should be snug around the baby. If using someone else's car seat, take the extra time to accurately adjust the straps, as a poorly fitted restraint can be dangerous in its own right. Shoulder straps should emerge from the slots level with the child's shoulders and should be moved upwards as the child grows.

As a rule, it is best to avoid second-hand car seats especially if they are over 10 years old. If you do decide to buy car seats second-hand, be very careful, and check that all harnesses and buckles are intact and that the seat is in good condition. In addition, verify that the model has not been recalled and that the seat has not been in an accident, and do not buy a car seat with an uncertain history. Be aware that older equipment may not meet current safety standards.

Installation

According to the Royal Automobile Club of Victoria (RACV), about 70% of child restraints are installed incorrectly. This could significantly reduce the restraint's ability to protect your child in a crash. Proper installation is crucial to getting the best crash protection from a restraint.

Correctly installing child restraints can be a complicated affair, especially for first time parents, so consider paying for an approved installer. All states offer restraint fitting services, some of whom will travel to you.

If fitting the seat yourself, carefully read and **follow the instructions**, especially the section on common mistakes. It is also advisable to have the seat checked for correct fit and stability at an accredited checkpoint after installation.

If it is necessary to move the car seat from one car to another on a regular basis have an authorized fitter teach you the correct way to move and re-install the car seat and buy a model that is light and easy to install.

Both the top **tether strap** and the seatbelt that keeps the restraint in position must be properly adjusted and without any slack. When tightening the seatbelt, push the child seat firmly into the car seat with your body weight, so that the car seat cushions are compressed. Depending on the position of the **anchor point**, the restraint may need extensions for the tether strap.

When to Replace

It is recommended that child safety seats be replaced following a moderate or severe crash in order to maintain a high level of crash protection for child passengers. The U.S.A. National Highway Traffic Safety Administration (NHTSA) maintains that child

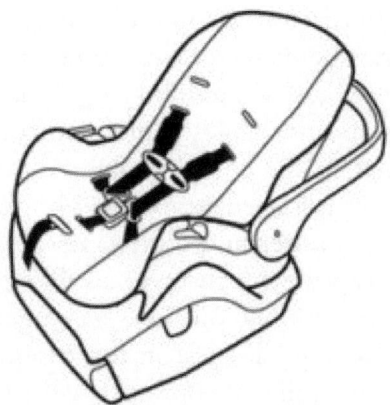

safety seats do not automatically need to be replaced following a minor crash.

Minor crashes are those that meet ALL of the following criteria:
- The vehicle was able to be driven away from the crash site;
- The vehicle door nearest the safety seat was undamaged;
- There were no injuries to any of the vehicle occupants;
- The air bags (if present) did not deploy; AND
- There is no visible damage to the safety seat.

Seat Types

Infant only, rear-facing car seat or capsule

Rear-facing infant car seats are designed for babies from newborn to 9–12kg and are tilted to support baby's neck and spine in the event of an impact. These seats must only be fitted to rear seats as it is illegal for a rear-facing restraint to be used where an exploding airbag may be deployed. There have been horrific infant injuries and even deaths related to airbags.

Follow the manufacturers' height and weight guidelines for each particular seat, rather than using age alone and keep baby in the safer rear-facing position as long as possible. It is time to move to a forward-facing seat when baby has reached the weight limit and can sit independently with good head control.

When using a rear-facing infant restraint, the shoulder straps should be at shoulder height or just above, whereas the shoulder straps in forward-facing restraints can be up to 25mm below the child's shoulders. The harness must not be twisted and should be adjusted to a snug fit as a loose harness won't perform well in a crash, and can lead to other problems, such as the child freeing their arms. If you can fit more than one finger between the straps and your child, the harness isn't tight enough.

Young babies are particularly vulnerable to heat and sun exposure, so shade should be provided if installing the restraint next to a window. Approved window screens are very effective at blocking out the sun while preserving visibility out of the car. These shades are preferable to car seat hoods or bonnets which reduce air circulation around baby and can promote over-heating.

In colder weather, dress baby warmly but be careful of placing a blanket over baby in the car seat. Rear-facing seats make it impossible to properly supervise a baby from the front seat, even with the use of a baby mirror, and any loose blanket can slip over the baby's face and become a suffocation risk.

Capsules have the advantage of being removable from the base unit and so allow parents to carry the capsule and baby from the car. This can be convenient when running errands as the baby can remain undisturbed throughout the trip. It can however, be tempting to leave a sleeping baby in the capsule for a prolonged period, but this is not recommended and can be dangerous. Capsules are not designed to fulfil a cot function and babies should not be left in the curled configuration for prolonged periods. Leaving a baby asleep and unsupervised in a capsule can also pose a suffocation risk. No one likes waking a sleeping baby but in this case it is the only safe option.

Convertible Rear-to-forward Facing Car Seat

Convertible seats are designed to protect children from birth through to approximately 18kg. These are designed to be either rear, or forward-facing depending on your child's size and age. They are a more economical option, if less portable, than the capsules.

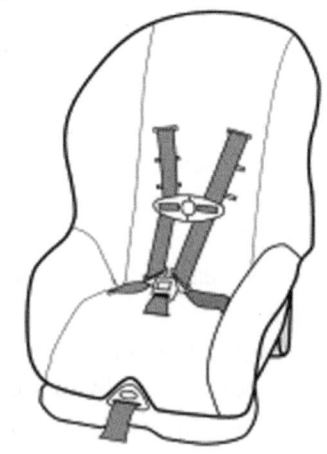

Infant car seats are usually designed to have a 5-point harness which should always be placed through the slots at, or up to 25mm below, the baby's shoulders. All harness straps should be untwisted and fit snugly, especially over the shoulder and thigh areas. A general guide to harness fit is that no more than one finger should fit under the straps at the collarbones.

One of the most important features of the five-point harness is the crotch strap which prevents children submarining with an impact or sudden braking. Submarining is when a child slips under the lap straps of the harness and onto the floor and can be prevented by the use of a crotch strap. This means that babies should always be dressed with their legs free as this will allow the crotch strap to be effectively buckled and tight.

For safe use of the car seat, a baby's head should be at least 6 centimetres below the top of the car seat. It is time to move up to a booster seat when the child has reached the height or weight limit, the harness is stretched to the limit, their ears are above the top of the seat and/or their neck is no longer supported.

Booster Seat

When a child reaches the maximum weight allowed for their infant car seat or the child's ears have reached the top of the seat, they will need to be transferred to a booster seat. These children are still too small to be safely restrained in an adult seatbelt alone.

It is illegal to use a booster seat with a lap belt alone, instead a lap/sash belt or preferably a five-point harness. Further, the addition of a crotch strap helps to prevent submarining or the slipping of a child from under the harness and onto the floor.

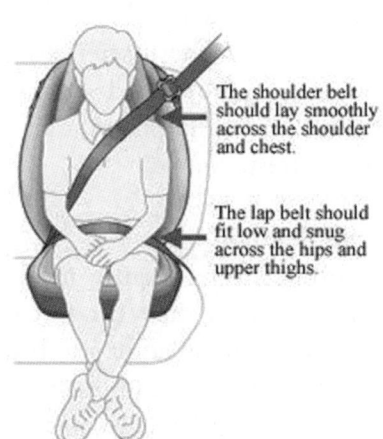

The shoulder belt should lay smoothly across the shoulder and chest.

The lap belt should fit low and snug across the hips and upper thighs.

The lap belt must be fitted low and tight across a child's hips, while the shoulder belt should lay flat and snug across their shoulder and should be clear of the neck or face. All straps and belts must lie flat and should be regularly untwisted.

Support to a child's head is critical and should be given by the top of the booster or alternatively, by the vehicle seat or headrest. If using a booster seat with no backrest, ensure the vehicle seat has a built-in headrest. Children should never be left with their head poking above a backrest as this will leave them at risk of severe head and neck injuries in the event of an accident.

Many full-back boosters have the additional safety feature of padded side wings located on the headrest. These offer a significant degree of side-impact protection missing from a vehicle headrest.

Adult Seatbelt

Children are frequently moved too soon from their car seat or booster seat to an adult seat belt. Governments around Australia have now legislated to prevent this by stipulating that all children under seven years must travel using a car seat or booster seat. But even these laws may not go far enough as children's size and development vary greatly and for most this means that they are not likely to correctly fit an adult seat belt until somewhere between the ages of 8 and 12 years, and at approximately 36kg in weight.

As a general guide, children can stop using booster seats when they are big enough to use the lap/shoulder belt with their back resting against the seat and with their legs bent comfortably over the edge of the seat. A 5-step test (shown below) has been developed to guide parents in the timing of their child's transition to an adult seat belt.

Demonstrating further that this transition is not simply a function of age is a recent study from Starship Children's Hospital in NZ which specifically showed that for children aged between 4 and 12 years:
- All 4 and 5 year olds required a car seat or booster seat
- 90% of 6, 7, and 8 year olds required booster seats

- 50% of 9 and 10 year olds required booster seats
- 10% of 11 and 12 year olds still required booster seats.

When fastening a child into a lap/sash seat belt, the lap belt should rest low and over the top of the thighs and not across the stomach. The shoulder or sash belt should lie across the middle of the chest and away from the child's neck and face. This should be possible when the child reaches approximately 150cms in height.

The sash strap should never be fastened behind a child's back or under his arm, as this is not a secure restraint and can cause injury in itself during an accident. If the sash does not sit securely across a child's chest then they are not ready for an adult belt.

Children who are too small for a seat belt are often uncomfortable and so are more likely than older children to use the seat belt incorrectly by placing the sash under their arm, or behind their back. Since seat belts are not meant to perform like this, the injuries your child may suffer in an accident could be life threatening.

Lap Belts

The lap belt alone, without a sash or shoulder component, is considered dangerous and is not recommended. During an impact, the lap belt is forced into the body, virtually folding the passenger in two and risking spinal injuries as well as burst injuries to internal organs. Furthermore, the lap belt offers no protection to the upper body which account for 65% of body mass in a child under 5 years. The addition of a sash belt aids in keeping the passenger's body upright, and stops them from travelling so far forwards.

Is your Child Ready for an Adult Seat Belt?
The 5-step test
This simple test has been adopted by SafetyBeltSafe U.S.A.

1. Does the child sit all the way back against the car seat?
2. Do the child's knees bend comfortably at the edge of the seat?
3. Does the belt cross the shoulder between the neck and arm?
4. Is the lap belt as low as possible, touching the thighs?

> 5. Can the child stay seated like this for the whole trip?
>
> If you answered 'no' to any of these questions, your child requires a booster seat to make both the shoulder belt and the lap belt fit correctly.

Children and airbags

Airbags are designed to protect adults by opening explosively however, this same mechanism can lead to head and spinal injuries in children who are positioned at an inappropriate height. In fact, infants and young children have been injured or even killed in the front seat of cars where an airbag deployed and consequently it is illegal in Australia to use a rear-facing restraint in a position where it will be hit by an exploding airbag, namely, the front seat.

Car Seats at a Glance

Weight	Height	Approximate Age	Restraint Type	Comment
Birth–9kg		up to 12 months	Rear-facing capsule	Use away from airbag
9–18kg		1–4 years	Forward-facing seat	
18–36kg	<145cm	Pre-school–8 years	Booster seat	
> 36kg	>150cm	>8 years old	Adult seat belt	Children < 12 years are safest in back seat

** Always check the manufacturer's recommendations for individual weight and size limits.

- If still confused about choice of seat for your child use the Royal Automobile Club of Victoria (RACV)'s Restraint calculator found at www.racv.com.au

PART 3

Baby Equipment and Toys

Indoor Baby Equipment

THE MIND-BOGGLING ARRAY of baby equipment currently on the market can leave new parents confused and overwhelmed as they are bombarded with promises of a smarter, happier and safer baby through the use some whizz-bang piece of kit. Naturally we all want the best for our children and by exploiting the premise that parents will always do more and buy more for their children than they ever will for themselves, the baby market remains ever-buoyant.

But not everything is as it seems and many baby gadgets are nothing more than gimmicks in disguise; they sound good on paper, look sleek and inviting but in the end, prove to be nothing more than an expensive piece of baby art. More importantly, some of the best-looking baby equipment may turn out to be some of the most dangerous and may lead to serious injury.

Accidents related to baby equipment are commonly attributable to one of the following factors;
- Design faults
- Improper assembly
- Improper use
- Poor maintenance
- Equipment failure

General Guidelines

When shopping for baby, begin with the essentials such as cots, prams and high chairs and buy the sturdiest and safest equipment your budget will allow. Optional extras can be purchased later as required or desired. Prioritise safety and function above convenience or gadget features; well-designed equipment is priceless.

When buying any baby equipment, don't assume that because a brand is well-known and on the shelf that this automatically means it's safe. Look for an Australian safety standard sticker and thoroughly research particular brands and their safety records. In particular, visit consumer websites such as the Australian Competition and Consumer Commission (ACCC) and the U.S. government-run Consumer Product Safety Commission (CSPC) to check for product recalls.

Nowadays, it seems that almost everything is delivered in a flat-pack requiring many hours of care and construction and baby equipment is no different. It is essential, therefore that parents take the time to thoroughly read all assembly instructions as putting together a high chair or safety gate incorrectly may have dire consequences.

Similarly, always read the manufacturers height and weight recommendations for equipment as using equipment unsuitable for a child's size may cause serious injury.

The safety features of a certain product may not be immediately obvious and we have all had episodes of hand-to-hand combat whilst trying to decode the inner workings of a pram or a high chair. It is vital therefore, that the instructions for use are also read prior to using any new equipment as one of the main causes of equipment-related injury is improper use.

Certain pieces of baby equipment have a way of becoming family favourites resulting in frequent and heavy use. It becomes important therefore that regular surveillance for wear be performed and that any maintenance be performed.

As a general rule, care should be taken when buying equipment second-hand, especially if the source and history of the item are unknown. Check that all harnesses and buckles are intact and that the item is in good condition without too many signs of wear. Check that the model has not been recalled and be aware that older equipment may not have all of the desired safety features.

When using any equipment with your baby, there is no safety feature so childproof that it can substitute for vigilant adult supervision.

High Chairs

High chairs are the safest place to feed a baby and manufacturers have generally honed designs to keep up with current safety recommendations.

Many high chair injuries relate to improper use, most commonly through the failure to adequately harness a child, resulting in falls and head injuries. According to the CSPC, nearly 9000 children in the U.S. suffered injuries related to high chairs in 2007, with most relating to falls. A baby must never be left unattended in a high chair and in particular older babies who can be surprisingly resourceful escape artists; all the safety features in the world cannot replace adult supervision. If leaving the room, roll the chair with you and then re-engage the brakes.

The commonest cause of death related to high chairs however, is from children sliding under the tray table and being strangled between table and chair seat.

In short, babies in high chairs need to be adequately harnessed and supervised.

High chairs should not be used until babies are over 6 months of age, have good head control and can sit well. Many high chairs are designed to have a reclining back for younger babies but should be locked securely in position before seating the baby and the height or recline of a high chair should never be adjusted with a baby in place. If the reclining feature of a high chair is used for babies who exceed the manufacturer's weight recommendations for this feature, it may lead to backwards tipping and serious injury.

Chair design should be wide-based and stable to resist tipping with any wheels having easy-to-use wheel locks. Wheels must be locked when the chair is in use especially in the presence of older siblings, many of whom just love to drive the baby around and possibly into danger. Look for any small pieces on the chair or tray table which may break off and risk choking.

High chairs must have a sturdy five-point harness which is adjusted for a snug fit and kept fully engaged at every use. Harness clasps must be sturdy and difficult for children to undo and the harness should not be attached to the tray table as it may be disengaged, dragging the baby with it. Merely engaging the waist strap without shoulder and crotch straps can be deadly, as baby may slip down under the strap and strangle. A simple crotch strap can help prevent this with some designers going further by placing a solid, vertical post between the baby's legs. This post may also prevent a baby slipping under the tray table possibly trapping his head between tray and chair seat.

When sliding the tray table into place, make sure that baby's fingers are not trapped and test that the table is securely locked into position. Do not be tempted to use the tray table as a substitute safety harness as it is not designed as a restraint with deaths reported from babies slipping underneath and strangling. It is an idea to store the high chair with tray table locked in place to prevent children climbing onto the seat and falling.

Many high chairs are collapsible for easy storage and so must opened out and locked in position prior to placing the baby; these locks can be tested by pressing firmly on the seat of the chair. These folding high chairs should have no 'pinch points' or exposed hinges to entrap little fingers.

Children should never be allowed to climb into a high chair themselves, as it may overbalance or tip, and once there, they may also stand and fall before being harnessed.

Consideration must be given as to placement of the high chair and it should never be placed near curtain cords, windows or walls as children may climb out, pull things in or push off from the wall and tip over. For obvious reasons high chairs must not be placed anywhere near steps or level changes.

If placing the high chair at the dining table, clear all hot drinks and food, as well as any hazardous utensils from immediate reach and never underestimate the arm span of a determined baby.

Similarly, clear the floor around a high chair before removing baby as you may slip on dropped food whilst carrying the baby. Do not move or lift a high chair with a baby in place as they are top heavy and can tip over.

When choosing a high chair, thought should be given to ease of cleaning of the frame, its harnesses and coverings, as well as the tray table. Look for removable seat covers and tray tables to facilitate cleaning of dropped food scraps as retained scraps compromise hygiene and if ingested are a food-poisoning risk. Dual tray tables, with a removable upper tray also aids with cleaning.

Regularly test all adjustable, reclining and locking mechanisms to ensure safe functioning and look for any sharp edges or protrusions, missing screws or any hidden grime.

Bouncers/Bouncinettes

These bouncing baby recliners can be a godsend for new parents as they can soothe a restless baby, lull a tired baby into a nap or simply free up adult hands for other tasks. There are also more involved models which are powered to rock, swing or vibrate to calm a restive baby.

But in 2007 the CSPC reported over 2000 infants within the USA were injured in bouncer seats, the majority of which fell from tables or other raised surfaces. Given the rocking or bouncing nature of such bouncers, a baby's movements can rock the chair to the edge of a table or counter top independent of where they were originally placed.

As a consequence, bouncers must only ever be used at floor level, avoiding the temptation to place them at eye level e.g. on a table. In particular never place the bouncer on a kitchen bench whilst cooking; not only is there a falls risk but also a substantial burns risk whilst you are distracted.

It is just as dangerous to place the bouncer on a soft surface such as a bed, couch or cushion as the seat may tip and trap the baby, causing suffocation. These seats should always be positioned away from heaters,

THE SAFETY BUBBLE

dangling cords and power outlets and must never be used as car seats.

Bouncer seats are a great way of keeping a baby close without having to hold them directly but they should not be used as a baby-sitting device and are no substitute for snuggle time. The American Academy of Pediatrics (AAP) notes that babies should spend only 20–30 minutes at a time in a bouncer. Excessive use of such seats places babies at increased risk of positional plagiocephaly or flattened head syndrome where babies develop a flat area on the spot of persistent pressure e.g. the back of the head.

Manufacturers always include recommended weight limits for bouncers (usually from 18–30lbs / 8–14kgs) and any baby who exceeds this weight limit can tip the bouncer. Similarly, it is important to read manufacturers' instructions for correct bouncer assembly and use, particularly when suspending the chair from a frame for rocking.

Choose a bouncer with a base or rear support which is wider than the seat itself to resist tipping and test the stability of models in the store by pressing down on the bouncer from different positions. In addition, the chair should stay in place and resist traveling when rocked back and forth. To aid stability the underside of the base should have rubber pads or other non-slip surfaces applied. Before placing baby in the bouncer look for any sharp edges, protrusions or exposed 'pinch point' hinges.

When using a bouncer secure baby with a 5-point or 3-point harness. In particular, younger babies should have a 5-point harness as the shoulder straps help limit sideways sag. The crotch strap must always be engaged to stop baby sliding down through and under the waist strap and possibly strangling. Check all fasteners and clasps on harnesses to see that they're strong, secure, and easy to work, and that they won't stick into your baby.

Entertaining a young baby can be difficult but dot not be tempted to tie or clip toys onto the harness or frame of a bouncer chair as the strings can become entangled around baby and may pose a strangulation risk. A safer option is to purchase a seat with an integrated toy bar which is sturdy on testing and stays firmly in place if swiped at. These should either have toys which are firmly attached or alternatively, are designed to safely detach without significant force being applied.

No matter how sturdy a toy bar is however, it should never be used as a handle to carry baby and bouncer; it is not designed to take such weight and may snap suddenly.

In general, a bouncer should not be carried whilst holding a baby even by the carrying handle as it can overbalance and tip baby out. Take baby out and then replace him into the chair at its new location; it takes an extra few minutes but may save a serious injury.

Do not tuck a baby into a bouncer using heavy blankets which may be pulled by older infants and may end up covering their face. If using the bouncer outside, make sure there is shelter or a canopy for UV protection and ensure the baby is wearing suitable sunscreen and a hat.

Second-hand or older bouncer chairs should be viewed with a critical eye and any seat which is damaged or incomplete should not be used.

In addition, some bouncer seats have been recalled in recent years; problems have included seats with an unstable base, kickstands that may not hold the seat stationary, toys or parts that may break off from the toy bar, and toy bars that suddenly become loose causing cuts and bruises. Always check consumer websites such as the ACCC or CSPC for recall listings.

Regardless of how secure a bouncer chair may be it is essential to keep a close eye on baby even if harnessed. Infants can wriggle in the bouncer and even newborns can slide or sag to one side and may suffocate or fall.

Stop using the bouncer as soon as baby can roll and sit unassisted as they will roll sideways or forward to escape, and will tip the chair.

Baby Walkers

It is safe to say that few pieces of baby equipment have sparked as much controversy as the baby walker; a round metal or plastic frame on wheels housing a suspended seat which is propelled by a baby's movement. It has been attacked on both safety and developmental grounds and has been heavily regulated in many countries; it is now illegal to import or sell walkers in Canada.

According to Relay Health, over one third of all infants placed in baby walkers will require emergency medical care and in Australia, baby walkers accounted for 12% of nursery furniture injuries presenting to Westmead Hospital in 2004.

Whilst not illegal in Australia, the sale of baby walkers are governed by safety regulations which are based on the American Society for Testing and Materials (ASTM) F977-00 Standard and include requirements covering stability of the walker, falls prevention and safety labelling.

A second-generation voluntary safety standard was issued for walkers in 1997 to protect against stairway falls. According to this standard, walkers must have a bottom friction strip made of rubberized material to stop the walker if its wheels drop away at the edge of a step. In the US, walker-related incidents have declined since the 1997 standard was introduced. The American Consumer Product Safety Commission (CPSC) estimates that in 1992, walkers were involved in 25,700 injuries to children younger than 15 months who were treated in hospital emergency rooms. In 2003 (the latest government data), the number dropped to 3,200 such injuries, an 88 percent reduction.

Despite these extensive regulations, it is impossible to guarantee that every baby walker sold within Australia adheres to the standard, thus parents are responsible for educating themselves of the possible risks, checking any purchases for safety features, and supervising babies diligently to ensure that any use of baby walkers is as safe as possible.

Concerns

The major safety concerns for baby walkers stem from the increased mobility of these babies facilitating access to stairs and other uneven surfaces. Serious injuries have occurred from tipping and falls, including head injuries, burns, lacerations and broken limbs. Walkers may also allow babies to reach higher surfaces and unexpectedly access hot drinks, ovens, irons, poisons or other dangerous objects.

Constant supervision of any children using baby walkers is essential as babies travel quickly in walkers (~7–10 cms/second); walkers should never be a 'set and forget' or be used to amuse baby whilst you are engaged in another activity.

Walkers give babies a dangerous degree of freedom, potentially allowing them to enter rooms and areas of the home or garden which may be hazardous. If a baby accesses wet areas or swimming pools there is a very real risk of them toppling face down into water and drowning. Water hazards may be as seemingly benign as a toilet, nappy bucket or dog bowl.

Developmentally walkers do not aid in walking, in fact, studies suggest that they may do the opposite, delaying walking by stopping babies developing balance, as well as upper leg and hip muscle strength. They also keep baby from floor play and pulling themselves up as much; an essential pre-amble to those first steps. In addition, some experts suggest that walkers seem to lessen a baby's desire to walk, perhaps by providing an easy alternative.

When they do start walking, these babies may also develop abnormal weight-bearing and gait, with findings which suggest they tend to lean forward and take shorter steps.

Consequently, any time spent in walkers should be limited to under 20 minutes at a time.

Childproofing Guidelines

To aid in stability, it is important to buy a walker model which has a wheelbase longer and wider than the frame. In addition, the frame should be wider than the doorways to stop babies traveling into another room without supervision.

Stairs are the natural enemy of the mobile baby, and walkers can prove a fast track to disaster if babies are able to manoever towards a staircase. Hence, walker must be fitted with a gripper on the under-surface of the base. Grippers are rubberised, anti-slip strips which are designed to stick on the edge of a step as the walker tips and so helps to impede any falls. Whilst these strips may give a parent an essential few extra seconds to reach a teetering baby, they are by no means foolproof and babies should never be

THE SAFETY BUBBLE

placed in a walker if in a room with even a few stairs.

Walker seats should be adjusted so that they are not sitting too high or too low with baby's toes just touching the ground, as this will avoid excessive weight bearing in infants who are not developmentally ready.

Look for a walker which is sturdy and stable and ensure that the folding mechanism is strong and easy to use. Before babies are placed in a walker, the frame must be firmly locked in place to prevent collapse, this can be tested by pushing down firmly on the seat. Older X-framed models are notorious for amputating fingers and should never be used and as a general rule do not use second hand walkers of indeterminate age as they will not meet current safety standards. A thorough check over the frame and seat will reveal any exposed springs or hinges, any 'pinch points' or any sharp edges.

Baby walkers cannot be used as a baby carrier as they can overbalance, or have the seat give way leading to falls and serious injury. Similarly, baby walkers should not be used as rolling entertainment centres by tying extra toys to the frame as they can become entangled in the wheels causing tipping or may twist around baby's neck causing strangulation. Many walkers are fitted with toys which are secured to the frame during manufacture and these must be secure, have no small parts and cannot be broken off.

Setting up a safe space for walker use is essential and begins with securing the exits and closing the doors. The use of safety gates to guard doorways and stairs is not advised as many accidents with walkers have occurred despite the presence of a safety gate due to the speed and momentum of the walker causing gates to open on impact. Consequently baby walkers must not be used in rooms with access to even a small set of stairs, even if guarded with baby gates.

Floors must be level with no drop-offs which may cause the walker to tip and so should also be free of rugs and other objects. In addition the floors should not be wet or slippery.

Walkers may also roll up against hot stoves or heaters and should not be used in these rooms; high chairs may be used as a safer alternative. It is easy to underestimate a baby's grasp particularly if they are slightly elevated in a walker, and all tables and counters should be cleared of dangerous objects even if they seem too high for baby to reach.

Similarly any dangling curtain or electrical cords should be secured up high to prevent a speeding baby becoming entangled.

Using a walker outside can prove infinitely more treacherous and is not recommended. Outdoor walkers can fall off decks, into potholes or into swimming pools not to mention possible access to roadways and beyond.

A much safer alternative to baby walkers is the stationary activity centre where an infant sits within a stationary play unit surround by securely attached toys and buttons. Some models can also be suspended in a doorway.

Jolly Jumper/Doorway Jumper

Baby jumpers or jolly jumpers are hung either in a doorway or on a customised frame and that allow pre-walking babies to bounce themselves off the floor. They consist of a suspended seat or sling which is attached to a spring-loaded cable. Accidents may occur when the cable or clasps give way allowing the jumper to collapse to the floor. Previously, some doorway jumpers have been recalled due to fracture of the plastic clamp which holds the jumper to a doorframe and also due to clamps detaching from the cable.

It is therefore essential to check a jumper before purchase for sturdiness and strength of materials and joins, and to always check with consumer sites for product recalls.

Each jumper will have the manufacturer's height and weight guides which must not be exceeded as this may cause snapping of the cables or safety straps. Most jumpers are suitable for babies up to 11kg and 75cms.

Before use, all clamps, springs and cables should be checked before each use as something may have moved or loosened. Once in position, the jumper should be firmly pulled on to check all attachments and to ensure that the frame or doorway can support a child's weight.

It is important to check that the width of any doorway is enough to accommodate the range of the jumper. If jiggling too vigorously, a baby may bump into the side of the doorframe causing injury.

Some jumpers may be purchased with a customised frame from which they are suspended. It is critical to ensure that any such frame is made of strong and durable materials, and has been well designed to resist tipping. Before hanging the jumper in a frame all hinge points must be locked and concealed and the frame should be tested before use. This process involves checking that the frame does not collapse under weight and that it is well balanced and will not topple.

Carers must ensure that no springs, hinges or sharp protrusions are within reach of the baby and that any springs or hinges are concealed or have a protective cover. Bear in mind that a baby's reach may be enhanced in a jumper by some element of side to side swinging. Some more elaborate jumpers have activity centres attached and should be checked for loose toys and other choking hazards.

Doorway jumpers are not appropriate for young babies or newborns and babies must be able to hold their head and weight-bear without collapse before being placed in jumpers. Further, the height of the jumper should be adjusted so that only baby's toes are on the floor and not the flat of the foot; too much weight placed prematurely through an infant's feet and legs may be harmful.

Prolonged use of jolly jumpers may exhaust a young baby and they should not be used for longer than 15 minutes at a time. If a baby is becoming restless or grumpy in the jumper they should be removed immediately. Interestingly, a few babies do not like the motion of jumpers and seem to get 'seasick', so if your baby has never enjoyed being placed in a jumper chances are that they are feeling a little green and it is time to abandon the activity completely.

Babies must always be directly supervised when using a jolly jumper and it cannot be used to babysit whilst carers are occupied by other tasks or in other rooms.

Babies may become tangled, or may swing themselves into objects or doorframes. Equally, older children should not be asked to supervise and should not be left alone with babies in a jumper as they do not understand the possible dangers. The most common temptation for an older sibling is that they want to push the jumper and have it function as a baby swing; a potentially lethal activity.

Jumpers must never be left hanging in the frame or doorway between uses as older children can become entangled and strangle. Babies should stop using the jumper once they can stand or walk.

Baby Gates

Gates are a core element of many home childproofing designs, so it is essential to choose a gate which enhances safety rather than provides another potential hazard.

There are two main types of child safety gate; pressure mounted and the more fixed hardware or wall mounted. A pressure mounted gate has a pressure bar along the top which exerts outward force to lodge the gate between two walls or two sides of a doorframe. Even the sturdiest of pressure-mounted gates are not suitable for the top of stairs as they may give way if enough force is placed against them and stairs must always be guarded by hardware-mounted gates which are screwed directly into walls or doorways. Gates that swing out should never be used at the top of stairs. So that if a child pushes from the top the gate will not swing open over the stairs. Install pressure-mounted gates with the pressure bar on the side away from children.

Whichever gate mechanism is chosen, it is essential that all gates are securely anchored, and this must be checked regularly by pushing against the gate to ensure that attachments have not loosened.

For maximal effectiveness, all gates must be sized accurately to the doorway or gap with most gating systems having extensions available if required. If a gate is too small for the opening, it will leave dangerous gaps which may entrap body parts, risk strangulation or allow a child to squeeze through. The gap between wall and gate should be

THE SAFETY BUBBLE

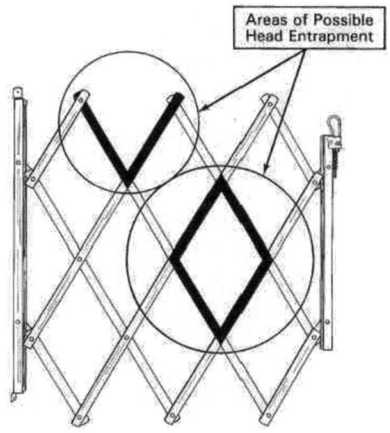

Areas of Possible Head Entrapment

<100mm to avoid entrapment of digits, limbs or heads. There should be no more than 2.5–5cm between the floor and bottom of the gate to prevent a child sliding underneath.

In general, most gates have a straight top edge with rigid vertical bars or a fine mesh screen below. Mesh must be fine calibre with holes no more than 0.6cm to prevent finger entrapment or use as a foothold for climbing. Vertical slats should be non-flexible and no more than 6cms apart to avoid footholds and entrapment of body parts. This distance is based on the average width of a baby's feet and arms.

There are a few design features to check off before purchasing any safety gate. Gates should be made of sturdy materials and have no sharp edges, exposed hinges or climbing footholds. Any gaps or lattice should be non-collapsible and less than 38mm in diameter.

Gates which are easy to use are far more likely to be used properly and constantly. After all, gates are only effective when they are securely closed and so should never be left disengaged or propped open, even for a minute.

In general, a baby gate should be self-closing and self-latching, with a solid mechanism that does not open even when bounced on, and which cannot be pulled open once closed. Test the gate in-store by pushing and pulling on it to see if it moves or opens. The opening latch should be simple to use one-handed when carrying something or someone, but should not be simple to use if under the age of two.

Accordion-style gates have not been sold since 1985, but can still be found as second-hand items. They have large V-shaped holes which have been involved in episodes of finger and limb entrapment as well as strangulation. This style of lattice also creates footholds for climbing.

It is never too early to install child safety gates and they should be well in place by the time a baby starts rolling. Crawling tends to begin suddenly one day and can catch parents unawares so be prepared! Discontinue using the gate when the youngest child is approximately two years old as any gate should be greater than three quarters of the child's height. Older siblings should be taught not to open the gate themselves as they will inevitably leave it open on occasion. If safe to do so, older children may step over gates, but must never climb up a gate.

Keep large toys and furniture away from safety gates to prevent a child using them to climb over.

Gates may also be used to reliably separate dogs and crawling babies. Infants are fascinated by animals and will chase them relentlessly often resulting in a sudden confrontation. It is far better to keep the two separated by a gate interspersed with short periods of tightly-controlled contact until the baby is older. More detail on childproofing pets can be found in Chapter 8.

Dummies/Pacifiers

Dummies or pacifiers are commonly used to comfort and settle children but can also be a potential baby hazard. Poorly designed or manufactured pacifiers can break into small parts which in turn may cause choking. There have also been reports of the entire dummy being inhaled and then blocking a baby's airway.

Consequently, consumer associations in Australia, U.S.A. and others have introduced strict safety standards for all dummies and these provide parents with a number of criteria to check off before buying a particular pacifier.

The shield of the dummy should not be small or flexible enough to be sucked into an infant's mouth, and there should be two ventilation holes on either side of the teat to allow breathing if dummy is breathed in. Avoid designs with large handles or protrusions which may force the dummy into the mouth if a baby falls forwards.

Ensure the dummy does not break up and produce small parts and test them regularly by pulling on the handles, teats and shields to make sure it does not come apart.

There should be no sharp parts or protrusions on the dummy as lacerations and bruising can be caused if a baby topples face wards.

Dummy teats are generally made of silicone or rubber. Silicone is thought to be more durable, however, some people find rubber teats softer than their silicone counterparts. Rubber teats in particular should be checked regularly for perishing or fragmentation. In addition, rubber teats should not contain > 20ppb of nitrosamines, a potentially cancer-causing compound. Latex allergy is related to prolonged exposure and some have suggested this as a reason to avoid rubber dummies. Ultimately, much of the information is anecdotal and the choice comes down to parental and infant preference.

Dummies should be inspected regularly for signs of wear and tear as any defects may harbour germs. All damaged pacifiers must be disposed of and replaced.

Clean and/or sterilise a dummy regularly by boiling it for 5 minutes (any longer can cause damage) or by simply cleaning it in hot, soapy water and air drying. Squeeze out any water from the teat after cleaning, as stagnant water can harbour microbes.

Always carry a spare rather than replacing a dummy from the floor as the 'five-minute rule' cannot apply to babies still building their immune system.

As tempting as it is to stop dummies dropping on the floor, never affix a dummy to a cot, pram or a child's neck or clothing as it can entangle and cause injury or strangulation.

As far as possible supervise your baby with a dummy and do not leave a baby alone with a dummy if they cannot remove it themselves.

Playpens

These high-sided, enclosed play areas have been a perennial favourite among parents as they allow for containment of a baby within a 'safe zone'. While there is some merit in this approach, not all playpens are created equal, and playpens must be well-designed and assembled correctly to maximise their childproofing potential. In addition, playpens should never be used as a substitute for supervision as unexpected injury can still occur even in an enclosed space. Children must never be left unattended in a playpen.

Both assembly instructions as well as manufacturer's height and weight recommendations must be carefully followed, placing a baby in a playpen when they are too heavy or too tall risks escape, tipping and collapse of the structure.

A playpen should be of solid and sturdy construction and if using a suspended playpen, (similar in design to a portable cot), it should be wide-based, heavy and stable. In other words, the playpen should not tip if the sides are lent upon.

The sides of the enclosure should be at least 50cms high to stop infants flipping themselves out, and walls should be free of structures such as horizontal bars which might provide a foothold for climbing. Any vertical rails should be spaced 6cms apart to stop entrapment of limbs or head and the horizontal top rails should be padded to protect against bumps.

If the playpen is collapsible, make sure it is locked in position before placing baby as collapse of the playpen with baby inside risks suffocation. Test this by pressing down firmly on the base. Any frame-locking devices should be shielded or out of reach of babies to avoid them collapsing the frame or trapping their fingers within the mechanism.

Playpens with mesh sides must be made of strong netting consisting of holes no larger than 0.6cm to keep small fingers and buttons from getting caught, leaving children entrapped or dangling. In addition, mesh playpens often have a drop-side which must not be left down as it can roll back and form a pocket which becomes a suffocation risk

Be mindful of where the playpen is placed within a room by creating a safe zone around the playpen, free from potential hazards. Avoid areas near heaters, fires or stairs and watch for dangling cords which can strangle or may be used to pull objects into the playpen. Steer clear of corners under heavy pictures or laden shelves do not leave the playpen near curtains or windows in case of climbing.

Never place large toys, cushions or pillows inside a playpen as they may be used for climbing, while blankets and other bedding in the playpen pose a suffocation risk. Similarly, toys should not be strung across the top, or hung from the sides of a playpen as children may become entangled or even strangle.

Some playpens are designed to double as portable cots and can be used for naps. If employing the enclosure as a cot, use only the mattress provided by the manufacturer as this will be firm and well-fitted. Any other blankets or mattresses may be too soft, or leave gaps which risk suffocation.

Any piece of equipment used as frequently and robustly as a playpen requires regular maintenance. Check for loose threads, protruding staples or missing screws and ensure that there are no holes in mesh sides. Any breaches in the padding should be immediately repaired. Be aware that wooden playpens may also produce splinters.

Stop using the playpen when your child can climb out or tip it over, which for most types will be when they are over approximately 86 centimetres in height.

Out and About Baby Equipment

As any parent will tell you, the only feat more difficult than caring for a newborn at home, is taking baby on the road. That first outing can rival a military operation in its planning and sheer scale, with anxious parents toting ridiculous amounts of baby equipment to prepare for any eventuality.

The majority of out and about baby equipment relates to navigating a baby safely and efficiently through the world, and can be distilled into 4 main items; prams, car seats, baby slings, and portable restaurant chairs. Car seats in particular, are so central to a modern baby's safety that it warrants closer inspection and is detailed in Chapter 16.

As with indoor baby equipment, the safety of outdoor baby equipment relates primarily to knowing the features to look for and those to avoid. Look for equipment which is well-designed and constructed and which carries an Australian safety standard approval sticker. Before shopping, research the various brands and features which are most appropriate for your family and should also include searching consumer websites for product recalls.

Be judicious in the use of second-hand items as safety standards are rapidly evolving and are often prompted by the lessons learnt from previous models.

Once equipment has been purchased, childproofing consists of the proper assembly and responsible use of items, as well as its ongoing maintenance. Finally, no matter how many safety bells and whistles are attached to a piece of baby equipment, there is nothing which matches the childproofing power of vigilant adult supervision; without this, even the safest piece of equipment is a potential hazard.

Prams

Previously, most pram-related injuries resulted from poor design and a lack of safety features, but under regulatory pressure, manufacturers have largely addressed these design and construction faults and most modern prams have an abundance of in-built safeguards. Sadly, however, children are still injured in prams everyday, with the majority of injuries related both to the inappropriate use of a pram and to a failure to engage the available safety features e.g, not engaging the brake or not fastening the harness.

The most common accidents occur when children stand up in a pram and fall out, when the pram tips or when the pram rolls into danger or out of control. According to the CSPC, in a recent one year period in the U.S.A. an estimated 14,400 children less than 5 years old were treated in hospital Emergency Rooms for stroller-related injuries. Most of the reported injuries were from falls and tipping of the pram, and most resulted in head injury. It is logical to assume that there were many more minor injuries treated at home.

The safety features of some contemporary prams may appear complex at first, and before buying, parents should have the store attendant demonstrate and discuss the various features of each pram. Do not assume that because it is on the shop floor and is a well-known brand, that it is safety-approved; look for a sticker with the Australian Standard (AS 2088) safety approval.

Undoubtedly, the most important part of childproofing your pram is to never, ever, leave a child unattended in a pram, for any reason, or for any length of time as most accidents occur in under a minute.

Brakes

Applying the brakes on a pram should involve a simple, accessible mechanism which can be applied in a single-action but is equally difficult for a child to disengage.

Foot-activated brakes are safer than hand mechanisms as brakes on or about the pram handle can be inadvertently activated. It is preferable that prams should have rear brakes installed with left and right wheel linkage with reports also suggesting that pedals which are coloured red give emphasis and are safer.

The brake must be engaged when placing a child in or out of the stroller, and should always be applied whenever the pram is stopped even if on flat ground and even if just 'for a second'. Simply stopping to tie a shoelace or answer a phone can be distracting enough to allow a pram to roll away.

If out walking, park the pram parallel to railway lines, roads, rivers and other hazards as the risks associated with it rolling away are lessened. Similarly, when parking the pram on a slope, park it across (i.e. at right angles) to the slope, engage the brake, lock the front wheel and keep the wrist strap on.

When loading a baby into the car, hold the pram while unlocking the car to stop it rolling away and then strap the child into their car seat before stowing the pram.

Wheels

Much has been made by pram manufacturers of the advantages of three versus four wheels, but in fact it is the stability of the entire design and not simply the number of wheels that matters. A wide wheel-base is the best way to achieve maximal pram stability and the pram must be tested for ease of tipping before purchase.

Equally, wheels are the key to a pram's manoeuvrability, and in-store testing should include a one-handed obstacle course to ensure easy single-hand steering. The front wheels should swivel freely for easy manoeuvrability, but if moving at speed (e.g. running) the front wheel/s should lock into a straight-forward position to help with pram control. Similarly, the front wheels should be put into the straight position when parked on a slope, with the pram parked across, rather than down the slope.

Tyres may be pneumatic or solid, with the majority of solid wheels being plastic. The choice is entirely dependent on the how and where the pram will be used. Pneumatic tyres rule the off-road terrain, and are superior on bumpy or unmade surfaces, but they are also bulkier, puncture-prone and require inflating at intervals. If sporting pneumatic tyres, it is essential to carry a puncture repair kit and a pump.

On the other hand, solid plastic wheels are more robust, but lack the grip and shock-absorbance of the pneumatic tyres; they are eminently suited to a quiet stroll through the shopping mall.

As a general rule, large wheels navigate steps, bumps and kerbs better than smaller wheels, with less chance of tipping.

Many models include detachable wheels as an aid to the transport and storage of prams. Regular checks should be made to ensure that such wheels are locked securely in place.

Ensure that wheels cannot be reached from the pram seat, especially in twin 'double decker' prams where one child is seated low to the ground and between the back wheels. If the lower child can reach the wheel, make sure it is covered with a wheel guard.

Wrist Straps

Wrist straps are available on many stroller models and serve to anchor the pram handle to your wrist. This will protect against a runaway pram should you lose your grip for any reason and are a essential childproofing device when out and about near roads and waterways; children have been lost from prams rolling into rivers and onto roads.

It is easy to make a habit of wearing the wrist strap each time you use the pram, like putting a seatbelt on before driving the car, and it becomes especially pertinent if running with the pram.

Wrist straps should be short in length and anchored securely to the handle of the pram. Long straps risk strangulation and will allow the pram to travel beyond arms reach.

Five-point Safety Harness

A good quality 5-point harness is essential to the safety of any pram, the five points being: one strap over each shoulder, one from each side of the waist and one through the crotch.

Ensure that the harness and clasps are robust mechanisms which will not snap or be easily undone by little hands. It is important not to compromise on the quality of a safety harness as over-balancing a pram can be as easy as a pothole or shopping bags and ensuring that your baby is strapped in securely can be the difference between a scare and a serious injury.

All straps must be adjustable and should fit snugly around the child; a loose harness not only allows a child to lean and tip the pram, and also risks strangulation. After fastening the harness, tug firmly to make sure that the seat does not pull away from the frame.

The pram harness must be used with *every* trip, even if a child protests. Many people meticulously harness their very young babies, but are far less consistent as children get older. In fact, once children can stand, wriggle and squirm, there is a much greater risk of the pram tipping, or of children climbing out.

Frame

Most modern prams are collapsible for easy transport, and central to such mechanisms must be easy-to-use, reliable frame locks and release buttons. Choose a pram which opens or closes using a one or two step process and avoid multi-step, multi-button systems; all steps should all be intuitive and easily remembered. Salespeople are well-practised and will make the opening and collapsing of any pram look easy, so always try it yourself.

The frame should be solid and have no exposed hinges or other pinch points to entrap little fingers, so look for models with hinge covers and hidden frame joints.

To check that the pram is properly locked in the open position, push down firmly on the seat before placing a child as children have suffocated in collapsed prams.

Adjustable Backrest

Prams with a reclining backrest are a parental favourite as they accommodate a sleeping baby (also a parental favourite), but they must be used with care. Always supervise a baby asleep in a pram to ensure that their face does not become covered either by bedding or clothing, or by sliding into a corner or up against the pram side. If baby is asleep in the pram on arrival back home, it can be tempting to leave them there rather to risk a messy transition to the cot. As a rule, however, it is better to risk waking a sleeping baby than to risk leaving them to sleep in an unsupervised pram.

Always ensure that the pram cannot tip backwards when the backrest is in the fully reclined position and never place heavy bags on the handle of the pram as this will further shift the centre of gravity backwards.

Some new strollers have a baby capsule or car seat which attaches directly to the frame of the pram. The seat must be designed to fit a particular pram and must be properly secured and locked into the frame before moving.

Only use the custom insert or mattress designed for a particular model of pram as this should guarantee a firm mattress which is precisely fitted to the edge of the pram, leaving no dangerous gaps. Avoid using a blanket to create a softer surface for baby especially with the newborn bassinette attachments as this can produce suffocation.

Accessories

In an Australian climate, well-fitted rain and sun covers for the pram are essential, especially for UV protection. Buy brand-specific covers or check that a universal cover is designed to fit your pram model. Using either poorly-fitting pram covers or even blankets clipped to the hood with pegs is unsafe and risks suffocation, particularly because when walking behind the pram, the free edge of the blanket cannot be adequately seen.

Prams should have a see-through hatch in the sun canopy which allows parents to monitor a child in the pram below.

Choose a pram with accessible under-seat storage for parcels and bags to avoid hanging shopping bags or handbags over the back of the pram; not only can this tip the pram, but they are also an easy target for thieves.

Drink holders which fit to the pram handle or frame should not be used for any hot drinks and drinks such as coffee should never be drunk over a pram or above a child. Baby skin is particularly thin and fragile and it takes only a few seconds of skin exposure from scalding liquids for serious burns to occur.

Durability and Reliability

Prams epitomize the phrase 'wear and tear' and cheaper prams cost less by compromising on the quality of fittings which will usually unravel sooner rather than later. So prioritise safety over looks and buy the best quality materials your budget will allow. It can be useful to buy one great quality pram for heavy use and a lighter, cheaper one for less rigorous trips.

Be sure to check the manufacturers' height and weight recommendations as children who are too big or too small for a stroller are at greater risk of injury from poorly fitting harnesses and tipping.

Older children will often want to climb in, or play on the pram so teach them the one-person-to-a-pram rule, and never let them push a baby around in the pram without an adult holding onto the pram with them or with the wrist strap on.

Easy cleaning of a pram is essential given its messy passengers and this process is aided by the presence of minimal nooks and crannies, easily removable parts and washable fabrics.

Out and About

When taking a pram out and about, it is best to avoid rough terrain, escalators and stairs where possible, as these surfaces only increase the risk of tipping, and of jarring a young baby. Instead use an elevator and if there is no elevator present then remove the baby from the pram completely and seek help to carry the pram independently.

It is important to choose the right pram for the job in that compact, light weight strollers are not designed for heavy outdoor use and can be unstable; stick to the footpaths and shopping centres with such prams.

Be very careful of distractions such as a mobile phone when pushing a stroller. If you must answer the phone, engage the brake, have the wrist strap on, keep a hand on the handle and do not turn away from the pram as it only takes a second of inattention for a pram to roll into trouble.

Similarly, it is dangerous to attach a dog leash to the pram as even the smallest of dogs can lead to interference, tipping or pulling of the pram. A poorly behaved dog can also be a distraction which takes attention and hands away from the pram.

If travelling by train with a pram, stand well back from the edge of the station platform whilst waiting and park the pram parallel to the track with the brake engaged. As always, at least one hand should be on the handle constantly and the wrist strap should be in use. Once on the train, it is advisable to travel in the carriages nearest to the guard so that they can see clearly that you are on and off safely.

Maintenance

Prams should be checked regularly for any broken straps, sharp edges, loose or missing screws or faulty brakes. Any faulty components should be replaced or taken to an authorised repairer, and should not be subjected to a potentially dangerous home repair job. Prams should never be used with a defect, even a simple broken strap or wobbly wheel can be the prelude to an accident.

Remember to hold onto receipts and to use warranties for repairs wherever possible.

Jogging Prams

These days, may people like to run with their babies in the pram and it is great way to stay fit and show your baby the world. Be sure, however, to buy a pram specifically designed to be used as a running pram as not all 3-wheelers are designed as such despite popular perception. Choice magazine recently found that only five of the eleven 3-wheel prams tested were actually recommended by the manufacturers for jogging. It is essential, therefore to clarify this point with the retailer or manufacturer before purchase.

Running prams are generally wide-based for stability and have larger, pneumatic wheels. Some models also having extra suspension to prevent jarring. The front wheels or wheel of a jogging model must also lock in the straight forward position to prevent swivelling and swerving of the pram at speed.

Babies less than 12 months old are particularly sensitive to jarring and bouncing on rough

terrain especially at speed, so choose a smoother running route for smaller babies and always run with the wrist strap on.

Baby Number Two

If planning a future sibling, it is economically prudent to research prams which can grow with your family and will accommodate a toddler seat or skateboard. It is important to buy a pram specifically designed to accommodate two children rather than to simply 'make do'. Older children should not be carried on the sun canopy or over the wheel arch of a single pram as this will overload and overbalance the pram and may collapse the canopy completely.

Baby-carrying Harnesses and Slings

The idea of carrying a baby close to the body has gained enormous popularity in recent years; it is convenient, cuddly and by most accounts, good for baby. As a result, many different types of baby-carrying harnesses have been developed, which can be broadly grouped into three distinct styles; slings, carriers and backpacks.

Slings: consist of a wide piece of fabric which is placed over one shoulder and is worn across the torso

Carriers: have 2 shoulder straps ($\pm$ hip straps) which support a deep fabric seat and padded headrest

Backpack: has a deep fabric seat supported by a rigid aluminium frame which is worn on the back

All of these baby designs have their merits and the choice of carrier should be an individual one based on each family's specific requirements and preferences. When choosing a carrier, consider the age and development of your child, the times you will be using it and your own physical requirements. Try a few different carriers and choose the most comfortable as this inevitably means that you are more likely to use it correctly and safely.

As with many baby products, there is an initial learning curve involved with the safe use of baby carriers and there can be a bit of trial and error before parents feel confident to carry babies this way.

There are three main causes of injury with baby carriers:

Faulty design: Parents cannot simply rely on the reassurance of a big brand. Some carriers have had product recalls after design faults such as defective buckles led to injury.

Incorrect sizing: The size and weight recommendations from the manufacturers must be carefully heeded. Some carriers are not suitable for newborns and if a baby is too small for the carrier they can fall through leg holes or side gaps. Conversely, if babies are too large, buckles and straps may snap causing a baby to fall. As babies are top heavy, falls from a height are more likely to result in head injury.

Improper usage: When choosing a carrier, parents should focus on simplicity of design and ease of use. Drops and falls are most likely during placement and removal of the baby. Carers must practice, practice, practice with the sling until they are confident with its use. When starting out, it is helpful to use a second person to assist in the loading or unloading of the baby.

Instructions should be carefully read before use as even one misplaced strap or unsecured buckle can put a baby at risk. Further, if a baby is fussing and crying in the carrier he is probably uncomfortable and should be repositioned and the sling checked for any pinching or protruding parts.

Carrier Guidelines

All carriers must be carefully adjusted to fit both adult and baby with all alterations being made prior to placing the baby within the carrier. Check that the straps are firmly fixed and cannot slip to ensure that baby is snug, secure and cannot fall out. If major alterations are needed once baby is in place, it is safest to remove them from the carrier before correcting buckles or straps.

If a carrier is to be used by several different adults, it should be carefully adjusted to each individual before introducing the baby. If possible, have a separate carrier for each adult to avoid frequent alterations.

When wearing the carrier it should be easy to reach and to use one hand to affect minor adjustments to the straps. After completing the carrier fitting, there must be no loose cords or long straps to become entangled around the baby.

Carrying a baby against your body may increase his core temperature and babies must be dressed appropriately for ambient temperature. In addition, carrier straps may need further adjustment according to the thickness of a baby's clothing. When out and about, check a baby's temperature throughout the journey and avoid going outside on extremely hot days. Slings made of a breathable fabric will also aid in air circulation.

Before leaving the house with a baby in a carrier, look in the mirror to check placement and position of the baby. In particular, ensure that babies can breathe properly and that their airways are not obstructed by cloth or straps. This is especially important with younger, inward facing babies whose faces can become buried in bulky clothing. Ensure that there is adequate air circulation around a baby's face and do not place anything over the top of the carrier in an effort to shield them from lighting. In babies less than six months, there should be firm, padded head support made from strong, durable materials.

Instead, to protect babies from the elements use hats, sunscreen, coats and umbrellas, and in the case of backpacks, custom-made sunshades are often available.

Young babies often fall asleep in carriers but should never be transferred to a cot whilst still strapped into a carrier or sling as the risk of strangulation or suffocation is simply too high.

Frequently used items such as carriers should be checked before each use for damage or looseness and second-hand carriers in particular, may be worn and should be carefully checked for buckle and fabric wear. In addition, check that these models have not been recalled and still meet local safety standards.

Slings

Baby slings must be made of strong but breathable fabric. If designed so that fabric is secured through metal rings, the steel used must be greater than 6mm thick. Some ⅛ inch rings have snapped and been associated with serious injury.

The safest mechanism is a two-ring system with the fabric being pulled and tightened around the rings before placing the baby in the sling. This will minimise the risk of fabric slipping through the rings.

Alternatively, if the sling is a knotted design, the knots should be secure and tested before putting baby in sling.

The correct positioning of a baby within the sling is critical to their safety and is related to their age and size. In general, very young babies are placed within the sling and across the body of the adult. Check the instructions for photographs of the correct positioning and in particular, ensure that the baby's chin is not pressed into their chest as this can cause neck strain and is a suffocation risk. Look into the sling often whilst carrying the infant to make sure your passenger has not slipped into a dangerous posture.

Older babies may be carried in slings on the hip but must be snugly fitted against the body of the adult. In addition the fabric should be pulled taut to eliminate any gaps which may allow a baby to slip through.

Backpacks

Backpacks are only appropriate for children over six months of age who can sit upright with decent core strength and can also support their own head and neck.

Any backpack with a rigid frame should have a kickstand to ensure stability when loading or unloading a baby and one hand should remain on the pack at all times to prevent tipping. Toddlers should be loaded and buckled into a backpack before it is placed onto an adult's back, with a second person available to assist in safely placing the carrier in position. Adults attempting to place the backpack behind them without help risk tipping or dropping of the pack, while a child left in a free-standing backpack will almost certainly topple.

All frameworks must be durable and sturdy and if any part of the metal frame contacts the baby it must be well-padded. Similarly, the folding mechanisms and hinges should all be hidden to avoid pinching. Look for a model with a waist/hip strap as these distribute the weight and offer more stability.

When walking around with a baby backpack, be aware that the baby's head will be sitting higher than your own and so overhead objects such as doorframes and branches can be a hazard.

Safe Use of a Baby Carrier

It is always tempting to resume your normal activities once your baby is snug within a carrier, but some activities put your baby at increased risk of injury and should be avoided.

Never cook or drink hot beverages with your baby in a sling or carrier as burns can occur from spills or from brushing them against a hot appliance. Similarly, do not undertake any activities which may bounce or jar your baby such as running, jumping or climbing.

Curious babies tend to reach for anything held in your hand and it is easy to underestimate a child's reach. When using a carrier or sling, avoid hot or dangerous objects, full bench tops or hazardous appliances.

It is important to recognise that carrying a baby this way changes an adult's balance, centre of gravity and view. Balance may not be as good while wearing a carrier, so it is important to wear comfortable, slip-resistant shoes and to hold on where possible e.g. going down stairs. When bending to pick something up, bend your knees into a squat rather than bending from the waist as baby can fall out of the sling.

When you are walking with a baby in the sling or carrier, watch for uneven surfaces as your view of the ground is impaired which may precipitate tripping. Also, remember that your turning circle is now bigger and so leave more space around you when passing through doors or spinning around as baby's head or limbs can get caught on corners and doors.

Take extra care when using a baby carrier on any moving vehicle such as a train, plane or bus; amongst other hazards, your altered centre of gravity can impair balance and lead to falls.

In general, do not wear slings or carriers when:
- Cooking
- Drinking alcohol or hot drinks
- Driving
- Standing on stools or ladders
- Using sharp knives
- Using heavy machinery e.g. lawnmowers, shredders
- Jogging
- Riding a bike
- Reaching overhead for things

Portable Restaurant Chairs

Whether taking your toddler to a friend's house for dinner or to a restaurant for brunch, there are a number of portable chairs which help parents sit their children safely at a table.

There are 2 basic types of portable seats; one which attaches directly to a table and another which anchors to a chair; both have their advantages and disadvantages.

Table-based seats are designed to be securely fastened to a table and are generally suitable for younger, lighter babies. Their use of counter-traction to ensure a strong attachment means that they risk unbalancing any table which is too small or too light to support the weight of a child. In some cases, this can lead to tipping or flipping of the table. Always ensure that a table is sturdy and balanced enough to hold the weight of your child.

The chair-based seat acts as a booster seat on an adult chair and so must be securely anchored around the back of the chair to prevent slipping. With the wide variety of chairs used in restaurants and houses, some portable seat designs will not safely adapt to the size and shape of a certain chair and so should not be used. If in doubt, try attaching the child seat to a chair and then assess for fit and stability. Do not be tempted to 'make do' and to attach a baby seat to a clearly inappropriate chair as this will only put a child at risk; for example, chairs with a rounded wooden top to the backrest will allow some toddler seats to slip off and are clearly not suitable.

Portable Seat Guidelines

Before safely using a portable seat, a baby must be able to sit unsupported and have adequate head control, both of which are not reliably present until over six months of age.

Portable chairs should be made from sturdy, durable materials and have slip-resistant footprints wherever they contact the table or anchor chair. All hinging related to collapsing the chair for transport should be concealed and pinch-proof and rigid frames should be well-padded.

These seats must also be fitted with strong lap and crotch straps and secured with good quality clasps. The crotch strap is particularly important to prevent babies from slipping through the waistband and out of the chair. The harness must be engaged at all times as children, especially toddlers, will try to stand or lean out of the chair.

Always read and adhere to the manufacturer's height and weight recommendations for a specific chair and do not exceed set limits, as putting too big or too small a child in a portable seat can lead to severe injury.

Test that the restaurant seat is properly secured to an anchor chair or table by pressing down firmly on the seat before placing a baby. When positioning the chair, ensure that your baby cannot reach dangerous objects on the table in front of them and maintain a clear zone free of knives, hot drinks, glass and the like.

Another tip if using a table-based system is to carefully place the seat of a full-size chair under the suspended seat of the portable chair to limit the fall should the table tip. This chair however, must not be placed directly under the baby's dangling feet as they may use it to push up and out of their seat.

Toys

THE U.S. CONSUMER PROducts Safety Commission (CPSC) states that in 2008 there were approximately 235,300 toy-related injuries serious enough to require emergency room treatment, with 35% of these relating to children under 5 years old. Ride-on toys such as bicycles, tricycles and scooters were involved in 26% of these injuries.

Comparable Australian statistics are not readily available but are likely to follow similar injury patterns with falls being the commonest cause of toy-related injury, ahead of swallowing and choking on small parts.

Toddlers under 3 years are most at risk of toy injury as they begin to move around and discover their world. The main dangers stem from their tendency to explore with their mouths with no sense of fear.

In U.S. there are >150,000 different types of toys on the shelves, with 5000 new toys introduced every year. Australia is similarly inundated with new products, and the increasing number of cheap imported toys appearing in discount stores is of particular concern.

Despite extensive toy-safety legislation and strict safety standards throughout Australia, it is simply impossible for inspectors to guarantee safety on such a large scale; ultimately then, it is up to parents to choose toys responsibly. This strict government regulation means that most toys are 'safe' but it is important to recognise that any toy can become dangerous if broken or misused.

Accidents related to toys are commonly attributable to one of the following factors:
- Poorly designed e.g. sharp edges, pinch points
- Inherently dangerous e.g. explosive or projectile toys
- Poorly made and break easily; small part production, chemicals
- Misuse and abuse; wrongly assembled or used incorrectly
- Age and developmentally inappropriate
- Poorly supervised play; teaching children to play safely

When buying toys, don't assume that because a brand is well-known that it is automatically safe. Research brands and in particular any product recalls on consumer websites such as the U.S. CSPC and the ACCC.

Similarly, finding a product on the shelf, does not mean it has safety standard approval. Look for an Australian Safety Standard sticker (AS/NZS ISO 8124.1:2002) but be aware that certain toys are not covered under federal safety regulations e.g. Australian exclusions include playground equipment, crayons and play doh. Under this standard, during testing a toy must not release a small part which is an ingestion or inhalation hazard. Small parts are generally recognised as anything which can fit into a 35mm film canister.

Always remember that there is no safety measure which substitutes for vigilant adult supervision, part of which should include teaching children about safe play.

General Toy Childproofing Guidelines

Ensure that all assembly and use instructions are read before handing toys to a child; two of the main causes of toy-related injury are improper assembly or use.

Check all toys for sharp edges and protrusions and if there is any doubt about a toy's safety then discard it completely. In particular, do not try to tape or glue parts of a toy back together as this will inevitably increase the risk of injury.

Make sure toys are not too heavy for younger children to play with and that they will not be injured if the toy falls on them, and do not let children play with toys near stairs, water or traffic.

Children usually learn not to mouth objects between 4–5 years old, but for younger children small parts pose a danger for choking, inhalation, or lodgement in nose, ears or throat. Contrary to popular myth, not all swallowed objects 'pass' without problems, any sharp or toxic objects can cause serious complications if swallowed, as can products containing small magnets.

It is essential that toys do not produce small parts. Small parts are often produced through the taking apart or misuse of toys by older children and it is essential therefore, to educate children and to make sure toys are age-appropriate so as to lessen the chance of misuse. If a baby is still mouthing objects it is also important to limit toys to those which can be washed or wiped.

Toys with bells attached can be choking hazards and should not be given to babies still mouthing. In general, all bells should have the ringing mechanism completely enclosed.

In a family with a number of children, it is important to teach older children to keep inappropriate toys away from their younger siblings and to play with them in a separate space or when the baby is asleep.

The packaging for toys is becoming increasingly elaborate and often contains screws, staples, plastic and wires which may be left lying around in the excitement of unwrapping a new toy. These pieces however, pose serious choking, ingestion and other hazards and must be removed from toys and discarded immediately. Plastic bags should be knotted before disposal to prevent them being placed by children over their head or face.

As much as possible, it is advisable to contain toys within a designated play room or smaller area within the main living room so as to keep traffic and family areas clear of tripping hazards. Be especially vigilant in keeping toys clear of stairs and walkways.

Extra care should be taken when using second hand toys as older toys may not meet modern safety standards or may have been recalled. Check carefully that they are in good condition.

Batteries
Young children, especially mouthing babies, should not be allowed access to batteries as they can leak toxic acid. Ensure all battery compartments are secured with screws and cannot be opened easily and if a toy's battery compartment is broken, it should be discarded. Home-made or taped repairs are unsound and often focus a child's attention to this area.

Loose Strings, Ribbons or Cords
Loose strings, ribbons or cords may appear attached to many different toys and can cause strangulation. Pull-along toys should have short strings which are not long enough to be wound around a child's neck.

Toys must not be tied to pram sides or baby's clothing as they can become entangled around a baby's neck, especially when in a pram or carseat and out of direct sight of an adult. Similarly, toys should not be strung across playpens or cots as they may become taut across a child's neck.

Balls
Balls for children under 6 years should be greater than 7.5cms in diameter and as a general guide; the smaller the child the larger the ball should be.

Furry or Plush Toys
Plush toys are harder to clean, collect dust and shed fur which can be an asthma trigger. Read labels to establish the composition of such toys before buying and preferentially choose those which can be immersed and washed properly.

Inspect regularly for breaks in the seams or holes as the inner stuffing can extrude and be a choking hazard. This is especially important if there is a small sound chip or battery concealed inside. It is best to avoid toys with bean-type fillings for young children as these can spill and cause choking.

Avoid cuddly toys with glued-on plastic eyes or nose as these can be broken or chewed off and so pose a choking hazard. Similarly, remove ribbons from around the necks of soft toys to avoid strangulation.

Toys with any poles or sticks attached are a danger to young children. They can poke themselves or others in the eyes and if toddler is crawling or walking with a stick in their mouth, they may fall causing the stick to lodge in the throat or mouth.

Magnets

A current trend is for toys containing small magnets, often no bigger than a few millimetres in diameter. They are most commonly seen in construction toys, jewellery and some soft toys. These magnets appear to children as lollies if they fall out of toys and can pose a major choking hazard.

In addition if more than one of these small magnets is swallowed they can be attracted to each other through the bowel wall and cause intestinal twisting and blockage.

Balloons

Balloons are a major cause of choking in children. Uninflated or deflated latex balloons pose the greatest threat and if inhaled can block the entire airway and be difficult to remove. Immediately dispose of deflated balloons and do not leave them forgotten on the floor to slowly deflate over days.

Older children can also inhale balloons when trying to inflate them and all children less than 8 years old should be supervised if playing with balloons. They should also be taught not to place balloons over or near their face or mouth.

Consider using Mylar (the shiny, non-rubber) balloons as a safer alternative to latex for young children.

Noisy Toys

Toys with a loud sound component can be dangerous to an infants hearing with instances of hearing loss related to such toys having been reported. To assess, hold the toy next to your own ear and if it is too shrill or loud for you to tolerate at close quarters, do not give it to your child.

Bath Toys

Bath toys should be washable and sealed to stop water collecting inside as stagnant water leads to mould growth. In particular, beware of squirty toys as water and mould will collect inside and these toys should be changed regularly. Some mould collections may been seen by holding bath toys up to the light, and looking for dark patches, if these are present, discard the toy immediately.

Squishy, soft bath toys may also contain the potentially harmful substance phthalates (see below).

Water Toys

All kids love playing with toys in the swimming pool, however, these toys can pose a very real danger and must always be used under strict adult supervision. These water toys should never be mistaken or misused as flotation devices as they are neither designed nor guaranteed as such.

Some of these pool toys can tip a child and can also make it difficult for them to right themselves, trapping them underwater.

All pool toys and float aids should be deflated and stored in a childproof cupboard or shed as they attract children to the pool.

For more information about childproofing pools and pool areas see Chapter 12.

Toy Guns

Toy guns which shoot projectiles carry the risk of eye injuries as well as the risk of younger children choking on the expelled projectiles. Many of these 'toy' guns such as BB or pellet guns are in fact high-powered, potentially lethal devices and should not be given to children.

Toy guns are often associated with loud snapping or popping noises which can damage a child's hearing and it has been shown that 'cap' guns held less than 12 inches/30cms from ears can affect hearing.

There are a lot of well-publicised concerns regarding the developmental impact of allowing children to play with guns and other violent toys. It can normalise violence and may make it easier for a child to mistake a real firearm for a toy.

The American Academy of Pediatrics (AAP) notes that 'studies in recent years have raised questions about the effect playing with toy firearms has on a child's developing personality. Playing with toy weapons and firearms may cause more aggressive and violent behaviour in some children'.

In general, many people are moving away from giving violent toys such as guns to children.

Chemistry Sets

Chemistry sets are interesting and educational toys, but when used inappropriately they can also pose the risk of fires, explosions, poisoning, burns and eye injuries. They are not suitable for children under 12 years and should only be used under strict adult supervision and when younger children are not present. These sets should not be stored within reach of children or in bedrooms to prevent unsupervised use.

Sports Equipment

Sporting equipment should always be given and used with the appropriate protective gear so that the two elements are immediately associated. It should always be a condition of use that protection be worn.

Bats, hard balls, pucks etc should not be left around the house or yard but should be stored in a childproof cupboard or cage and be used by younger children only when supervised.

Computer Games and Online Gaming

Gaming is an increasingly popular and complex part of the toy world and parents must educate themselves about suitable and age-appropriate games before allowing children to play. This is most effectively done by playing the game yourself before letting your children play to ensure that it has merit beyond senseless violence.

Gaming consoles should be set up in common areas rather than in children's bedrooms; this encourages monitoring of activities and behaviours. Most consoles have parental control features which can be used to narrow the range of activities available to young children; for example, internet capabilities may be disabled.

Parents should familiarise themselves with the local rating system for games which in Australia is similar to film ratings and consists of: G, PG, M, MA 15+ and soon the to be instated R18+.

Online gaming is increasingly popular with children and has its own myriad of safety issues, including the sharing of personal details inappropriately. Supervise and educate your children about safe online behaviours.

Maintenance
All toys should have regular safety surveillance as well as maintenance. They should be cleaned regularly in hot soapy water where possible or wiped down with non-toxic cleaning detergents (e.g. water /vinegar).

Examine toys regularly for cracks, splinters, missing parts, sharp edges or other damage and discard broken toys. Home-spun repairs are often sub-standard and leave toys vulnerable to small part production, collapse or sharp edges.

Dispose of any toys with exposed electronics or batteries especially those with broken battery compartments. Taping the compartment lid in place is inadequate and leaves babies with free access to potentially dangerous battery acids.

Toy Storage and Toyboxes
Teach children to clear the floor of toys regularly to prevent tripping and to store their toys safely.

Store baby and toddler toys on low shelves to discourage climbing, conversely, store older children's toys at a higher level off the ground so that they are not easily accessible to a younger sibling.

All free-standing storage units such as shelves, chest-of-drawers and wardrobes should be bolted securely to the wall to stop toppling, especially if climbed on. A simple 'L'-shaped metal brace secured to a stud is adequate. Teach children never to climb up on shelving but rather to use a step or if too young, to ask for help.

Do not store toys in the original packaging as they will often contain plastic, staple, wires and other hazardous materials.

Toyboxes are a great and accessible place to store toys for younger children and should be of sturdy construction. They must be fitted with slow-closing hinges to prevent the lid slamming onto little heads or fingers.

There should always be cut-outs at both ends of the toy box to allow for ventilation should the child climb or fall in and toyboxes must never be lockable.

The safest way to store toys is in an open topped basket or

plastic container with curved corners. Some plastic containers also come with a loose, fitting, non-sealing lid.

Trampolines

Trampolines are an increasingly popular part of Australasian backyards with parents being lured by the apparent safety of modern design modifications to the traditional trampoline. Whilst desirable, these changes to trampoline construction are no substitute for close parental supervision; trampolines continue to be associated with high injury rates, especially from limb fractures and spinal injuries.

In general, it is not recommended that children under 6 years old use a full size trampoline. In addition, only one child at a time should be on the trampoline to minimise the chance of awkward bounces and collisions.

Trampolines should preferably be spring free or if not available, should at least have padded, covered springs to minimise the risk of pinch injury or of falling through gaps. Choose trampolines with a netting enclosure to prevent a child bouncing off the mat and onto the ground.

Do not have a ladder to the trampoline, as this gives access to the under 6's. As a general rule, if children cannot get up onto the tramp on their own, they are too young to use it.

Place the trampoline away from eaves, trees and pools and for greater stability, sink the base of the trampoline into the ground. In addition, inspect the trampoline regularly for wear and repair as required.

It is essential to teach children to use the trampoline safely, including entering and exiting safely, ensuring the zipper on the net is completely closed before jumping, and jumping in the centre of the mat and not on the sides. Do not allow somersaults as these risk awkward falls onto the neck and head, risking paralysis. Have children remove their shoes and socks before trampolining as bare feet grip better.

Chemicals in Toys and Baby Bottles

There is an increasing amount of interest in the chemical content and safety of children's toys. It has long been known that lead toys are harmful and with the growth of plastics in toy manufacture, two further compounds, BPA and phthalates are gaining attention as potentially harmful.

The chemical content of toys is an evolving area with government legislation and regulation inevitably lagging behind. It therefore becomes the responsibility of parents to stay informed of the current evidence regarding the content of toys.

BPA

BPA or Bisphenol-A is a building block used in the manufacture of PVC and other polycarbonate plastics. It is commonly found in food storage containers, baby bottles, toys, rattles, teethers and CDs and also forms part of the epoxy resin lining of food cans and bottle tops.

The real problem is that BPA becomes unstable in heat and in very acidic or alkaline environments. Therefore, it can leach out of plastics when it comes into contact with some detergents, bleaches and when heated in microwaves, sterilisers or dishwashers.

Evidence is only now emerging as to how long term exposure to chemicals such as BPA may affect human beings. In various animal studies and now human studies, BPA has been linked with neural and hormonal derangements and has been implicated in some cancers (including breast cancer), impaired immune function, early puberty, obesity, diabetes and hyperactivity in children.

A study published in the Journal of the American Medical Association (JAMA) where the urine of over 1500 people was tested for BPA showed that 90% of them had detectable levels of BPA. In all people the BPA levels were within the recommended range set by the FDA, but over the level found to be harmful in animal studies. Particularly worrying, was that the 25% of this group with the highest BPA levels had 3 times the incidence of heart disease, 2.4 times the incidence of diabetes and had higher levels of some liver enzymes when corrected for other factors.

While evidence is still being compiled and research is ongoing, there is little doubt that exposing a baby from birth to this potentially dangerous chemical is undesirable.

It is illegal to sell toys

containing BPA in the U.S.A. since the Consumer Product Safety Act of 2008, and Canada has also banned the sale of baby bottles containing BPA and has listed BPA as a toxic substance.

In June 2010, the Australian government announced the voluntary phase-out by Australian retailers of plastic baby bottles containing BPA. Toys however, are not covered under this phase-out and continue to be a potential risk to mouthing babies.

Reducing exposure to BPA

Manufacturers are not currently required to state whether their product contains BPA, but they are usually marked with a number 7 recycling code on the bottom of bottles and toys.

Another clue is that BPA is usually contained in clear plastic products, so if objects are cloudy or soft plastic, they are more likely to be BPA-free.

Given all of the recent publicity on BPA, manufacturers have begun to state clearly on packaging when a product *does not* contain BPA, so look for BPA-free products such as baby bottles.

Further protection can be found by choosing food in cardboard or glass containers rather than canned goods. In addition, avoid microwaving polycarbonate plastic food containers and instead use glass, porcelain or stainless steel containers when heating food in the microwave or on the stovetop.

Phthalates

Phthalates are oily, colourless, and odourless compounds which are used, primarily to make PVC more flexible. These compounds are therefore common in toys such as rubber ducks, dolls and balls, but are also found in baby shampoos, lotions, medicines, and perfumes.

The potential health effects of phthalates which have been raised by scientists include early onset puberty, low sperm counts as well as in-utero effects such as abnormal genital development and premature delivery.

This potential harm caused by phthalates is particularly worrying in the case of baby toys, where constant mouthing of toys could lead to an increased dose exposure.

In early 2009 the U.S.A. joined the European Union

in banning phthalates in children's toys, whilst in Australia, the use of phthalates in toys is currently under review by the Australia's National Industrial Chemicals Notification and Assessment Scheme (NICNAS). In January 2010, the Australian Minister for Competition Policy and Consumer Affairs (ACCC) announced a temporary ban for a period of eighteen months, on products containing greater than 1% of the phthalate Diethylhexyl phthalate (DEHP).

Lead

Health officials have long sought to reduce children's exposure to lead, however despite this, the fight is still far from won as evidenced by the recent mass recalls in the U.S. of popular toys from such characters as Thomas the Tank Engine, Nemo, Dora the Explorer and Sesame Street.

Lead is especially toxic to the brains of young children with even a single exposure to a high dose (e.g. swallowing a piece of metal jewellery containing lead) can lead to permanent neurological and behavioural damage. More chronic exposure to low doses of lead can lead to reduced IQ, attention deficit hyperactivity, and problems with fine motor skills and coordination. In short, no safe level of lead exposure has been identified.

Despite most countries outlawing lead in toys, there continues to be cases of importation and sale of lead-containing toys. The most common sources of lead in toys are from lead paint and cheap costume jewellery, but it has also been found in bibs and vinyl lunchboxes.

To screen a piece of jewellery for lead, use a home lead tester available from the local hardware store. It is also best to simply throw away heavy, cheap jewellery and to avoid giving jewellery to young children who place items readily in their mouths. In addition, look for unpainted toys or toys which state that the coating is lead-free.

Be particularly cautious in the use of second-hand or older, painted baby furniture or toys which may pre-date the introduction of lead-free paint.

Age Appropriate Toy Buying Guide

The age guides printed on toy packaging are recommendations

linked to child development and safety and not IQ, and so should be carefully heeded. A child may well be *smart* enough to play with a certain toy, but may not be physically or cognitively developed enough to safely play with it. Challenging a younger child with an age-inappropriate toy can lead to injury or death.

Be aware that age-appropriateness works equally both ways, as a toy which is also too simple for an older child may be misused and so is more likely to lead to injury.

0–6 months

At this age, infants explore the world with their mouths and at 3 months babies begin to grasp and hold things on their own. Consequently the main risks come from choking, poisoning and sharp edges.

Avoid toys which can produce small parts, break easily or have sharp edges and toys with strings or cords longer than 30cms should also be avoided.

Suitable toys:
- Mobile with high contrast colours and patterns, musical if possible. Hang out of reach
- Baby gym with hanging toys for non-mobile babies
- Hand held toys and rattles as babies are near-sighted
- Music box or plush toy
- Unbreakable mirror; babies are fascinated by their reflection
- Soft books with high-contrast patterns
- Sensory toys which tweets when pressed
- Wrist rattles
- Push and pull toys with short string
- Large blocks
- Washable bath toys and squeaky toys

6–12 months

By 6 months, babies can usually sit up and are able to reach for, and grasp objects they desire. Everything is explored with the mouth and all toys should be chosen with this in mind.

Suitable toys:
- Washable bath toys and squeaky toys
- Plush toys
- Soft balls
- Push and pull toys with short strings
- Strong rattles
- Mobile with high contrast

colours and patterns, musical if possible. Hang out of reach
- Sturdy musical instruments such as castanets, tambourines, drums, keyboards etc.
- Activity centre with hanging, spinning or musical toys
- Board books
- Activity quilts and mats
- Wooden blocks
- Electronic activity toys which encourage new skills

12–24 months

By 12 months toddlers are mobile and reaching upwards. They are still placing objects in the mouth and are relentlessly curious. Creativity and imagination are beginning to surface.

Suitable toys:
- Large solid toys e.g. trains
- Push-pull toys with short string
- Blocks
- Balls
- Bucket and spade
- Kitchen pots and pans
- Ride on-toys
- Musical toys or CD player
- Board books and folding-flap books
- Activity centre

- Musical instruments
- Simple and large jigsaws
- Plastic tea set
- Play doh or non-toxic modelling clay

2–3 years

Two year olds are fearless, independent and curious; they move at speed and can climb. Toys which stimulate their creativity are the key to retaining their interest.

Suitable toys:
- Peg boards
- Activity centres
- Ride-in or ride-on toys and bikes
- Non-toxic paints, crayons and pencils
- Small table and chairs
- Large component construction sets
- Large Lego sets
- Longer and more wordy books
- Musical instruments
- Sturdy car, train or similar sets
- Blackboard
- Jigsaws
- Tea sets
- Play doh or non-toxic modelling clay
- Dress-up clothes

Bikes and Trikes

What greater rite of passage than a child's first bike? Time was when this meant a cumbersome frame with a set of rickety, uneven training wheels. Fast forward to the new millennium and there are a dazzling array of shiny, lightweight bikes with 1001 gears, steering bars, adjustable seats and even sunshades. But inevitably, helping your child to be a safe bike-rider involves distilling the hype down to a few basic truths.

Bicycles are a childhood staple, but the risks of such toys are significant with the Centre for Accident Research and Road Safety in Queensland stating that bicycles are the most common consumer product causing injury in children. In NSW, half of all hospitalisations from injuries in the 5–14 age group are for bicycle-related injuries.

The most common injury sustained during road bicycle accidents is head injury and despite a reduction in such injuries since the introduction of mandatory bike helmets, some children still refuse to wear helmets. Other common bicycle injuries include lacerations and limb fractures, with the most common mechanism of bike-injury being through collision with another vehicle or object.

Learning to ride a bike can be a precarious time for a child and as a consequence, they are often closely supervised by an adult during this initial period. In addition, most children will practice riding well away from busy roads and pathways all of which makes them less likely to suffer a serious injury related to their bike.

In fact, the greater danger lies with older children who ride more independently, but whose motor and cognitive skills are still developing along with their sense of danger and ability to make informed judgements. In findings from the Western Australian Injury Surveillance system, the 10–13 year age group accounted for the highest number of bicycle road traumas at 52.7%, whilst children aged less than 5 years accounted for only 4.3%.

The role of gender within bicycle injury remains a consistent and compelling finding from many studies, with boys being 2 to 4 times more likely than girls to present to hospital with a bike-related injury.

Childproofing Bicycles

To begin, ensure that any bicycle purchased has an Australian Safety Standard sticker, especially in these days of cheaper imports. Secondly, bicycles should be sized appropriately for each child and adjusted regularly as one of the major causes of falls from a bike is related to children riding bikes which are too big.

All bikes should have appropriate safety equipment fitted including; brakes, reflectors, lights, bell or horn and visibility devices such as flags or reflective tape.

Bicycles must also be regularly maintained to maximise safety and minimise the risk of a mechanical failure leading to an accident.

Helmets should be worn for every ride, everyday, but as children grow older their compliance may wane. This falls under that eternal parental conundrum of how to show a child to safely in a world full of distractions and peer groups. It may help to lead through example by riding together as a family and so reinforcing safety messages as well as having fun.

Teach children not to forget UV protection when riding, including sunscreen and helmet visors.

Ultimately however, there is no safety measure which

substitutes for the proper supervision of young children on bikes and for teaching older children to ride safely and responsibly on the roads.

There is no magic age after which children should begin to ride bikes independently and it can vary widely depending on physical development and maturity of each individual child. Most children >6 years old, however, do possess the motor skills to safely mount a bike, balance and pedal. The use of training wheels is optional but may be useful in children lacking initial confidence.

It is not recommended that children under 10 ride unsupervised in public areas such as roadways and footpaths, as they may not have the road knowledge or motor skills to navigate these areas safely. Older children should participate in a bike safety course which covers road rules before being allowed to ride in public areas.

With bike prices sky-rocketing it is tempting to buy second-hand, but care must be taken before doing so, and a knowing eye must be passed carefully over any such bikes to ensure that they are in good condition and have not been left to rust in the shed. Be aware that older models may not meet modern safety standards and always check on consumer websites that the model has not been recalled.

As a rule, never use a second hand helmet from an uncertain source, as it may have been in an accident and have damaged protective layers.

Bike-buying Guide

Buying the right bike for your child should be all about great fit and appropriate safety equipment. This does not have to mean buying the most expensive bike in the shop as long as you know what to look for and what to avoid.

It is critical to buy a bike of appropriate size for a child (see below), as buying a larger bike for children 'to grow into' is extremely dangerous and vastly increases the risk of injury. Always read and respect, therefore, the manufacturer's age and size recommendations as a guide to buying the right bike.

Consider your child's current riding abilities and choose a bike which accommodates this skill set, and always buy a bike suitable for the *type* of riding your child wishes to undertake e.g. BMX or mountain bike riding.

At first, children's bikes should not have gears as this can distract them and make riding too complex; young children need only concentrate on the pedals. There should also be a chain guard to enclose the chain wheel and upper run of the chain.

Avoid slippery plastic pedals and instead look for rubber-treated pedals or metal pedals with serrated edges for grip. Ideally pedals should also have tread on both sides. Fixed toe-clips are another way of securing foothold, but in young children are more likely to lead to injury. These may be difficult for young children to master.

Wheel rims should be aluminium as they have 5 times shorter braking distances than chrome-plated steel rims; use a magnet to tell the difference as the magnet will not stick to aluminium.

In general, bikes for children under 7 years should have foot (coaster) brakes rather than hand brakes as young children do not have the hand strength to safely engage hand-brakes. For children older than 7 years bikes should have hand and foot brakes to familiarise them with handbrakes before graduating to bigger bikes with handbrakes alone. Always check hand and foot brakes for fast, easy stopping without instability or jamming.

Fit
It is universally agreed that correct sizing of a bicycle is critical; when a bike is too big children cannot safely reach the ground, pedals or controls. Conversely, when a child has grown out of a bike they are forced to stand up on the pedals and may lose balance.

The best approach when buying a new bike is to tap into the expertise of specialised bike shop staff as they are experts in safe sizing and fit. This does not necessarily mean you have to pay more, but knowing the right size bike for your child will allow you to shop around for a competitive price.

A child should be able to sit on the seat and have their feet resting flat on the ground without tipping the bike. There should also be a 3cm space between the crossbar of a frame and the child standing with both feet flat on ground. This space should be more (approx. 5cm) for BMX or mountain bikes. For girls' bikes, make the measurements using an imaginary line where a cross bar would be.

The handlebars should be positioned at approximately the same height as the seat and should be no higher than the child's shoulders. They should be able to comfortably reach the handlebars with a slightly bent arm whilst sitting on the seat. Ensure children can also reach and adequately grasp any handbrakes without stretching.

If your child is using training wheels, be sure that they are sturdy and can be raised or adjusted as their skills improve.

As always, it is important to monitor and adjust fit on a child's bicycle as they grow; if in doubt return the bike to the store and ask for help in re-sizing.

Safe Riding

Much of making children safe whilst biking lies in teaching them how to ride safely within different settings and situations. According to the WA Childhood Injury Surveillance Systems, almost 12% of road trauma presentations were by children who sustained injuries whilst riding a bicycle on the roadway. Of these, 82% of accidents also involved a car.

Interestingly, the weekends did not see an increase in bicycle accidents, instead, the injury rate peaked on Tuesdays. Injuries did spike however, in the after school hours of 4–6pm, while no injuries were recorded between 6.00am and 8am.

Guide to Kid's Bike Sizes		
Age	**Child's Height**	**Bike Wheel Size**
Age 2–5	26–34 inches/65–85cms	12 inches/30cm
Age 4–8	34–42 inches/85–106cms	16 inches/40cms
Age 6–9	42–48 inches/106–121cms	18 inches/45cms
Age 8–12	48–56 inches/124–142cms	20 inches/50cms
Youth	56–62 inches/142–157cms	24 inches/60cms

As a general guide, children under the age of ten years should not be allowed to cycle unsupervised on public roads as they do not possess the road knowledge, the judgement, nor the bike skills required to safely negotiate traffic. Riding on the roads requires a sophisticated mix of physical and mental skills. Children can however, be taught the rules of the road from an early age, including the meaning of road signs, as well as how to interact with other traffic, including bicycles.

Younger children should be taught to ride in graduated riding environments, each one more complex than the last and where possible should always use cycle paths rather than roads. In Australia children under 12 years can legally ride on the footpath.

Parents can promote good riding as well as fitness by riding safely with their children and following road rules.

Important Road Rules to Teach Children:

- Stop at all signs and signals equivalent to a car
- Always yield to pedestrians and cars
- Ride in the same direction as cars, never against
- Use bike lanes and paths where possible rather than the footpath except for children less than 10 years old.
- If riding on the footpath be especially aware of cars leaving driveways
- Children should never ride at dusk or in the dark
- Never ride with headphones on as it shuts out important sounds from the surrounds
- Always stop and look for traffic in both directions when leaving driveway, laneway or curb
- Children should avoid riding in the wet
- Only one person should ride on the bike at a time. Never share a bike as it can lead to over-balancing
- Don't carry objects in arms or on handlebars while riding. Both hands should be on the handlebars. Use a backpack or bike carrier which also allows the bike to remain balanced.
- Do not ride in and out of cars
- Look out for hazards such as potholes, manhole covers,

puddles, gravel and leaves. Alert all riders behind you.
- Ride single file in a group
- Walk bike across intersections using crossings and with traffic signals
- Pass other bikes or people on the right in Australia, ring the bell, and say 'on your right'
- Look carefully before changing lanes and use left and right turn signals

Bike Maintenance

Children's bikes live a pretty hard existence; often left outside in the elements, and ridden under all sorts of conditions, they are prone to some wear and tear. Where possible, bikes should be kept indoors or in a garage as moisture will cause rust and weaken parts; at the very least they should be stored undercover.

It is important that parents regularly monitor a child's bike and perform safety checks on them at least once per season. The bike should be checked for loose parts and screws and the frame inspected for cracks. In addition the brakes must be tested and checked for frayed cables and worn brake pads.

Tyres ought to be inflated to the pressure recommended on the sidewall and any worn tyres replaced. Wobbly wheels can render the whole bike unstable and must be aligned for better control. Wheels must be able to spin freely without rubbing against framework or mudflaps. Older children can be shown how to use a puncture kit and may test their skills on an old inner tube.

Regularly assess a growing child's handlebars and seat to ensure that they do not require height adjustments or re-alignment due to movement. All bolts should be tightened regularly and any worn grips replaced. In particular, grips must cover the end of the handlebars.

Bicycle seats should be level, not move around and should have no tears or exposed springs.

Helmets

Approximately two thirds of bicycle deaths are due to head injuries with the use of bike helmets being shown to reduce the risk of head injury by up to 85%. And yet various Australian injury surveillance studies have consistently found that only a third of children suffering from bicycle road trauma are known to be wearing a helmet at the time of the accident. As a consequence, there is a high incidence of head injuries in this group. Further, in random surveys of helmet wearing at various locations, only 40–50% of children are wearing an approved bicycle helmet, and even fewer of these are wearing appropriately-fitted helmets.

These numbers come despite the introduction of Australian laws in 1989 mandating compulsory helmet wearing for all bicycle riders.

So why are children not wearing bicycle helmets? The answer is undoubtedly complex and multi-factorial spanning peer issues, pop culture and a sense of immortality. But much can be gained by parents from imprinting children at a young age to wear a helmet when riding their bike. If this is perceived as the norm, then perhaps children will be less likely to remove their helmet as they grow older.

All helmets should have the Australian Safety Standards sticker and be brightly coloured to aid in visibility. They should have good ventilation to promote air circulation and prevent overheating.

Replace any helmet made before 1999 as safety materials and standards have changed and always replace any helmet involved in an accident as it loses the ability to absorb impact.

Do not store bicycle helmets in the sun as the lining foam can degrade and check the foam regularly to ensure it is not crumbling.

Hats should not be worn underneath helmets as they may lead to slipping and movement of the helmet. For UV protection, instead wear a visor fitted to the helmet.

Children should not wear helmets when on playground equipment as the chin strap can become caught and may pose a strangulation risk.

Helmets must be fitted correctly to ensure proper position and function. They must also be regularly re-assessed and adjusted as a child grows. Helmets should sit level on the head and cover the forehead with the rim sitting just above the eyebrows. They should not sit tilted forwards or backwards and should not be able to move or slide on a child's

THE SAFETY BUBBLE

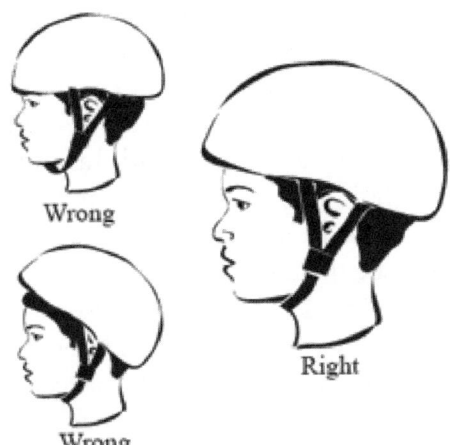

head; this means that inner linings and straps need adjustment to ensure a snug fit. Helmets must be fitted with strong, wide straps which fit securely under the chin and which form a V under the earlobes.

Clothing

Any bike clothing should be bright and light; bright for visibility and lightweight to stop overheating. Children should wear pants which are not too loose or flared as they can get caught in the chain leading to a serious spill.

Shoes must have closed toes for safety, and riders should never wear thongs, flip/flops, open toes, cleats or stops and must never ride barefoot. Rubber soled shoes are also preferable as they will grip onto pedals and prevent slippage.

If children are wearing a backpack whilst riding, there should be no straps dangling down as they may get caught in the wheels.

Child Bike Seats

Involving young children in family bike rides has become more feasible in recent years with the advent of child seats for adult bicycles. These seats may be mounted on the rear or in the front of the main bike seat and are suitable for children over 12 months old but less than 22kg in weight. Babies younger than

12 months do not have the head, neck and core strength required to safely withstand the rigors of riding.

Any child seat should have a padded back which is high enough to support their head and neck and must be fitted with a 5-point harness complete with childproof clasps. Look for seats with moulded leg supports, spoke guards and foot straps to prevent dangling feet becoming caught in a wheel.

Be aware that the additional weight of a child in a bike seat also affects the balance and handling of the bike and so practise is essential before setting off on a long or difficult ride. This increase in weight on the bike also increases the braking distance and this must be factored in when navigating high traffic areas.

Children must be fitted with an infant or toddler helmet and should always have UV protection using helmet visors and sunscreen.

Bike Trailers

The American Academy of Pediatrics (AAP) recommends bike trailers as one of the safest ways to ride with young children. Trailers are low, mesh-covered seats supported by two or three wide-based wheels for stability, which are towed behind an adult bike. Trailers should only ever be pulled by adult riders, as older children are not equipped physically or cognitively to adjust real-time to the presence of the trailer.

Bike trailers should not be used to carry babies under 12 months as they are unsupervised and do not have the head control necessary to tolerate bumps and turns adequately. In addition, babies cannot safely wear helmets.

Trailers are designed to sit low to the ground both for stability and so that it is not far to fall a tumble does occur. Always test the stability of a trailer in-store, before purchase by trying to tip it over and look for a flexible joint and release mechanism which will disengage the trailer and leave it upright should the bike fall over.

Children should be secured in a trailer with a proper 5-point harness fitted with childproof latches. Remember that children in a bike trailer are largely unsupervised whilst in motion, making it all the more important that they are firmly secured.

When attaching the trailer to the cycle, ensure that the trailer is spaced far enough behind the bike so that the child cannot lean and reach the back wheel of the bike. Trailers should also be fitted with UV and rain protective canopies as well as reflectors and a tall flag for visibility. It should to go without saying that any children riding in a bike trailer must be fitted with a helmet and should always wear sunscreen.

When riding a bike with an attached trailer remember that it is wider than the bike and can clip objects or curbs, so use a wider berth around objects and corners. In addition, sharp turns should be avoided as even the sturdiest trailer may tip.

Tricycles

Tricycles are sturdy, wide-based three-wheel bikes which are appropriate for toddlers. Many modern tricycles are fitted with safety harnesses, foot rests and even sun canopies. These features can be utilised as age-appropriate and then adjusted as a child grows.

Many tricycles also have a removable push-handle from which parents can control and in some cases, steer the trike whilst walking behind. These handles are a safety essential helping parents to intervene if required when children are riding on footpaths and crossing roadways.

Tricycles should be sized in a similar manner to larger bikes with children's feet able to touch the ground when seated. If this is not the case, the child is too small to safely get on and off the bike, and they will also struggle to control the bikes momentum.

Given that tricycles are used predominantly for toddlers with fairly primitive motor skills, they should be used away from slopes, stairs and changes in level.

Another useful safety feature is the ability to lock or restrict the steering on a tricycle which can prevent jack-knifing and allow children to learn to ride without the complexities of steering.

Balance Bikes

Balance bikes are lightweight pedal-less bikes which allow young children to scoot their feet along the ground to gather speed and to then to raise their feet and 'coast'. The increased stability imparted by a low centre of gravity allows for use from 18 months of age.

The theory behind such bikes is that balance, co-ordination and steering are all mastered before adding the complex mechanics of pedalling. Enthusiasts insist that balance bike graduates transition quicker to a two-wheeled bike without the need for training wheels.

Many balance bikes also have restricted steering to stop the bike jack-knifing at speed. Most are fitted with pneumatic or solid rubber wheels, however some cheaper models have solid plastic wheels which can slip or wobble on uneven surfaces and so should be avoided.

One potential concern with balance bikes is the absence of brakes on many models with children expected to drag their feet for stopping, even at speed.

Further, the Australian standard requires that children's bikes have at least two braking systems, of which one must be a back-pedal brake (where brakes are activated when you pedal backwards). With no pedals on the balance bike some models are fitted with a single handbrake fitted to the front or rear wheel, which may not be ideal as handbrakes are not recommended for young children as they do not have the hand strength required for safe operation.

With increasing popularity the market is being flooded with cheap balance-bike imports, but with no requirement for formal safety testing parents should look for sturdy construction and adequate safety features. Cheaper aluminium-framed bikes can have poor weld joins with spikes protruding.

_# PART 4

Travelling

Grandparents and Visiting

Visiting a friend or going to Grandma's house is always a special adventure for young children, but it can also be an uncontrolled, and often child unfriendly environment.

The degree of childproofing appropriate to different situations will depend on the amount of time a child is likely to spend visiting; it may be a one-off visit to a friend's home who also has children requiring little mobile childproofing, or it may be that a grandparent is about to undertake day care duties a few days a week which requires more extensive childproofing strategies.

It is possible to take some childproofing on the road, and to carry a childproofing kit which consists of:

- Plastic electrical outlet covers
- Wire twist ties to secure electrical and curtain cords
- Masking or duct tape
- Corner guards

Undoubtedly, however, the most effective portable safety device is 20/20 childproof vision with the ability to rapidly identify and neutralise any child hazards on arrival.

No matter the length of a visit, when taking young children into a non-home environment, diligent supervision must be taken up a notch. It is easy to become distracted when catching up with friends or relatives, but without the childproofing comforts of home, parents must be constantly aware of a child's location and activity.

Quick Childproofing

Before the occasional visit, it is best to call grandma to discuss how to prepare her home. If it is a short visit, concentrate in preparing one room, such as the living room and closing the doors to restrict access beyond this room; in particular close bathroom and laundry doors and lock any doors with access to garages or the outside.

Have Grandparents pack away all of the precious ornament and artwork which may be within reach, and to clear all floors and surfaces of choking hazards such as pins, paperclips and coins.

All pets should be excluded from the space, especially if unaccustomed to children, and the water and food bowls placed out of reach.

One of the main sources of childhood injury whilst visiting is from handbags left on the floor or on low tables; these often contain choking hazards and may also contain lighters, or medications. Older people often replace childproof caps on medication bottles with ones that are easier to open, and for a small child such tablets can seem like lollies. In young babies and toddler only a small dose of some medications can prove fatal. All handbags must be kept in a high cupboard or in another room behind closed doors as it never ceases to amaze how high a determined toddler can reach.

Houseplants must also be moved to high surfaces and any stray or dangling leaves removed to guard against poisoning or choking.

After arriving at Grandma's house, perform a hands and knees sweep yourself, even if done subtly under the guise of playing with baby; look in particular for stray choking hazards and dangling electrical or curtain cords. Any such cords can be wound up and secured out of reach using twist ties or string. Similarly, tape shut any low drawers or cupboards in the vicinity.

The best way to stop a child getting into mischief is to keep them occupied and so bring a generous supply of toys and distractions, and if a regular visitor, keep a basket of toys at Grandma's house. Clear a good amount of floor space by moving any coffee tables and other furniture to the edge of the room; this also protects baby from any sharp table corners. Any exposed corners should then be covered with a bumper if available, or even a washcloth taped in place. Glass coffee tables should be completely removed from the room.

Stairs must be off-limits, either behind closed doors, or by the use of gates; tension gates which use spring pressure to hold in place can be carried around as temporary barriers where required, however, these are unsuitable for use at the top of stairs as they can give way if pushed on with great force.

More extensive childproofing will be necessary if grandparents are to assume more of the day-to-day care of young children, including the provision of safe sleeping arrangements. Avoid the use of the family heirloom cot as it is unlikely to measure up to modern safety standards (see Chapter 1), and never allow a baby to sleep in the middle of an adult bed as this risks suffocation. Instead, bring your own portable cot or purchase a more permanent cot for the purpose.

Travel

Travelling with excited children can be fun, and with some simple preparation, it can also be safe. Childproofing in an environment outside your own home, state or country relies on parents being able to identify and neutralise any hazards.

Prepare a simple childproofing kit prior to departure, filled with a few essentials which may be used to childproof in particular hotel rooms.

Contents may include:
- Masking or duct tape (preferably duct tape as children may tear through masking tape)
- Electrical plug covers (which maybe accessed online for different countries)
- Corner bumpers
- String or garbage bag ties
- Anti-slip decals for the bath

Flying with Children

Airports

Airports can become the Achilles heel of any family holiday if parents are forced to wait for hours in various queues with over-excited and over-tired children. So as much as possible, fly in the morning when children are less fatigued and research airport facilities online before leaving home.

These days it is possible to perform much of the check-in

and seat allocation procedures online, the day before departure. Take advantage of these e-check-in facilities as much as possible to minismise the time spent queuing once at the airport. In an ideal situation, all that will be left to do at the airport is to self-check any luggage.

Many airlines also have self-check-in stations within the airport terminal, but if none of these e-options are suitable, then arrive at the airport early to minimise the risk of lengthy lines leading to a missed flight. If checking in directly with the airline, ask if the flight is full as they will sometimes block out a vacant seat next to you; this is especially useful if travelling with a child under 2 on your lap. To increase your chances of success, choose to fly on quieter days, perhaps mid-week.

In general, everything takes longer with children in tow and so allowing plenty of time for security checks etc. is a good idea.

If travelling with another adult, formally allocate duties and ensure that one adult is reponsible for supervising the children while the other one takes care of the check-in duties.

If travelling as a solo parent, be extra vigilant about watching children, even when partially distracted by other activities. Some people prefer using reins or harnesses, or to keep children strapped into prams or slings until boarding; airlines will check such items from the gate lounge.

Airports are huge spaces full of people and one-way exits, losing a child can send your plans and the airport into chaos. It is a good idea to fit travelling children with identification bracelets stating their name, your phone number and the number of someone not travelling should your mobile phone be turned off.

Have children pack their own backpacks or bags with favourite toys, snacks and drinks, but do not make them too bulky or heavy as parents inevitably wind up carrying such items.

Keep eyes and ears out for any special arrangements for people travelling with small children, such as fast-track customs points or early boarding call for planes.

Aeroplanes

Before booking a trip away, visit your chosen airlines website online as most have a section dedicated to travelling with children, which clearly outline any requirements or restrictions.

Childproofing an aeroplane is firstly about safely seating your child and then about preventing them from running amok and harming themselves during flight. Safely seating an infant in aircraft is a difficult subject; much has been made of the dangers associated with merely holding babies on an adult lap as this has been found to be dangerous during periods of turbulence and emergency landings. According to the Federal Aviation Authority (FAA) in the U.S. poorly restrained children have been needlessly injured in emergencies from being thrown around the cabin.

The Civil Aviation Safety Authority (CASA), recommends that infants are seated in an approved car restraint system including rear-facing restraints where appropriate. There are also authorised aviation restraint systems such as the Kidsflysafe CARES system from the U.S. which is pre-approved by most airlines for use, whereas car seats must be taken into some airlines at least 24 hours prior to departure to be approved for in-flight use. In addition, using a car seat means both purchansing a separate airline seat for a baby and also means carrying a rather bulky child restraint through the airport and on-board, which may be difficult if flying with multiple young children and will require some pre-planning.

Some airlines provide a belly-extension belt which anchors the baby to an adult's lap, the 'belly-belt' but these have been banned by the FAA as too dangerous especially in the event of emergency landings where babys have become human airbags for adult passengers.

Booster seats are not permitted to be used with standard airline seating as they require a shoulder harness system, and in general, once a child has outgrown their full-harness child restraint, it is safe for them to use the aircraft seat and lap belt.

Most airlines provide a limited number of bassinets which attach to the bulkhead and these must be booked well in advance, and are subject to strict weight and height limits which make them suitable only for infants under 6–8 months of age.

Entertaining children for an entire flight is nigh on impossible for certain age-groups; young babies will usually spend at least some of the flight sleeping, whilst older children can be well entertained with adequate snacks in combination with electronic media such as hand-held games and movies viewed on portable DVD players or ipads.

But it is wiggly, squirmy toddlers who have the most trouble settling on long flights as they are too old to sleep much and are too young to settle and watch a movie. Moreover, their modus operandi is usually to go-go-go! Have a bag full of goodies and snacks which can be brought out one by one, and for a little more excitement, wrap a few new toys as presents; the novelty factor can provide extra distraction-value.

Airlines discourage people from allowing their toddlers to walk the aisles or stand in front of the seat, but this is far from realistic as many parents towards the end of a long flight are left pacing the plane with restless toddlers. Look for some relief from kind cabin crew and accept all offers of help; similarly, ignore all glares of disapproval.

Take the largest carry-on bag allowed and better yet, use one which slings over your back and allows you to have both hands free to deal with children. Pack a smaller plastic bag with one nappy, wipes and a nappy sack and place in the seat pocket in front of you as an easy carry to the small airline toilet.

Provide as many familiar snacks as possible for children on flights and be aware that the first rule of flying with children is that the snacks will always run out before the flight does! If feeding them food or baby bottles from the plane's galley, check the temperature yourself before feeding it to children, as they often heat food to a much higher temperature.

Dress children like colourful onions; in layers of bright and distinctive clothing which is easy to spot in a crowd. This will also allow you to put layers on and off as they require for temperature regulation. Infant sleeping bags are an easy way to keep babies warm and to transfer them without waking if required. Pack a change of clothing for unexpected spills and accidents.

Hotels

Hotels are all part of the holiday experience for parents and children, but it is also a whole new world of possibilities. Hotel rooms are no more dangerous than a home, but they are smaller with a higher concentration of furniture than most homes. So before relaxing and enjoying a holiday, parents should take a few minutes to childproof the room.

Before leaving on holiday, call the hotel to find out whether they offer any childproofing services as some will prepare the room prior to your arrival. In addition, some hotels will also provide a childproofing kit on request.

On arrival, take a few minutes to crawl around on all fours looking for any small or sharp objects missed by the cleaning staff, and to identify any other low hazards, this should include checking under the bed.

Begin childproofing by moving all furniture away from the windows and shift any sharp-edged or glass coffee tables to the corner; moving furniture can also create play space for children making them less likely to find trouble. Sharp corners on tables can also be softened using childproof bumpers or face washer cloths taped in place using duct tape. Seal unused drawers using tape and don't forget to lock or tape shut the minibar area as these often have bottle openers and glassware as well as alcohol.

Any breakable lamps, vases, bowls or ornaments should be stowed out of reach.

Secure all electrical sockets with simple plastic outlet covers or duct tape and unplug unneeded appliances such as lamps or alarm clocks, and wind any cords to prevent dangling and secure them with string or garbage ties. Cords which snake across the floor are a tripping risk and can be secured to the floor using tape. Be especially wary of hotel room coffee machines or kettles, which are often on low surfaces and may be pulled down by children; put such items away and if required, use them on a high surface and unplug them immediately after use.

Unplug any unused or easily accessible phones to avoid a hefty phone bill.

Check that all flat screen televisions are secured to a cabinet on the wall to minimise the risk of toppling and tape any doors on the entertainment cabinet.

Wind any long curtain or blind cords and fix them using string or ties, and discourage children from hiding amongst any long, flowing hotel curtains.

Windows and doors must all be securely locked and any balcony doors should also be kept locked; do not allow children free access to a balcony. It may be safer to request a room without a balcony until children are older. Latches and locks can also be taped over to further discourage tampering.

In 2000 the U.S. Consumer Products Safety Commission (CSPC) performed spot checks on 90 hotels across the U.S.A. and found that hotel-provided cots were woefully inadequate with unsafe mattresses and supports as well as loose hardware, sharp edges and pillows. If using a hotel cot, make sure it fits the Australian Standard with no more than 50–85mm between vertical slats, and has a firm mattress which fits snugly around the perimeter. Remove any pillows or blankets which may cause suffocation, If using a portable cot, press on the base to ensure the support is firm and that the frame locks securely in place. Check all cots for loose or missing screws, sharp edges or exposed hinges. Move the cot so that there is a safe zone around it and is not within reach of windows, cords, or heaters, and is not under heavy pictures or mirrors. For more information on cots, see Chapter 1.

The ensuite nature of hotel bathrooms makes access easier for children, and doors should remain closed when not in use. If there is a mechanism to lock the bathroom from the inside, place a folded towel over the top of the door when older children are inside to prevent them inadvertently locking themselves in. Younger children must always be supervised in the bathroom. Unplug any electrical appliances such as hair dryers and store them in secure drawers or the wardrobe. Use anti-slip decals for the bath and shower and put away all hazardous (often complimentary) products such as mouthwash, cosmetics and razor blades. Be especially vigilant about checking water temperature in the bathroom carefully as hot water thermostats are often set higher than the recommended 50°C. If the bathroom has a low bidet, be particularly careful to exclude children.

Appendix I

Baby CPR Guide

Remember ABC and 30 + 2

Educate yourself

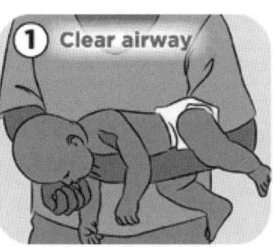

1. A = AIRWAY

Look in mouth & sweep with finger

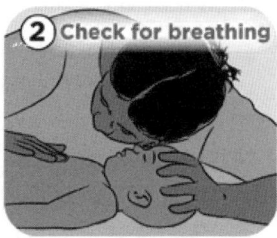

2. B = BREATHING

Listen, look and feel for breathing

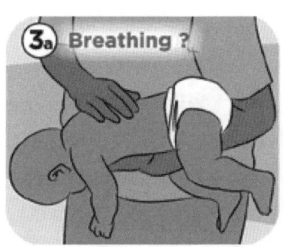

3a. If breathing place baby in recovery position

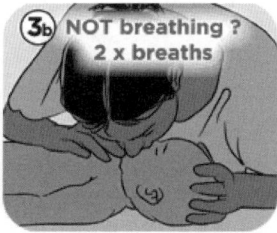

3b. If not breathing, lift chin, cover nose & mouth and blow for 1 second

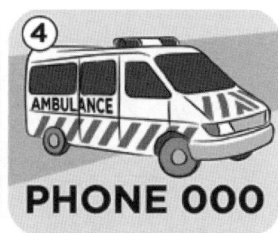

4. Call emergency number **.

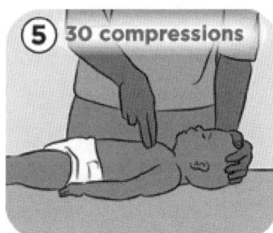

5. C = CIRCULATION Start 30 compressions with 2 fingers in centre

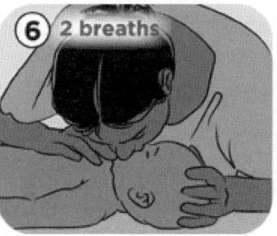

6. Repeat 30 + 2 until signs of life or help arrives

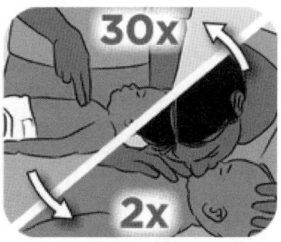

Click here to view baby & child CPR video

Appendix II

The Choking Child Guide

Remember 5 Front + 5 Back

1. PREVENTION. Keep small objects away from children

2. GET HELP. Call emergency number **

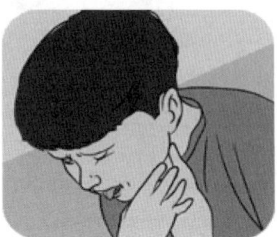

3. COUGH. Ask older child to cough

4. Sweep mouth to clear give 5 back blows with heel of hand

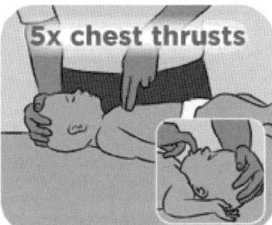

5. With 2 fingers give 5 chest thrusts

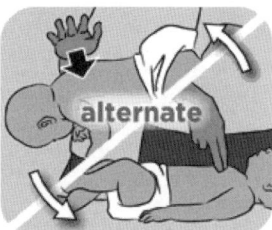

6. Repeat 5 FRONT & 5 BACK

Keep watch to see if object dislodges

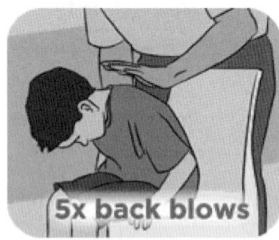

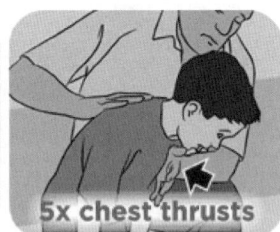

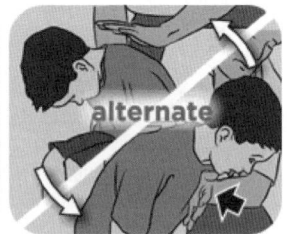

If baby or child becomes unconscious, commence CPR

Appendix III SIDS

SIDS Guidelines

SIDS stands for Sudden Infant Death Syndrome or Cot Death as it used to be known. Is frightening because it strikes babies predominantly under 6 months old, and seems random. It is the number one cause of death in infants < 1 year old, though statistically 1999 out of 2000 babies will not die of SIDS.

The cause of SIDS remains unknown, but research has uncovered factors which place babies at higher risk of SIDS. Many of these risk factors can be modified with a few simple guidelines, and since their introduction in 1991 the number of SIDS deaths have been greatly reduced.

What can you do?

1. **Always place a baby to sleep on their back, not on tummy or side.**
   Once over 6 months, babies will start rolling over themselves. The risk of SIDS in babies > 6 months in extremely low.
2. **Sleep baby with face uncovered.**
   Put baby's feet touching the bottom of the cot so they cannot slip under blankets. Consider the use of safe baby sleeping bags as they cannot fall over baby's face.
3. **Cigarette smoke before and after birth increases baby's risk of SIDS.**
   If mother smokes the risk of SIDS doubles, if father smokes also the risk doubles again. Don't smoke!
4. **Provide a safe sleeping environment.**
   Keep cot clear of bumpers, soft toys and pillows.
   Ensure the cot reaches safety standards and has a firm, well-fitted mattress.
5. **Sleep baby in their *own* sleeping environment next to parents bed for first 6 to 12 months.**
   For more information about SIDS and safe sleeping visit http://www.sidsandkids.org

Resources, References and Links

www.childproof.com.au

Raising Children network; www.raisingchildren.net.au

Kidsafe Australia; www.kidsafe.com.au

SIDS and Kids; www.sidsandkids.org

Victorian Injury Surveillance Unit; http://www.monash.edu.au/miri/research-areas/home-sport-and-leisure-safety/visu/

Royal Children's Hospital Safety Centre; www.rch.org.au/safetycentre

Australian Competition & Consumer Commission (ACCC); www.accc.gov.au or www.recalls.gov.au or www.productsafety.gov.au

Choice; www.choice.com.au

Vicroads; www.vicroads.vic.gov.au

U.S. Consumer Product Safety Commission; www.cspc.gov

Swim Australia; www.swimaustralia.org.au

Kids Alive – Do the five; www.kidsalive.com.au

The Petcare Information and Advisory Service; Petnet.com.au

Poisons Information; call 13 11 26 from anywhere in Australia

Westmead children's hospital; www.kidshealth.chw.edu.au

Women and Children's health Network; www.cyh.com